THE FABER BOOK OF MOVIE VERSE

The Faber Book of

MOVIE VERSE

edited by
Philip French and Ken Wlaschin

Introduction and Notes by
PHILIP FRENCH

faber and faber
LONDON · BOSTON

First published in Great Britain in 1993
by Faber and Faber Limited
3 Queen Square London WC1N 3AU

Photoset by Wilmaset Ltd, Wirral
Printed by Clays Ltd, St Ives plc

Philip French and Ken Wlaschin are hereby identified as
editors of this work in accordance with Section 77 of the
Copyright, Designs and Patents Act 1988

A CIP record for this book is available from the British Library

ISBN 0-571-16660-1

2 4 6 8 10 9 7 5 3 1

CONTENTS

I'd met Robert Graves at a party in Madrid. At first, I have to admit, I wasn't at all clear about who he was and I mistook him for some sort of scientist . . . When I first went to visit Robert on Majorca, I was determined to learn all about the work he did. 'You know, Robert,' I said, 'I really don't understand poetry.'

And he said, to the point as always, 'My darling, you're not supposed to understand it, you're supposed to enjoy it.' Poems are like people, he told me; there aren't that many authentic ones around.

Ava Gardner, *Ava: My Story*

INTRODUCTION:
A Poet and Pedant Overture

The cinema is a little more than, or very nearly, a hundred years old. It depends on whether you date its origin from the Kinetoscope, the peepshow device through which American viewers saw the brief products of Thomas Alva Edison's Kinetograph movie camera of 1891, or from Louis Lumière's Cinématographe, by means of which French audiences saw images projected on to a screen in 1895. During most of those hundred years poets and poetry have been associated with the movies. As a way of defining the scope of this book of verse *about* the cinema it might be useful to list the various connections.

First there is the so-called 'poetry of the cinema', a somewhat vague term used to describe evocative images or sequences that go beyond the dramatic, psychological and painterly to take on the mysterious haunting resonance and lyricism associated with poetry. We speak of directors as different from each other as Griffith, Ford, Flaherty, Mizoguchi and Lean as 'poets of the cinema'. The scenarios that silent film-makers wrote, and the published texts prepared by themselves or others after viewing the completed films, invariably look on the page, and read, like verse.

Second there is the cinema of poets – films directed or written by poets. Apollinaire and Vachel Lindsay were among the first to write enthusiastically of the unique possibilities of the new medium, but neither worked in the cinema, though in 1914 Apollinaire collaborated on an unfilmed screenplay. Many others, however, did get a chance to make films. The novelist and poet Gabriele D'Annunzio wrote the screenplay and highly poetic flash titles of *Cabiria*, the seminal Italian epic of 1914, thus beginning a national literary tradition that has carried on down to Pier Paolo Pasolini. In Russia, Vladimir Mayakovsky was deeply involved in the early Soviet cinema, as was his French contemporary, the poet and theorist Antonin Artaud, with the experimental cinema of his country. Artaud wrote the scenario for the avant-garde classic *La Coquille et le clergyman* (1927) and played Marat in Abel Gance's *Napoléon* (1927) and a sympathetic young priest in Carl Dreyer's *La Passion de Jeanne d'Arc* (1928). The poet Jacques Prévert, as screenwriter for Jean Renoir and Marcel Carné in the 1930s and 40s, helped create the style dubbed 'poetic realism'. Outside France – as a consequence of *Le Sang d'un poète* (1929), *La Belle et la bête* (1946) and *Orphée* (1950) – Jean Cocteau is

[1]

thought of primarily as a film-maker rather than as a poet. In Britain Dylan Thomas earned useful sums writing screenplays that failed to reach the screen (though several were published and a couple filmed posthumously) and W. H. Auden was drawn into the British documentary movement through his friendship with Benjamin Britten, writing verse commentaries for, most notably, Cavalcanti's *Coal Face* (1935) and Basil Wright's *Night Mail* (1936). John Grierson intended that Auden and Wright should co-direct *Air Mail to Australia*, a sequel to *Night Mail* (it was not made), and Auden worked as an assistant director on the 1935 GPO production *Calendar of the Year*. In the same year he provided verse sub-titles for a London Film Society screening of Dziga Vertov's *Three Songs of Lenin*.

These European authors were invited to write for the cinema because of their reputations as poets. In the United States, apart from such avant-garde poet–film-makers as Maya Deren and James Broughton who worked outside mainstream cinema, poets (other than lyric writers) have been engaged for their other literary gifts and despite their poetic reputations. One thinks of the movie critic and novelist James Agee, brought to Hollywood by John Huston, of Harry Brown, whose novels include *The Stars in their Courses* (*The Iliad* reworked as a Western, though when Howard Hawks filmed it in 1967 only Philoctetes as the wounded gunfighter Phil Tate remained from the original dramatis personae), and Dorothy Parker, who wrote in the 1920s that 'Men seldom make passes/At girls who wear glasses', anticipating the cherished Hollywood cliché 'You look beautiful without your glasses', a line that in endless variations reaches down to the 1992 Australian film *Strictly Ballroom*. Agee's film criticism in *The Nation* (he also wrote anonymously on the movies for *Time*) was the subject of a famous backhanded compliment from Auden in a letter to *The Nation*'s editors. 'I do not care for movies very much and I rarely see them', Auden wrote, but 'what he says is of such profound interest, expressed with such extraordinary wit and felicity, and so transcends its ostensible – to me rather unimportant – subject, that his articles belong in that very select class – the music critiques of Berlioz and Shaw are the only other members I know – of newspaper work that has permanent literary value.'

Agee wrote a couple of screenplays, but no poetry about the cinema. Brown wrote two poems about the movies included in this anthology. James Broughton contributed some occasional lines to the Edinburgh Film Festival programme after his films *Loony Tom* and *Mother's Day* had been screened there in 1951:

Come up through the heather where the Puritans glow
for it's culture time in the kilt-happy north.
All brows are now raised for a highminded view
of sonata, soprano, and picture show.

Bertolt Brecht, who scripted one important film made outside the movie industry (*Kühle Wampe*, 1932) before quitting Germany on the coming of the Third Reich, worked on his single major commercial production during his wartime Hollywood exile, Fritz Lang's *Hangmen Also Die* (1943). He was, however, cheated out of his main credit by a fellow communist, the American playwright John Wexley, whom Lang had brought in as a collaborator because of Brecht's poor English. Wexley successfully appealed to a Screenwriters' Guild arbitration board composed largely of communists and fellow travellers who had little regard for Brecht's reputation. Four years later Brecht was called before the House Un-American Activities Committee, made something of a mockery of the hearing and immediately left the United States for good.

Third, there is the cinema *about* poets. As fictional characters they tend to be mad, phoney, weak or wild like the characters played by Richard Basehart in *Repeat Performance* (1947), Richard Attenborough in *Only Two Can Play* (the 1962 version of Kingsley Amis's *That Uncertain Feeling*), Robert Morse in *The Loved One* (1965) and Sean Connery in *A Fine Madness* (1966). An odd exception is the whimsical philanthropist and author of verse for greetings cards, the aptly named Longfellow Deeds, played by Gary Cooper, the definitive populist hero of Capra's *Mr Deeds Goes to Town* (1937).

Real-life poets have been romanticized in a dotty, sometimes unintentionally comic fashion – Robert Browning and Elizabeth Barrett in *The Barretts of Wimpole Street* (1934), in which Fredric March and Norma Shearer as the poets are overshadowed by Charles Laughton as the monstrous Edward Moulton-Barrett; Shelley and Byron egging on Mary Shelley to elaborate a sequel to *Frankenstein* in the prelude to James Whale's scintillating *The Bride of Frankenstein* (1935); Ronald Colman as a swashbuckling revolutionary François Villon in *If I Were King* (1938); Shelley, Byron and company having a sexual and literary orgy in Switzerland in Ken Russell's *Gothic* (1986); Byron alone, represented as effete by Dennis Price in *The Bad Lord Byron* (1948) and big, bland and delightful to know by Richard Chamberlain in *Lady Caroline Lamb* (1972); Rip Torn as a pawkily humorous Walt Whitman in *Beautiful Dreamers* (1990). In Sally Potter's *Orlando* (1992), a screen version of the

Virginia Woolf novel, the eponymous heroine (who starts out as an Elizabethan hero) encounters Jonathan Swift, Alexander Pope and Joseph Addison, a trio of posturing male chauvinists, at a literary salon in 1750, somewhat anachronistically as all three were dead by then. Oscar Wilde has been variously impersonated by Robert Morley (Gregory Ratoff's *Oscar Wilde*, 1959), Peter Finch (Ken Hughes's *The Trials of Oscar Wilde*, 1960) and Nickolas Grace (Ken Russell's *Salome's Last Dance*, 1987). An encouragingly serious recent work in this area is Paul Turner's Welsh-language movie *Hedd Wynn* (1992), a celebration of the career of the Welsh poet Ellis Evans, who competed under the bardic pseudonym Hedd Wynn and won a posthumous ceremonial chair at the 1917 National Eisteddfod with a poem written in the trenches a few weeks before his death at Passchendaele. And we should not forget that Roger Corman, who produced and directed a series of elegant low-budget movies based on Edgar Allan Poe's tales and poems, put Poe on to a motorcycle to ride along with other counter-cultural figures in his bizarre psychedelic biker comedy *Gas-s-s-s! Or It Became Necessary to Destroy the World in Order to Save It* (1970). He was anticipated by D. W. Griffith, whose 1909 film *Edgar Allan Poe* concerns the poet selling 'The Raven' for practically nothing.

Imaginative treatment has been given on stage recently to Rimbaud and Verlaine (Christopher Hampton's *Total Eclipse*), Shakespeare and Ben Jonson (Edward Bond's *Bingo*), John Clare (Bond's *The Fool*), the Shelley–Byron set (Howard Brenton's *Bloody Poetry*), Ezra Pound (Bernard Kops's *The Cage*) and T. S. Eliot (Michael Hastings' *Tom and Viv*). None of these plays has reached the big screen. On the whole the cinema has done better by novelists, painters, playwrights, musicians, composers and even ballet dancers. Critics have occasionally had a look-in (Clifton Webb in *Laura*, George Sanders in *All About Eve*, the whole London theatrical Critics' Circle being murdered by Vincent Price as the vengeful Shakespearian actor in the 1973 horror flick *Theatre of Blood*). Indeed the French director André Téchiné even persuaded Roland Barthes to make his only screen appearance as William Makepeace Thackeray, to escort Charlotte Brontë around a very Gallic London in *Les Soeurs Brontë*. Television and the cinema have, of course, produced endless documentary essays on poets.

Fourth, there is 'the cinema of poetry'. This category includes verse drama, principally Shakespeare, but also the film versions of Rostand's *Cyrano de Bergerac*, Eliot's *Murder in the Cathedral* and most recently Derek Jarman's idiosyncratic treatment of Marlowe's *Edward II*. The

American playwright Maxwell Anderson sold a number of his verse plays to Hollywood, among them *Winterset* and *Key Largo*, but little of his original text reached the screen. Mainly, however, one is thinking of something less obvious – of movies based on poems. These were more common in the silent era when film-makers frequently took narrative poems, and sometimes lyrical ones, as their points of departure. The most famous is *A Fool There Was*, the 1915 William Fox production which took its title from the opening line of Rudyard Kipling's 'The Vampire', written in 1897 to accompany a painting exhibited that year by his cousin Philip Burne-Jones and subsequently adapted for the stage by Porter Emerson Browne. The movie launched the career of the Cincinnati-born Theodosia Goodman (under the screen name Theda Bara) and popular-ized the sexual connotation of 'vamp' as noun and verb.

There have been fewer such adaptations since the coming of sound. One celebrated example is the 1936 Warner Brothers film of *The Charge of the Light Brigade*, which is officially dedicated at the beginning to the memory of the Poet Laureate Alfred, Lord Tennyson, and superimposes lines from the poem over the concluding battle scene at Balaclava. Another is the 1939 George Stevens film inspired by Rudyard Kipling's *Gunga Din*. In this imperial adventure yarn an actor with a close resemblance to Kipling accompanies the climactic mission against the Indian insurrectionists in which Gunga Din dies gallantly, and is seen to compose the poem in the final sequence. The poem is then read by the colonel as the regimental *bhisti* is buried with full military honours. But Mrs Caroline Kipling, the poet's widow, objected to the representation of her late husband after she had sat in a preview audience that laughed at the scenes in which he appeared. As a result RKO's engineers used an optical printer to obliterate him not only from copies distributed in Britain, but also from subsequent American prints, though the original negative has recently been discovered and the film restored. (Thirty-six years later, Christopher Plummer convincingly impersonated Kipling in the framing sequences of John Huston's *The Man Who Would Be King*.) A year after *Gunga Din*, one of its stars, Cary Grant, appeared in *My Favourite Wife*, a screwball comedy remotely derived from Tennyson's *Enoch Arden*, as is hinted at in the hero being called Nick Arden.

There have also been movies made from James Moncur March's long verse narratives of the 1920s – *The Set-Up* (directed by Robert Wise in 1948) and *The Wild Party* (directed by James Ivory in 1976), neither bearing much resemblance to, or quoting from, the originals. March himself worked in movies through the 1930s (his screenwriting credits include *Hell's Angels* and *Journey's End*) but his offer to assist on the script of *The Set-Up* was rejected. Oddly, the scenario commissioned by Samuel Goldwyn from MacKinley Kantor for what became William Wyler's *The Best Years of Our Lives* (1947), the key homecoming picture of World War Two, was written in free verse and made over by Robert E. Sherwood into an eloquent prose screenplay. Sherwood, more than incidentally, was one of America's first important movie critics and a satirical verse commentator on the cultural scene before becoming a major playwright and screenwriter. An example of his comic verse is to be found in this book.

Fifth, and related to this, is what we might call 'poetry in the cinema', quotations used in titles, and poems quoted by characters. Quotations in titles almost invariably occur in films adapted from novels or plays: *Gone With the Wind* (from Ernest Dowson's 'Non Sum Qualis Eram Bonae Sub Regno Cynarae'), or *A Handful of Dust* (from Eliot's *The Waste Land*). It is rare for an original screenplay to use a quotation as its title, unless it be something as familiar as *To Be or Not To Be*, where the characters in Lubitsch's bitter 1942 comedy were members of a Polish troupe performing a Shakespearian repertoire at the outbreak of World War Two. The title is less apposite for the 1983 Mel Brooks remake where the hero is a song-and-dance man. Hitchcock's *Rich and Strange* (1932) takes it title from *The Tempest*; his thriller *North by North West* (1959) almost certainly derives its title from *Hamlet*, but punning on an American airline. The one notable aspect of *Silent Dust*, a minor 1949 British movie about an upper-class reprobate returning home after disreputable military service in World War Two, is that the lumbering title of the play on which it was based (*The Paragon*) should have been jettisoned in favour of a quotation from Thomas Gray's *Elegy Written in a Country Churchyard* ('Can Honour's voice provoke the silent dust'). At least two other films have titles from Gray's poem (*Paths of Glory* and *Far From the Madding Crowd*). Lindsay Anderson's 1968 movie *If* takes its title from Kipling's poem, though it is nowhere quoted. William Blake is not quoted in Michael Cimino's *Heaven's Gate*, but he is probably the source of the title (though it just might come from Shakespeare's *Cymbeline*). Among foreign movies, one of the most striking quotations is the line from Leopardi's poem 'Le Ricordanze' which provides the title for Luchino Visconti's *Vaghe Stelle dell'Orsa* (1965). The heroine's brother frequently quotes Leopardi and the poet's work and life illuminate the movie's themes. The Italian title translates as 'Misty Stars of the Great Bear', but the film was shown in

English-speaking countries under the meaningless title *Of a Thousand Delights*.

Graham Greene's dramatically named short story *The Lieutenant Died Last* underwent a dozen changes of title during production at Ealing Studios before being released as *Went the Day Well?* in 1943. An unattributed epigraph to this movie about English villagers defeating the disguised vanguard of a German invasion force follows the opening titles:

> Went the day well?
> We died and hardly knew it.

In writing the history of the film, Penelope Houston traced the epigraph to an anonymous poem that prefaced a collection of tributes to young people killed in the early years of World War Two to which the head of Ealing, Michael Balcon, had contributed a memoir of the studio's golden boy, Penn Tennyson, grandson of the Poet Laureate. The lines that gave the film its title were, in fact, written by John Maxwell Edmonds (1875–1958), a literary scholar and future Cambridge don, as one of a number of exemplary epitaphs for Great War graves officially commissioned in 1918 and published in *The Times Literary Supplement*. Another of his twelve lapidary inscriptions for World War One memorials eventually found its way onto a memorial at Kohima Cemetery in Assam for British soldiers who died in Burma:

> When you go home
> Tell them of us and say
> For your tomorrow
> We gave our today.

This epigraph appears at the end of *Yesterday's Enemy*, a sombre 1959 war film set in the Burma campaign, and suggested its title.

Among the notable cases of poems quoted in movies are Leslie Howard's delivery of John of Gaunt's 'This scepter'd isle' speech from *Richard II* at the end of *The Scarlet Pimpernel* (1934), and its companion piece, Howard's quotation from Rupert Brooke's 'Grantchester' in the parallel scene during the final sequence of his patriotic World War Two thriller *Pimpernel Smith*. As the disillusioned itinerant *littérateur* in *The Petrified Forest*, Howard also quotes from T. S. Eliot, and Howard's tragic death in 1943 is properly commemorated by Maurice Lindsay in this anthology. (In his *Memoirs of the Forties*, Julian Maclaren-Ross recalls a story submitted to *Horizon* during World War Two that contains 'a complete description in blank verse of the film *The Petrified Forest*'; it was rejected by Cyril Connolly because the author had a red beard.) With a dignity comparable to Howard's, Gene Hackman (as an ex-US army colonel) quotes *Julius Caesar* in the 1983 movie *Uncommon Valor* to inspire an intrepid band of former Special Service soldiers looking for Americans held in remote prison camps in south-east Asia. As Doc Holliday in John Ford's *My Darling Clementine*, Victor Mature prompts the drunken actor played by Alan Mowbray during a recitation from *Hamlet* in a saloon in Marshal Wyatt Earp's Tombstone, Arizona. In an earlier Ford film, *Stagecoach* (1939), immediately preceding his Western and his first in the sound era, the heroic drunk Doc Boone (Thomas Mitchell) takes leave of his censorious hatchet-faced landlady by ironically addressing her with Faustus's lines inspired by Helen of Troy, conjured up for him by Mephistopheles in Christopher Marlowe's *Doctor Faustus*.

The use of Christina Rossetti's sonnet 'Remembrance' in Robert Aldrich's *Kiss Me Deadly* (1955) is the subject of a fine poem by Gerald Burns included in this book. In Alan Rudolph's 1992 movie *Equinox*, the withdrawn heroine constantly clutches and reads from the collected works of Emily Dickinson. A black fan at a pick-up basketball game in a Los Angeles park in Ron Shelton's *White Men Can't Jump* (1992) celebrates a particularly graceful shot by proclaiming: 'A thing of beauty is a joy forever – John Keats said that man!' In Donald Siegel's Cold War thriller *Telefon* (1978), the brainwashed KGB assassins planted around America to be awoken in an emergency are triggered to go about their murderous tasks by hearing a couplet from Robert Frost's 'Stopping by Woods on a Snowy Evening' – 'But I have promises to keep, / And miles to go before I sleep'. In the film of *Oh, What a Lovely War*, an infantryman on the Western Front quotes Rupert Brooke's 1914 'The Soldier' ('If I should die, think only this of me: / That there's some corner of a foreign field / That is for ever England'), as if he were its author. In the 1990 David Puttnam movie *Memphis Belle*, a member of an American World War Two Flying Fortress crew, operating from a British base, passes off W. B. Yeats's 'An Irish Airman Foretells His Death' as his own work but subsequently attests to its true authorship. In *Once Upon a Honeymoon* (1942) Ginger Rogers and Cary Grant quote poems as part of their loving banter, he countering her lines from Browning's 'Pippa Passes' and *Hamlet* with a couplet from Irving Berlin and some doggerel of his own composition.

Apart from certain 1960s documentaries of public poetry readings, no movie – certainly no feature film – has given poetry so central a place as

Peter Weir's *Dead Poets Society*. His picture, set at the end of the Eisenhower Era in 1959, makes the teaching of literature a metaphor for spiritual liberation and has the teacher-hero, Robin Williams, insist that his pupils at a New England private school address him by way of Walt Whitman exhortation. In Woody Allen's *Hannah and Her Sisters*, Michael Caine buys his sister-in-law (Barbara Hershey) the complete poems of e. e. cummings as a token of esteem and a means of seduction, drawing her attention to a poem on page 112: 'your slightest look easily will / unclose me / though I have closed myself / as fingers, / you open always petal by petal myself . . .'

The sequence involving a specific poem that most readily springs to mind for middle-aged British moviegoers is in *The Way to the Stars*, Anthony Asquith's and Terence Rattigan's 1945 tribute to the RAF (the air force version of the navy's *In Which We Serve* and the army's *The Way Ahead*). Michael Redgrave, who published poetry as a Cambridge undergraduate, plays an RAF Squadron Leader and recites (and is established as the fictive author of) John Pudney's understated three-stanza poem 'For Johnny', making it, for a while at least, the best-known poem of World War Two:

> Do not despair
> For Johnny-head-in-air;
> He sleeps as sound
> As Johnny underground.

This poem had so penetrated the popular consciousness that in the 1960s, in his poem *Nostalgia – Now Threepence Off*, Adrian Mitchell could write that 'Johnny-head-in-air spends his days reporting flying saucers, the telephone receiver never cools from the heat of his hands'. 'For Johnny' is a rare example of a poem of some quality attributed to a fictitious character. Usually such work is mediocre, as with the portentous verse composed by the hero's disturbed sister in *The Prince of Tides* (1991), or intentionally bad, as is the case with the work of the effeminate Chicago journalist in *The Front Page* and the poems composed by Steve Martin in *The Man With Two Brains*.

Sixth, there is the poetry of cineastes – poems written by moviemakers not normally thought of as poets (as opposed to Fiona Pitt-Kethley, a former movie extra known solely for her verse). A couple are represented here – most notably the screenwriter I. A. L. Diamond observing post-war Hollywood before he attained fame through his collaboration with Billy Wilder; and the Irish writer-director Neil Jordan ruefully recording his first negotiations with Tinseltown over the 1988 comedy *High Spirits*. Most of them, however, deal with loftier matters of life and love rather than meditating in concrete terms on their craft. Among movie stars who have written, and in some cases published, verse are Rudolph Valentino, Mae West, James Stewart, Sebastian Shaw, Sarah Churchill, Marilyn Monroe, Leonard Nimoy, Klaus Kinski, Daniel Gélin and Richard Harris. During the Second World War, and before resuming his acting career, Captain D. van den Bogaerde of the Queen's Royal Regiment (subsequently known as Dirk Bogarde) published several poems in literary magazines, *The Times Literary Supplement* among them. His 1943 poem *Steel Cathedrals*, an evocation of railway stations in wartime, is a minor classic. He has written poetry in the half-century since then, but his published work has been restricted to fiction and autobiography. Among directors, Luis Buñuel, Humphrey Jennings and Andrei Tarkovsky have published poems of some merit. Between dictating his celebrated memoranda, the Hollywood mogul David O. Selznick dashed off verse over a period of fifty years, much of it directed to his various inamoratas, though in his lifetime he only published one short poem – a celebration of his first-born that appeared in *Good Housekeeping* in 1932.

Seven, there is the complex question of the influence of the cinema upon the technique of verse writing. The obvious effect of films on fiction during this century is the subject of a good deal of critical analysis. Less attention has been paid to the changes brought about in poetry, though Frank O'Hara is among the poets who acknowledge the stylistic influence of the movies on their work.

Finally we come to what is in fact the subject of this book, poems about the cinema, verse inspired by movies and moviegoing. Rudyard Kipling wrote what is generally regarded as the first significant work of fiction inspired by the cinema, his great story 'Mrs Bathhurst', published in 1904. The story is noted for its pared-down, elliptical modernity, for the now fashionable device of an eponymous figure who remains off-stage, for the early use of 'it' to characterize indefinable feminine allure, and not the least for the description of an early movie audience entranced by a film, and for the idea of a cinematic image (in this case a sequence from a newsreel) obsessing a particular viewer. Kipling was to write, some two decades later, one of the first, most scathing poems about Hollywood, 'Naaman's Song', which is related to his brief involvement with the film business.

But the first verses about the movies were written by fans and journalistic hacks in film magazines, trade journals and children's publications, a practice that continued up to the 1950s on both sides of the Atlantic in periodicals like *Photoplay* and *Picturegoer*. For years during the 1940s, the final item on the readers' letters page of *Picturegoer* was invariably a brief poem by Ralph Wotherspoon writing from London SW5; in the 25 December 1943 issue, for instance, the prolific Mr Wotherspoon wrote:

> Slightly forsaken, somewhat forlorn,
> Rather resembling a startled faun,
> Puckish and wistful, electric, neat,
> Scaling the heights on his dancing feet –
> Other performers might gladly share
> The motto Per Ardua ad Astaire.

A good, indeed superior, example of the popular verse from the early years of the century is Mabel Hayes's 'Too Awfully Exciting' published in the annual *Little Folks* in 1913 (reproduced overleaf). The same number of *Little Folks* features an illustrated poem called 'A Moving Picture' that must be among the first lines celebrating the superiority of the home movie over the static image:

> Fanny to snap the baby tried,
> But all she took as you will see,
> Was just a hammock, wall and sky,
> Some cushions and a tree.
> Their Uncle Ben, who saw them fall,
> Said gaily, with a heartless laugh,
> 'Really to take him well, you want
> A cinematograph!'

That was two years before Vachel Lindsay turned his attention to the movies, claiming them as part of the popular subject matter he sought for his celebratory verse. He was conscious of the new ground he was breaking in his poem on the death of John Bunny in 1915 and his tribute to Mae Marsh. His seminal *Art of the Motion Picture* appeared in 1915. Lindsay reviewed movies occasionally for the liberal *New Republic* and was not averse to using poetic comparisons. Writing about Mary Pickford's performance in *A Romance of the Redwoods* in 1917, he quoted W. B. Yeats – 'rhetoric is heard, poetry overheard' – and went on to say: 'For the first time in my knowledge, the acting of Mary Pickford is permitted by her directors to have divine accident in it, poetry overheard'. Shortly thereafter, the celebrant of the public school and the imperial

TOO AWFULLY EXCITING

A RECITATION

I DON'T know a thing that's more awfully thrilling
  Than one of those grand cinematograph plays;
When Aunt Kate and I went to see "The Red Hunters"
  I got so excited folks stared in amaze.

The hero was splendid! He strode in (in this way)
  So handsome and fierce, with his hand on his gun,
And he cried to the villain "Get out!"—you could see it—
  The wicked thing went with a scowl (like this one).

The heroine murmured (like this) "You have saved me!"
  They both got engaged just as fast as they could;
But the horrible villain was bent upon vengeance—
  He got some cruel Indians to wait in a wood.

They sharpened their tomahawks, creeping and creeping,
  While nearer and nearer the loving pair came;
He was holding his horse, they were talking and laughing,
  Not knowing a bit—oh, it did seem a shame!

I just couldn't stand it! I jumped up and shouted
  "Oh dear—do be careful—they'll kill you—look out!"
"Hush! Hush!" whispered Auntie, but I didn't care,
  For it quite seemed as if they had both heard me shout.

They just reached the town in the last nick of time,
  And the Indians, baffled, rode yelling away;
The two darling people stood there safe and happy—
  With all the breath left me I shouted "Hooray!"

He sprang to the saddle and caught her up with him,
  As all the wild Indians burst from the wood,
And off they went galloping—gallop—a-gallop—
  Their foes riding after as fast as they could.

I did feel so glad it had all ended nicely—
  Before I could stop it a tear had got loose;
We hurried away, with the people all smiling,
  And Auntie Kate said, "Well, you *are* a young goose!"

MABEL HAYES.

291

spirit, Sir Henry Newbolt, turned his attentions to where that ethos had led on the battlefields of the Great War in his poem 'The War Films'.

For much of the next half-century English-language poets reflected the general attitude of intellectuals in the western world towards the cinema – an acknowledgement that moviegoing was among the principal pastimes of urban man, that Charlie Chaplin had become one of the great figures of world history, that Hollywood was a universal symbol of dubious glamour and a source of cultural corruption. Also that film had fundamentally changed the way we experience the world, refining and redefining the syntax of vision, and that visiting the cinema provided a rich source of guilty pleasure.

A famous nostalgia boom occurred in the mid-1960s, coinciding and entwined with a sudden popularization and commercial exploitation of the avant-garde. The two strands came together most obviously in Pop Art. One feature of the nostalgia boom was a vogue for trivia competitions among undergraduates. Others were the seasons of Bogart pictures at the Brattle cinema, just off the Harvard campus in Cambridge, Mass., and the launching of the Nostalgia Book Club. *Newsweek* devoted a cover story to the subject, canvassing the opinions of sociologists and asking various celebrities why they had decided to look at the past and become collectors of twentieth-century memorabilia. The death of Marilyn Monroe in 1962, the assassination of President Kennedy in 1963 and the escalation of the Vietnam War were three of the factors adduced in explanation of this social tendency. Another factor, as far as the cinema is concerned, was the increasing domination of television and the closing of many of the great picture palaces in Britain and North America. One by one those cathedrals of the cinema, where movies had become a new religion and their stars gods and goddesses for two generations, put up their shutters or were deconsecrated as supermarkets and bingo halls. It is not entirely surprising that many small-town cinemas in the American South-West were turned into store-front churches for evangelical sects.

More positively, the French New Wave directors – Louis Malle, Claude Chabrol, François Truffaut, Jean-Luc Godard, Eric Rohmer and Jacques Rivette – had drawn attention to a cinematic tradition, principally that of Hollywood, that they had celebrated in their criticism and acknowledged as a major influence on their own movies.

It was at this point that film studies became important for the first time on university campuses across America (concentrating first on European cinema, then homing in on the native product); that Pauline Kael, a

Californian lured to the East Coast, became (in tandem with the British recruit Penelope Gilliatt) part of a two-woman team of movie critics that brought the *New Yorker* to parts of America that Harold Ross's Manhattan weekly had not previously reached; that publishers started commissioning books on the movies (nine out of ten books on the cinema have been published since 1967); and that poets felt themselves relaxing towards the cinematic experience, free, even obliged, to celebrate the movies, moviehouses and stars that had given them so much pleasure. It was in the 1960s that Randall Jarrell looked back to his idyllic childhood holidays in Hollywood and wrote 'The Lost World' sequence and John Hollander produced his eloquent elegy for the lost cinemas of Manhattan, 'Moviegoing'. Their poems and a number of others from the same period helped release a flood of movie verse that has continued to this day. It shows little sign of abating. A good many of our leading poets have had something to say about the cinema, but while there may be some surprise appearances in this book there are also equally surprising absences. John Betjeman, for example, didn't write anything on the movies, though he liked films and had favourite cinemas. Nor did Philip Larkin, though in a letter of 1941 he speaks of going to the cinema daily, and writing to his future biographer Andrew Motion in 1981 he says of Sylvia Plath: 'I see her as a kind of Hammer Films poet'.

In May 1983, I presented a half-hour programme of poems about the cinema called 'The Muse at the Movies' on BBC Radio Three. It was heard by my American co-editor, Ken Wlaschin, then the Director of Programmes at the National Film Theatre and Organizer of the London Film Festival. He too had been collecting movie poems. Resources were thus combined to produce this book. As to why the period of gestation should have been so long, this is a tedious story, though it has resulted in a much better collection than we would have compiled ten years ago.

Initially our intention was a book of poems accompanied by posters, paintings, stills and caricatures. The paintings would have included impressions of London cinemas by Walter Sickert, William Roberts and Frank Auerbach, and New York movie houses by Reginald Marsh and Edward Hopper. There would also have been John Minton's unfinished painting of 'The Death of James Dean' and R. B. Kitaj's painting of John Ford on his deathbed, Warhol's portraits of Monroe, Presley, Cagney and Elizabeth Taylor, the graphic artist and film critic Manny Farber's painting inspired by the Westerns of Budd Boetticher, Dali's 'The Face of Mae West', Harry Jackson's bronze statue of John Wayne, and so on. Among the photographs a prominent place would have been found for

Weegee's pictures of Hollywood and the Walker Evans photograph that occasioned Alan Ross's poem 'Walker Evans's Atlanta'.

When costed, such an enterprise proved altogether too ambitious. We were also to discover what extraordinary demands certain publishers and agents make on behalf of their clients, in some cases giving the impression that they are actively hostile to the production of large anthologies or to books of specialist interest. However, when dealing directly with the poets themselves we have met with nothing but enthusiasm and generosity.

Three categories of poems have been reluctantly excluded. The first is lyrics. Nothing written to be accompanied by music is to be found here. Such songs as the Henderson, Brown and DeSylva number 'If I Had a Talking Picture of You' (from the 1929 Fox production *Sunny Side Up*) and the Johnny Mercer–Richard A. Whiting song 'Hooray for Hollywood' (launched in the 1937 Warner Brothers film *Hollywood Hotel*) have been rejected. Likewise we have dropped the lyrics of Dory Previn's moving song 'Mary C. Brown and the Hollywood Sign' about the failed actress who committed suicide by jumping from the letter 'H' of the sign in the Hollywood hills

> 'cause she did not become a star
> she died in less than a minute and a half
> she looked a bit like Hedy Lamarr.

The Bernie Taupin–Elton John number 'Candle in the Wind' is among the more recent songs in this area that might have got in.

Certain songs contain just the odd couplet on the movies, so could hardly have been included anyway. One thinks of the lines from the acerbic female duet 'Take Him' putting down the eponymous hero of Rodgers and Hart's *Pal Joey*:

> His thoughts are seldom consecutive.
> He just can't write.
> I know a movie executive
> Who's twice as bright.

(Incidentally, *re* David Wagoner's epic poem on the death of John Dillinger, the last music Dillinger heard before the harps of heaven was the theme song of *Manhattan Melodrama* by Rodgers and Hart, which with a revised lyric became their perennial favourite, 'Blue Moon'.)

The major losses from this missing section are Cole Porter's lyrics for two witty songs from *Silk Stockings*, the 1955 Broadway musical version of Ernst Lubitsch's *Ninotchka* – 'Stereophonic Sound' and 'There's a

Hollywood That's Good'. The first is wonderfully funny about the mid-50s vogue for colour and widescreen, the second (which was dropped before the show got to New York) mocks Hollywood's moguls by rhyming 'Darryl' with 'apparel' and 'Cohn' with 'throne'. Both are to be found in *The Complete Lyrics of Cole Porter* (1983), edited by Robert Kimbell with a foreword by John Updike.

We have also decided to exclude poems in translation (though for historical reasons it is necessary to mention one of the earliest serious poems occasioned by the cinema – an Italian poem by Vincenzo Cecchetti, written in the Romanesco dialect and published on the front page of a Rome newspaper on 11 April 1897). So there is no place here for a couple of pieces by Yevgeny Yevtushenko, Stanislaw Grochowiak's charming poem on seeing *Hamlet* at an open-air cinema in the Polish countryside, or – and these are real losses – Paul Morand's poem on Hollywood and the deeply moving 'Oración por Marilyn Monroe', addressed to God by the Nicaraguan radical poet-priest Ernesto Cardenal. Paul Morand (1888–1972), diplomat, novelist and suave travel writer (his books include the 1934 satire on the movie business *France la doulce*), was one of the most socially observant French writers of the inter-war years. In the decade after the Great War he sometimes turned to verse, as in his 1928 commentary on a visit to the United States:

> Au loin, on voit Beverly Hill, et sur la droite
> la *Metro Goldwyn*, puis *Paramount*
> avec sa moitié de pacquebot au-dessus de la ville
> qui garde du soleil dans ses soutes
> à l'heure où toute la plaine est déjà dans l'ombre.
> On est bien, à cause du voisinage de la mer;
> on pense à toutes les jeunes filles belles, en province,
> qui se donneraient, pour être ici,
> aux jeunes gens du monde entier qui se croient des *sheiks*,
> bref à tous ceux qui ne savent pas
> qu'un studio, c'est ce qui ressemble le plus
> à une administration soviétique.

Ernesto Cardenal was an unflinching opponent of the Somoza regime, a minister in the Sandinista government and a sharp thorn in the side of the Vatican. Written shortly after her death, his sixty-one-line 'Prayer for Marilyn Monroe' features, after several withering references to 20th Century-Fox, the words:

Forgive her Lord, and likewise all of us
for this our 20th Century
and the mammoth Super-Production in whose making we all shared

The poem can be found in *Marilyn Monroe and Other Poems*, translated by Robert Pring-Mill (Search Press, London, 1975). It is one of numerous poems in a dozen languages about Monroe. Charlie Chaplin and Marilyn Monroe have inspired the two largest bodies of movie-star verse by far (at least so far), the former during his prime, the latter since her death.

The major poet not included in this book, because he wrote in German, is of course Bertolt Brecht. With characteristic directness, addressing a brutal experience described earlier in this introduction, he wrote a pithy poem called 'Hollywood':

> Every day, to earn my daily bread
> I go to the market where lies are bought
> Hopefully
> I take my place among the sellers.

That precise use of 'hopefully' by his translator Michael Hamburger might briefly endear Brecht to his British right-wing detractors for whom the proper deployment of 'hopefully' is a cultural shibboleth. Brecht's six-stanza 'Hollywood Elegies' has some eloquently withering lines (translated by John Willett): e.g. 'The village of Hollywood was planned according to the notion / People in these parts have of heaven'. But his 'Elegies' are doubly excluded, as is the poem 'Hollywood', for being in German and written for musical settings by Hanns Eisler. Brecht also wrote a poem after meeting Charlie Chaplin during his American exile, 'A Film of the Comedian Chaplin'. Brecht admired Chaplin and the poem probably refers to the 1914 one-reeler, *A Face on the Barroom Floor*. According to Hanns Eisler, Chaplin was baffled by Brecht's work. In Hollywood Brecht also composed an eight-line poem dedicated to 'Laughton's Belly' on the occasion of his initial meeting with the British actor in 1944 to discuss his play *Galileo*, in which Laughton eventually appeared in 1947 under the direction of Joseph Losey. After his return to Europe, Brecht wrote his most affecting movie poem, the eleven-line 'To the Actor P. L. in Exile'. The addressee is the great Hungarian-born German actor Peter Lorre (1904–64), who appeared on stage in Brecht's *Mann ist Mann* in 1931, became an international star the following year in Fritz Lang's *M* and was subsequently a popular character actor in Europe and Hollywood. Lorre was in Berlin in 1950 appearing in *Der*

Verlorene (The Lost One), the only film he directed, when he met Brecht again and inspired this poem.

The third area of exclusion is passing references to movies in larger works. In 1924, for example, in *Hugh Selwyn Mauberley*, Ezra Pound invokes the role of the movies in setting the post-war cultural agenda:

> The 'age demanded' chiefly a mould in plaster,
> Made with no loss of time,
> A prose kinema, not, not assuredly, alabaster
> Or the 'sculpture' of rhyme.

James Joyce, who returned to Dublin in 1915 to open Ireland's first purpose-built cinema, was influenced by the movies in writing *Ulysses* and has a couple of allusions to the cinema, one of them to the Marx Brothers, in *Finnegans Wake*, which is as much a poem as it is a novel. In *The Cocktail Party*, the 1949 play by Groucho Marx's friend and admirer T. S. Eliot, the smug British juvenile lead Peter Quilpe goes to Hollywood to work for the Jewish movie mogul Bela Szogody on what sounds like a faintly disguised film version of *Brideshead Revisited* while his former mistress, Celia Copplestone, takes the veil as a missionary nurse in Africa and is crucified by rebellious natives on an ant-hill. The play isn't well served by brief quotations. A typical exchange goes:

> JULIA: But give us your news;
>   Give us your news of the world, Peter.
>   We lead such a quiet life, here in London.
> PETER: You always did enjoy a leg-pull, Julia:
>   But you all know I'm working for Pan-Am-Eagle?
> EDWARD: No. Tell us, what is Pan-Am-Eagle?
> PETER: You must have been living a quiet life!
>   Don't you go to the movies?
> LAVINIA: Occasionally.

While mocking the movie business, *The Cocktail Party* became the most successful English verse drama of this century, largely through the casting of film stars in the central role of the charismatic psychiatrist, Sir Henry Harcourt-Reilly – Alec Guinness in the Edinburgh Festival première and subsequent London production, Rex Harrison on Broadway. Many members of the audience were unaware that the play was in verse; others, aware of the much advertised form, had trouble in recognizing it aurally.

In certain poems the cinema is just one item in the urban landscape. In World War Two poems about short periods of military leave by Michael

Barsley and R. N. Currey it is the absence of movies that contributes to the desolate scene. In 'Local Leave', Currey recalls how:

> I went
> Around closed shops in heavy sleety rain,
> Queued uselessly for flicks, came back again
> To spend my Saturday evening on the site.

In Barsley's 'Rural Sunday':

> The flicks are shut and a volunteer hut
> Is the only building alive,
> Where a colonel's niece in a smart two-piece
> Serves cups of tea till five.

In a lengthy, jocular, versified 'Last Will and Testament', published in their discursive, idiosyncratic *Letters From Iceland* (1938), one of the great travel books of the inter-war years, W. H. Auden and Louis MacNeice make comic bequests to hundreds of prominent (and obscure) friends, strangers and enemies in contemporary Britain. Then and now, the poem demands exegesis. In a section celebrating British cinema, Auden bequeaths:

> To the Post-Office Film Unit, a film on Sex
> And to Grierson, its director, something really big
> To sell, I offer my thanks and my respects.

Jointly, Auden and MacNeice proffer these bouquets and brickbats:

> We hope one honest conviction may at last be found
> For Alexander Korda and the Balcon Boys
> And the Stavisky Scandal in pictures and sound
>
> We leave to Alfred Hitchcock with sincerest praise
> Of *Sabotage*. To Berthold Viertel just the script
> For which he's waited all his passionate days.

Everyone was knocking the Korda clan and the Balcon brothers in the 1930s: there was unquestionably an undercurrent of antisemitism in these attacks which might be reflected in the idea of Hitchcock, the Catholic Cockney, making a film about the crooked French financier Serge Stavisky. Berthold Viertel is the Austrian director of the British movie *Little Friend* (1934) that inspired Christopher Isherwood's novel *Prater Violet*. His son, Peter Viertel, had his first screen credit on Hitchcock's first thriller with an American setting, *Saboteur* (1942), and went on to become a screenwriter and novelist of some distinction.

Hitchcock makes a notable glancing appearance in Oliver Reynolds' 'Synopticon', a lengthy poem about New Testament hermeneutics, published in his 1991 collection *The Oslo Train*. Reynolds compares the possible appearance of St Mark in the Gospel that bears his name with Alfred Hitchcock's brief appearance in his own movies (the specific reference is to *The Paradine Case*):

> Is that man with a cello
> Hitchcock
> Only a glimpse
> and already the plot's
> hurried on
> The man met by the disciples
> bearing a pitcher of water
> is it Mark
> When Jesus is arrested
> he's followed by a yonge man
> in Tyndale's version
> cloothed in lynnen
> apon the bare
> is it Mark

These are, however, a few lines from an eight-page poem. There is a rather longer film reference in the final section (called 'Movie') of Ron Perelman's book-length poem *Captive Audience*, an eloquent, complex meditation on the state of America in the summer of 1987, the time of Colonel Oliver North and the Iran-Contra scandal. In 'Movie' Perelman imagines a film featuring Cary Grant, Katharine Hepburn and Jacques Derrida:

> Cary Grant was married
> to Katharine Hepburn, a woman
> who thought Derrida was an idiot
> and repulsed his obscure advances
> whenever he came on the screen.
> But behind Grant's face and its
> European-savage-tamed-by-American-
> money smile (movies elongate
> the eternal sensual present

> of all adjectives) lay a nasty mortgage
> as big and secret
> as the reversed letters in Freud's
> middle name. So Grant had to
> in fact rent Derrida a room
> in his own home, which, however,
> Derrida actually owned . . .

Two other long poems of great merit with interesting references are the 'Autumn Journals' by Louis MacNeice, who has already been cited in this introduction for his collaboration with Auden. In the fifty-page 'Autumn Journal' of 1938, his poetic chronicle written at the time of the Munich Agreement, he says:

> Sleep quietly, Marx and Freud,
> The figureheads of our transition.
> Cagney, Lombard, Bing and Garbo,
> Sleep in your world of celluloid.

Fifteen years later MacNeice devotes part of the Third Canto of his 'Autumn Sequel' to the doubts he experienced while writing a commentary for the 1953 documentary on the conquest of Everest at Beaconsfield studio, now the home of the National Film and Television School:

> A weir of whirling celluloid. What price
> Should we demand for turning what was rare
> Into a cheap couvade or proxy paradise,
> Just one more travelogue to make the groundlings stare?

There are other fine poems we've reluctantly excluded because they contain only a passing reference to the movies. Some concern personal identifications with movie stars. In his autobiographical poem, 'A Start in Life', the poet Hugo Williams recalls confronting his father, the British stage and screen star Hugh Williams, and sheepishly admitting to, and being powerfully dissuaded from, an ambition to embark on an acting career:

> Of course I wanted to be an actor. I had the golden chain
> like Alain Delon. I could lift one eyebrow.
> I didn't wear any socks.
> I came home from France
> with a brush-cut and a sketch of myself
> and my father said 'WHAT ARE YOU GOING TO DO?'
> 'I'll let it grow out', I wanted to say.

In 'A White Christmas', Duncan Forbes (represented in this anthology by 'At the Regal') sets up a familiar scenario of lovers identifying with romantic couples on the screen:

> And is it a year now
> that you and I as it were
> played out *Dr Zhivago*,
> Lara and Omar Sharif
> walking in snow on snow
> and wondering what to believe?

Likewise, numerous reflective poems inevitably touch on the cinema in recreating recent social experience. A characteristic American example is Robert Pinsky's *An Explanation of America*, a meditative, book-length 'Poem to my Daughter', published in 1979. Pinsky's references to Disney, *Deep Throat*, 'the Jews who dream up the cowboy films', the Paramount cinema, 'the Alien or Creature of the movies', 'a movie Nazi' are strands in an immensely complex web of post-war American associations. In William Scammell's shorter, simpler, but equally evocative poem of post-war British life, 'Ancient and Modern' (published in his 1984 collection *Jouissance*), the poet looks back in eleven stanzas to various key aspects of Britain in the 1950s. The sixth stanza touches on the cinema:

> and BBC announcers
> said Churchill won applors
> and Rank rebuffed Jane Russell
> with young Diana Dors

In Scammell's most recent collection, *Bleeding Heart Yard*, a long poem about the various intrusions into the Lake District from Wordsworth to the present includes a reference to Ken Russell

> brandishing his Paniflex
> at Mother Nature's teeming sex.

Likewise there are references to the cinema scattered through the poetry of Allen Ginsberg, in for instance 'A Methadrine Vision in Hollywood' and 'Hiway Poesy: LA–Albuquerque–Texas–Wichita', where passing by the Petrified Forest he is reminded of 'Leslie Howard's scratchy '30s image'. There is even a passing evocation of the movies in *Flowers and Insects*, a 1987 collection of verse by Ted Hughes celebrating the wonders of nature. The opening poem, 'Narcissi', contains these splendid lines:

The Narcissi are untouchable
In a rustling, silent film
Of speeded up dancing
And laughing children
From the 1918 Armistice.
Their tiny faces are pinched
Under big, loose bows of pale ribbon.

We have also excluded prose poems about the cinema, of which there are quite a number. This rules out Edwin Brock's autobiographical 'How I Dated Deanna Durbin', which is written partly in prose and partly in verse. Sadly it has also led us to reject a poem by Robert Crawford (represented in this anthology by 'Talkies') called 'Bond', about an octogenarian Scot taking his dog to see James Bond movies:

A man in the row behind leant forward, gave a tap on the shoulder. 'Hey, mister, is yur dug enjoyin the pitchur?' 'Aye, son, can ye no tell? He's seen all the James Bonds. He feels it's a shame it's no still Sean Connery but.'

The poems we have included have been chosen from a much larger number to provide a comprehensive rather than a definitive anthology. Some border on greatness. A few flirt with banality. In differing degrees and in different ways we like them all. And our approach to movie poems is not unlike that of George MacBeth (an Oxford contemporary and longtime BBC colleague of mine) to poems about animals as expressed in the introduction to his 1965 *Penguin Book of Animal Verse*:

All good poems about animals are about something else as well. It may be divine providence or it may be human iniquity. The important point is that these qualities should be seen *through* the nature of animals . . . The main justification of this anthology can now be clearly stated. I am on the side of those who like poems about dogs because they like dogs rather than because they like poems. Subject matter . . . has been derided too virulently and too long.

We have presented the poems in eight sections, the titles of which are self-explanatory except perhaps for the one called 'Movies as Metaphor'. By this we mean the twentieth-century inclination to look at life or interpret experience as if we were seeing it as a movie. For example, Seamus Heaney's poem about Irish language scholars rendered in terms of a movie script, or William Plomer using to nightmare effect the moviegoing phrase derived from continuous daily performance of films, 'This is where we came in'. (In Terry Southern's misanthropic comic novel of the late 1950s, *The Magic Christian*, the millionaire practical joker Guy Grand inserts offensive, near-subliminal shots into famous films like *The Best Years of Our Lives* and *Mrs Miniver* to disconcert spectators. But when they remain in the cinema to confirm what they believe they've seen, they're confronted next time around with the innocent, original Hollywood film.)

Most of the poems might well have been accommodated without too much stretching under the 'Movie as Metaphor' rubric. Equally most would fit into two or more categories. Danny Abse's 'A Night Out', for instance, could have gone into the section on 'Movie Houses and Moviegoing' or the part devoted to 'Films and Genres'. We decided on the latter because of the vivid manner in which Dr Abse evokes Andrzej Munk's film *Passenger*; it thus sits well beside Elizabeth Jennings's poem about Andrzej Wajda's *Ashes and Diamonds*.

The poems in each section are organized on a partly chronological and partly thematic basis, but in a way that seems to us to make sense rather than to conform to a rigid formula. The first section, 'The Silent Cinema', for example, begins with a poem by Austin Dobson written before the coming of the cinema about one of the numerous persistence-of-vision contraptions that led up to the motion picture. It ends with a poem by Robert Crawford, published in 1992, about the coming of sound to Hollywood. In its context as the title poem of Crawford's latest collection, 'Talkies' can be read as a metaphor for the state of Scottish culture. The poems between either relate to silent movies or were written before the coming of sound and are ordered more or less according to the appearance of the artists and films to which they refer. The section 'The Stars and the Supporting Cast' begins with some general poems, and then adopts a chronological arrangement according to when, fairly roughly, the performers imposed themselves on the public. This is followed by some poems about the work of extras, and the section concludes with verses occasioned by the deaths of stars. A similar arrangement is to be found in the section 'Behind the Camera'. The grouping of 'Films and Genres' begins with a chronological arrangement of poems about movies made since the coming of sound, the chronology again determined by when the pictures came out, not when the poems were written. It leads on to poems about Westerns, horror films, disaster flicks, documentaries, newsreel, pornography and home movies. In the 'Movie Houses and Moviegoing' section, poems on childhood experience of the pictures are put together as are poems about specific cinemas and the closing of movie houses. The section on 'Movies as Metaphor' places together poems that draw on specific movie terms, and poems that use the cinema as a way of writing autobiography. Readers can infer from the poems themselves, the acknowledgements and the authors' ages (given in the index), as to when a poem was written.

Many people have helped and encouraged us during the long gestation of this book. I would like to acknowledge Ian McIntyre, George Fischer, Fraser Steel and the late George MacBeth, all of the BBC. Ken Wlaschin would wish to mention Victor di Suervo for his encouragement of this book in the form of a Hollywood stage production of 'Poetry Goes To the Movies' and the staffs of the American and British Film Institutes for their support. Many friends and acquaintances have drawn our attention to poems we might have overlooked, among them John Baxter, Kevin Brownlow, Owen Dudley Edwards, John Gross, Deac Rossell, David Robinson and Roger Savage. At Faber and Faber, the book was initially welcomed by Andrew Motion, then, after his departure, enthusiastically superintended by Tracey Scoffield of Faber's film department, with the new poetry editor, Christopher Reid, and the cinephile Matthew Evans, Chairman of Faber and a Governor of the British Film Institute, taking a benevolent interest. We would also like to thank Alison Truefitt for her sharp-eyed copy-editing.

The most important practical assistance in the realization of this book has come from Kersti French, who corresponded with poets, publishers, agents, editors and literary executors, often having to wheel, deal, wheedle and woo in order that a limited budget could produce a large anthology in which almost everything is in copyright. She also had to involve herself in detective work to trace the sources and copyright owners of obscure poems. Anyone not properly acknowledged should contact us.

The greatest thanks, of course, must go to the poets themselves. Their enthusiasm was a constant source of inspiration. Several of them suggested poems of their own of which we were unaware, and told friends to send us their work, often with mutually happy consequences.

All the poems are published exactly as they originally appeared except for Louis Simpson's 'Why Don't You Get Transferred, Dad?', which is the free-standing centrepiece of a three-part poem. We thought of including only part of Randall Jarrell's 'The Lost World', but decided the sequence was of a piece and all set in Hollywood.

The parenthetic notes after the titles (as in the poems by Vachel

Lindsay, Percy Cudlipp and John Updike) are as they originally appeared. So too are the jocular footnotes that accompany Edmund Wilson's 'The Playwright in Paradise' and Roger McGough's 'The Filmmaker (With Sub-titles)'. At the end of each section are notes on the poems, identifying the movies, directors and stars alluded to, and providing where appropriate a cultural, historical and industrial context. (An asterisk after the poet's name indicates that the poem has a note at the end of the section.)

This book may seem surprisingly bulky to many readers. But considering the number of poems that have come our way during the latter stages of compiling it, this is merely an interim anthology of verse about the cinema, though it is the first of its kind. Someone at this moment is surely responding in verse to *Bill & Ted's Excellent Adventure* and *Wayne's World*. The phrase 'Party on, dudes' must soon figure in a movie poem. Until it does, and gets to be on a par with Eliot's 'HURRY UP PLEASE IT'S TIME' and 'It's them pills I took, to bring it off' from *The Waste Land* (or *Tom & Ez's Excellent Adventure*), we cannot yet respectably sign off with so demotic a salutation.

Philip French, London
October 1992

I

The Silent Cinema

The Toyman

With Verse, is Form the first, or Sense?
Hereon men waste their Eloquence.

'Sense (cry the one Side), Sense, of course.
How can you lend your Theme its Force?
How can you be direct and clear,
Concise, and (most of all) sincere,
If you must pen your Strain sublime
In Bonds of Measure and of Rhyme?
Who ever heard true Grief relate
Its heartfelt Woes in "six" and "eight"?
Or felt his manly Bosom swell
Beneath a French-made *Villanelle?*
How can your *Mens divinior* sing
Within the Sonnet's scanty Ring,
Where she must chant her Orphic Tale
In just so many Lines, or fail? . . .'

'Form is the first (the Others bawl);
If not, why write in Verse at all?
Why not your throbbing Thoughts expose
(If verse be such Restraint) in Prose?
For surely if you speak your Soul
Most freely where there's least Control,
It follows you must speak it best
By Rhyme (or Reason) unreprest.
Blest Hour! be not delayed too long,
When Britain frees her Slaves of Song;
And barred no more by Lack of Skill,
The Mob may crowd *Parnassus* Hill! . . .'

Just at this Point – for you must know,
All this was but the To-and-fro
Of MATT and DICK who played with Thought,
And lingered longer than they ought
(So pleasant 'tis to tap one's Box

And trifle round a Paradox!) –
There came – but I forgot to say,
'Twas in the Mall, the Month was May –
There came a Fellow where they sat,
His Elf-locks peeping through his Hat,
Who bore a Basket. Straight his Load
He set upon the Ground, and showed
His newest Toy – a Card with Strings.
On this side was a Bird with Wings,
On that, a Cage. You twirled, and lo!
The Twain were one.
                    Said MATT, 'E'en so.
Here's the Solution in a Word:–
Form is the Cage and Sense the Bird.
The Poet twirls them in his Mind,
And wins the Trick with both combined.'

Austin Dobson*

Still Life

It was believed
a sneeze set loose your soul
just as sure as a camera
could steal it.

Consider then that Tom Edison
made a movie of a man
sneezing.

We can watch him now.
The motion of that old picture
is still
the same, but strange
(as old pictures are)
over and over. He is only shades
of white or black, and to us
as to deaf Tom

[30]

years ago, the man is silent
sneeze
after sneeze after sneeze.

We watch him now
and repeatedly it is still
not clear to us
just what we've seen:
a man's loss, a camera's gain,
or in the end nothing at all.

James Hazard*

Epitaph for John Bunny, Motion-Picture Comedian

(In which he is remembered in similitude, by reference to Yorick, the king's jester,
who died when Hamlet and Ophelia were children)

Yorick is dead. Boy Hamlet walks forlorn
Beneath the battlements of Elsinore.
Where are those oddities and capers now
That used to 'set the table on a roar'?

And do his bauble-bells beyond the clouds
Ring out, and shake with mirth the planets bright?
No doubt he brings the blessed dead good cheer,
But silence broods on Elsinore tonight.

That little elf, Ophelia, eight years old,
Upon her battered doll's staunch bosom weeps.
('O best of men, that wove glad fairy-tales.')
With tear-burned face, at last the darling sleeps.

Hamlet himself could not give cheer or help,
Though firm and brave, with his boy-face controlled.
For every game they started out to play
Yorick invented in the days of old.

[31]

The times are out of joint! O cursed spite!
The noble jester Yorick comes no more.
And Hamlet hides his tears in boyish pride
By some lone turret-stair of Elsinore.

Vachel Lindsay*

To Mr Mack Sennett, on His Animated Pictures

SENNETT! Regard, I pray, our cinema –
    Its endless reels of rancid agonies,
The drear dilemmas of its formula.
    There is no laughter in Los Angeles.

CHAPLIN, arouse! Up, up, my HAROLD LLOYD!
    Ah, where is CONKLIN? MABEL NORMAND, where?
Only the coils of Technicolored FREUD
    Discharge their nonsense on the shuddering air.

Betimes a notice strikes the casual eye:
    'You'll scream, you'll yell, you'll whoop at A or B!
You'll foam and froth and faint at X and Y!'
    Let others titter. They amuse not me.

Ah, no. I'll bid old memories arise,
    Let the dead pan of LANGDON soothe my soul,
Watch TURPIN ROLL HIS INDEPENDENT EYES,
    And the flung custard seek its human goal.

Morris Bishop*

Mae Marsh, Motion Picture Actress

(In *Man's Genesis*, *The Wild Girl of the Sierras*, *The Wharf Rat*,
A Girl of the Paris Streets, etc.)

I

The arts are old, old as the stones
From which man carved the sphinx austere.
Deep are the days the old arts bring:
Ten thousand years of yesteryear.

II

She is madonna in an art
As wild and young as her sweet eyes:
A frail dew flower from this hot lamp
That is today's divine surprise.

Despite raw lights and gloating mobs
She is not seared: a picture still:
Rare silk the fine director's hand
May weave for magic if he will.

When ancient films have crumbled like
Papyrus rolls of Egypt's day,
Let the dust speak: 'Her pride was high,
All but the artist hid away:

'Kin to the myriad artist clan
Since time began, whose work is dear.'
The deep new ages come with her,
Tomorrow's years of yesteryear.

Vachel Lindsay*

Elegy on the Heroine of Childhood

in memory of Pearl White
'. . . We died in you, and offered
Sweets to the Gods . . .'

Who flung this world? What gangs proclaimed a truce,
Spinning the streets from bootlaces come loose?
What iron hoop in darkness slid
Chased by electric heels which hid
Cold faces behind pamphlets of the time?
Why was I left? What stairs had I to climb?

Four words catch hold. Dead exile, you would excite
In the red darkness, through the filtered light,
Our round, terrified eyes, when some
Demon of the rocks would come
And lock you in his house of moving walls:
You taught us first how loudly a pin falls.

From penny rows, when we began to spell,
We watched you, at the time when Arras fell,
Saw you, as in a death-ray seen,
Ride the real fear on a propped screen,
Where, through revolting brass, and darkness' bands,
Gaping, we groped with unawakened hands.

A sea-swung murmur, and a shout. Like shags
Under carved gods, with sweets in cone-shaped bags,
Tucked in to-morrow's unpaid fears,
Rucked there before the unguarded years,
We watched you, doomed, drowned, daggered, hurled from sight,
Fade from your clipped death in the tottering light.

Frantic, a blunted pattern showed you freed.
Week back to week I tread with nightmare speed,
Find the small entrance to large days,
Charging the chocolates from the trays,
Where, trailing or climbing the railing, we mobbed the dark
Of Pandemonium near Cwmdonkin Park.

Children return to mourn you. I retrace
Their steps to childhood's jealousies, a place

[34]

Of urchin hatred, shaken fists;
I drink the poison of the mists
To see you, a clear ghost before true day,
A girl, through wrestling clothes, caps flung in play.

From school's spiked railings, glass-topped, cat-walked walls,
From albums strewn, the streets' strange funerals,
We run to join the queue's coiled peel
Tapering, storming the Bastille,
Tumbling, with collars torn and scattered ties,
To thumbscrewed terror and the sea of eyes.

Night falls. The railing on which fast we pressed
Bears you, thumb-printed, to a death unguessed,
Before the time when you should rise
Venus to adolescent eyes,
A mermaid drying from your acid bath
Catching our lechery on a flying path.

Who has not seen the falling of a star?
Black liquorice made you bright before the War.
You glittered where the tongue was curled
Around the sweet fear of this world.
Doom's serial writing sprang upon the wall
Blind with a rush of light. We saw you fall.

How near, how far, how very faintly comes
Your tempest through a tambourine of crumbs,
Whose eye by darkness sanctified,
Is brilliant with my boyhood's slide.
How silently at last the reel runs back
Through your three hundred deaths, now Death wears black.

Vernon Watkins*

Ode to Felix

At that tired eye-level point where
Impulse buying starts, he
Was there in flush, banked rows in
The supermarket: Felix the Cat.

Two dozen cat-food packets, patterned
For sales appeal, repeated two
Dozen static gestures of his face who
Almost first made cartoons animate.

I remembered that black-and-white
Stroll, brought back on the t.v. screen
About twenty years after: undoubtedly
Smart for its time, the commentator said.

Yes, he had all the possibilities
Already, little early Felix. His
Famous walk was even then the quaint, quick
Cartoon swagger, his features were

The easy prototype of all
Those smirking descendants, capering
In slick, flourished lines, richer
For the primary colours, and running on

Down and down a million celluloid frames
Hand-painted in endless studio rows by
Patient, paid artists reducing everything to
That clear-cut, lucid world, while

Elsewhere other grown men sound-tracked
The basic squawk. — This way was
The world infested by your
Charming animal kingdom, Felix, having

Driven out real beasts. Numberless
American children responded to
The uncle-funny voices, actually came
To look like Mickey Mouse. In the

Demure eyes of innumerable
Homely girls and wives lived
Bambi's primal innocence. Felix,
You were first of all those lovably

Blundering and resourceless dogs and
Elephants who helped to make our
Gross and failing natures bearable.
You set off Li'l Abner, firm and strait,

Shouldering over fields with no effort, as in
Our own fulfilment dreams, you
Tamed with Snow White all our dwarfs
And witches, you helped to paint

Donald Duck on the fuselage of
The bomber for Hiroshima. If today
A man in the *Sunday Times* Colour
Supplement makes t.v. commercials

To pay to make his very own cartoon
Satirizing agencies, the credit's
Partly yours, and you can be proud to think your
Walt Disney voted for Goldwater . . .

I would not buy your food, I have no cat.
I can pass on down the stacked and shining
Aisles to other violences (the frozen red
Chops glossed in cellophane on puce, plastic trays)

But I'm not to pass without that sense, again,
Of one of my more elementary sorts of
Going mad: Your thousands of representatives,
Felix, walking into my world, writing my

Morning letters, modulating from the shapes
Of strangers outside the house, answering
My alarm calls for Fire, Police, *Ambulance*. In
That last nightmare trap and maze, they

Strut and chirp their obscene, unstoppable
Platitudes, Felix, while I run round and
Round and round to destroy their pert, joking smiles
And scream my own voice hoarse into their cute squeak.

Alan Brownjohn*

The War Films

O living pictures of the dead,
O songs without a sound,

[37]

O fellowship whose phantom tread
   Hallows a phantom ground –
How in a gleam have these revealed
   The faith we had not found.

We have sought God in a cloudy Heaven,
   We have passed by God on earth:
His seven sins and his sorrows seven,
   His wayworn mood and mirth,
Like a ragged cloak have hid from us
   The secret of his birth.

Brother of men, when now I see
   The lads go forth in line,
Thou knowest my heart is hungry in me
   As for thy bread and wine:
Thou knowest my heart is bowed in me
   To take their death for mine.

Henry Newbolt

Picture-Show

And still they come and go: and this is all I know –
That from the gloom I watch an endless picture-show,
Where wild or listless faces flicker on their way,
With glad or grievous hearts I'll never understand
Because Time spins so fast, and they've no time to stay
Beyond the moment's gesture of a lifted hand.

And still, between the shadow and the blinding flame,
The brave despair of men flings onward, ever the same
As in those doom-lit years that wait them, and have been . . .
And life is just the picture dancing on a screen.

Siegfried Sassoon

A War Film

I saw,
With a catch of the breath and the heart's uplifting,
Sorrow and pride,
The 'week's great draw' –
The Mons Retreat;
The 'Old Contemptibles' who fought, and died,
The horror and the anguish and the glory.

As in a dream,
Still hearing machine-guns rattle and shells scream,
I came out into the street.

When the day was done,
My little son
Wondered at bath-time why I kissed him so,
Naked upon my knee.
How could he know
The sudden terror that assaulted me? . . .
The body I had borne
Nine moons beneath my heart,
A part of me . . .
If, someday,
It should be taken away
To War. Tortured. Torn.
Slain.
Rotting in No Man's Land, out in the rain –
My little son . . .
Yet all those men had mothers, every one.

How should he know
Why I kissed and kissed and kissed him, crooning his name?
He thought that I was daft.
He thought it was a game,
And laughed, and laughed.

Teresa Hooley

The Vampfollowers

A Fool there was, and he paid his Coin
To a dark-eyed Dame, from the Ten-der-loin.
He took her out to a West Coast Town,
Dressed her up in a Form-fit Gown,
Filled her Eyes with Bel-la-Don-na,
And said, 'Now, Kid, for-get your Hon-na,
For, Hence-forth, you're a scar-let Scamp —
A reg-u-lar, red-lipped, black-souled Vamp.'
She signed his Con-tract, for she was Meek,
He made her Fa-mous with-in a Week;
And when I tell you his Pro-fits, you'll
A-gree that, per-haps, he wasn't a Fool.

                                    Robert E. Sherwood*

Viva Vamp, Vale Vamp

Oh for the days when vamps were vamps,
Not just a bevy of bulbous scamps.
The vintage vamp was serpentine,
Was madder music and stronger wine.
She ate her bedazzled victims whole,
Body and bank account and soul;
Yet, to lure a bishop from his crosier
She needed no pectoral exposure,
But trapped the prelate passing by
With her melting mouth and harem eye.
A gob of lipstick and mascara
Was weapon enough for Theda Bara;
Pola Negri and Lya de Putti
And sister vampires, when on duty,
Carnivorous night-blooming lilies,
They flaunted neither falsies nor realies.

Oh, whither have the vampires drifted?
All are endowed, but few are gifted.
Tape measures now select the talent
To stimulate the loutish gallant
Who has wits enough, but only just,
To stamp and whistle at a bust.
O modern vamp, I quit my seat,
Throw down my cards and call you cheat;
You could not take a trick, in fact,
Unless the deck were brazenly stacked.

Ogden Nash

To a Movie Child

Oh, little loving Movie Child,
   What woes are yours to carry!
Your mother gets a little riled
   And throws you from the ferry!
The dastard villains, scowling black,
   To show how much they hate you,
Affix you to a railroad track
   Where trains may decimate you.
Although your sentiments are pure
   As William Jennings Bryan's,
The Arab sheiks are always sure
   To feed you to the lions.

I've seen a widow, pale and wild,
   Amid the flames that burned her,
Observing, 'Fireman, save my child!'
   And lo! The fireman spurned her.
I've seen you penned inside a lair
   By some base-hearted sinner,
About the time a grizzly bear
   Was coming home to dinner.
I've seen you smiling with delight
   While busily unwrapping

A big round stick of dynamite,
   Whose fuse was brightly snapping.

And always you have worn a smile
   So tender and forgiving,
To show that you were free from guile
   And felt the joy of living.
Though scheming scoundrels plainly spoke
   The evil they intended,
You treated them like gentlefolk
   And never seemed offended.
Full many an hour you've beguiled,
   Full many a thrill I owe you;
But you're so good, dear Movie Child,
   I would not care to know you.

                    James Montague

Caligari by Dreamlight

In the willow garden the silent wraith
drifts by like a lonely blot of steam.
Eyes like cigarette burns.

Now we plunge the cruel diagonals,
the ancient town layered like an artichoke.
Shadow sleeps on the skin of light.
Always some of us are mad,
sometimes all of us are mad.
There is one of us who never wakes.

Help help I am in the black box
Mouth stuffed with deadly truth
Another me who cannot speak

Within the gnawed book the secret crawls
like a silverfish; when the Doctor grins
darkness slathers the windows.

I carry over the rooftops my white bride.
I shall lie in my coffin with folded arms.
I will not do what you say.
Put the Doctor away.

Fred Chappell*

Dream Song 222

It *was* a difficult crime to re-enact,
Fatty's; if crime it were. Was he so made
as to be dangerous?
or if she'd gone to the john beforehand might
in the middle of his love she have been all right
or was there shoved ice?

This burning to sheathe it which so many males
so often and all over suffer: why?
Is it: to make or kill
is jungle-like what constitutes my I,
so let's thrust? When both crimes lead into wails,
at once or later. Tales

told of these truths stand up like goldenglow
head-high, and around the planet men are erect
and girls lie ready:
a bounce, toward pain. Melons, they say, though,
are best – I don't know if that's correct –
as well as infertile, it's said.

John Berryman*

Chaplinesque

We make our meek adjustments,
Contented with such random consolations
As the wind deposits
In slithered and too ample pockets.

For we can still love the world, who find
A famished kitten on the step, and know
Recesses for it from the fury of the street,
Or warm torn elbow coverts.

We will sidestep, and to the final smirk
Dally the doom of that inevitable thumb
That slowly chafes its puckered index toward us,
Facing the dull squint with what innocence
And what surprise!

And yet these fine collapses are not lies
More than the pirouettes of any pliant cane;
Our obsequies are, in a way, no enterprise.
We can evade you, and all else but the heart:
What blame to us if the heart live on.

The game enforces smirks; but we have seen
The moon in lonely alleys make
A grail of laughter of an empty ash can,
And through all sound of gaiety and quest
Have heard a kitten in the wilderness.

Hart Crane*

Chaplin

The sun, a heavy spider, spins in the thirsty sky.
The wind hides under cactus leaves, in empty doorways. Only the wry

small shadow accompanies Hamlet-Petrouchka Chaplin across the plain,
the wry small sniggering shadow preceding, then in train.

[44]

The cavalcade has passed towards impossible horizons again;
but still the mask – the quick-flick fanfare of the cane remains.

The diminuendo of footsteps even is done
but there remain (Don Quixote) hat, cane, smile and sun.

Goliaths fall before the sling, but craftier ones than these
are ambushed – malice of sliding mats, revolving doors, strings in the dark
    and falling trees.

God kicks us in the pants and sets banana-skins on stairs;
and tall sombreroed centaurs win the tulip lips and aureoled hair,

while we, craned from the gallery, throw our cardboard flowers
and our feet jerk to tunes not played for ours.

                                                    A. S. J. Tessimond

Buster Keaton & the Cops

Stone Face is the likeness of all lovers.
Under a flower cart he keeps his seat,
hiding his hopes from the crowd
until some clown discovers
his hat in the cop-cluttered street.

The officers fall on their knees
in the flowers and find his hiding-place.
He remains undismayed.
He rubs his cuffs and dusts his collar.
The cops crawl up and greet him face to face.

He throws his roses in their eyes.
In retreat he duels for his life,
with daffodils he clouts their clubs.
He creeps from his cart, he tries
to lose them in the lilies which he spills.

When he impeccably plucks his hat
and races through the swirling street,
his shirt-tail hangs unfurled
and waves goodbye to his heart
and goodbye to the fragrant world.

                              George Keithley*

The Aristocrat

Buster with his pork-pie hat above
That stone face, no fist, cop's foot, not curled
Lip, no eyes like angry marbles could
Dislodge or nudge the stiff agreement of
That fragile pair, possessed of authority because,
Silent within, at once self-amusing
And self-amused, he kept the personal style
That keeps through common nonsense an iron grace.

In vaudeville with a knockabout act he bent
Body to will, objects into props,
Renewing the aristocratic tradition of
Anything for the laugh. We are a mob in darkness,
Roaring our dangerous approval at the one
Who fights us, grave of face, to keep his hat.

                              John Bricuth

Buster Keaton

Into the frenzy of falling bodies
and chaos of pastry, apollonian
and sober even as an infant,
he came, just as decades later
he would calmly step into a frame
and never leave. In the curious

oracle of his face, distant and mute
and abstracted perfect as statuary,
the lesson of his life could be seen:

Patience. Be humble. Believe in grace
and miracles of our own foolish making.
Words are mostly waste. Laughter,
like love, is a rigorous discipline.
Think slow. Act fast. Persevere.

After the sacred grove of Hollywood
has babbled, flushed, and scattered,
his image quietly endures, surviving
even when the small boat of his career
launches bottomward sudden as an anchor,
his body stubborn as a buoy or pile
fixed on the horizon, until he sinks
(soon to return, grave-faced) beneath
his flat hat floating on the water.

Or angled over some final tombstone:
the god of light, poetry, and movies
still laughs at that one, Buster.

Michael McFee

In the Days of Rin-Tin-Tin

In the days of Rin-Tin-Tin
There was no such thing as sin,
No boymade mischief worth God's wrath
And the good dog dogged the badman's path.

In the nights, the deliquescent horn of Bix
Gave presentiments of the pleasures of sex;
In the Ostrich Walk we walked by twos –
Ja-da, jing-jing, what could we lose?

The Elders mastered The Market, Mah-jongg,
Readily admitted the Victorians wrong,
While Caligari hobbled with his stick and his ghoul
And overtook the Little Fellow on his way to school.

                              Daniel Hoffman*

The Bright Reel Theatre

O Bright Reel Theatre (now The Barricade)
Where Shostakovich played for silent films,
Your programmes are as deeply buried as
The movie Freud saw in New York before
The First World War. But then what images
(Even of love I scarcely understood)
I saw myself, that in the secret dark
Made my throat ache with unshed tears, the acts
Of characters colourless and dumb as though
In dreams! And now such personages seem
Like the real named and nameless of the past.
With me will die a regiment of the dead;
Though some I'll leave. As Shostakovich said:
'We must remember, no matter how hard it is.'

                              Roy Fuller*

Naaman's Song

('Aunt Ellen')

'Go, wash thyself in Jordan – go, wash thee and be clean!'
Nay, not for any Prophet will I plunge a toe therein!
For the banks of curious Jordan are parcelled into sites,
Commanded and embellished and patrolled by Israelites.

There rise her timeless capitals of Empires daily born,
Whose plinths are laid at midnight, and whose streets are packed at morn;
And here come hired youths and maids that feign to love or sin
In tones like rusty razor-blades to tunes like smitten tin.

And here be merry murtherings, and steeds with fiery hooves;
And furious hordes with guns and swords, and clamberings over rooves;
And horrid tumblings down from Heaven, and flights with wheels and
    wings;
And always one weak virgin who is chased through all these things.

And here is mock of faith and truth, for children to behold;
And every door of ancient dirt reopened to the old;
With every word that taints the speech, and show that weakens thought;
And Israel watcheth over each, and – doth not watch for nought . . .

But Pharpar – but Abana – which Hermon launcheth down –
They perish fighting desert-sands beyond Damascus-town.
But yet their pulse is of the snows – their strength is from on high –
And, if they cannot cure my woes, a leper will I die!

Rudyard Kipling*

At a Private Showing in 1982

This loving attention to the details:
faces by Bosch and Bruegel,
the mélange of torture tools,
the carpentry of the stake,
the Catherine wheel,
the bars, spires, gibbets, pikes –
I confess my heart sank
when they brought out the second reel . . .

Anorectic Jeanne d'Arc,
how long it takes her
to burn to death in this picture!
When monks fast, it is called ascetic.
The film beamed on the dining-room wall
of an old brownstone

[49]

undergoing gentrification on Capitol Hill,
glass shards and daffodils
on alternate lawns,
harpsichord, bare board table,
cheese, nuts, jug wine,

and striding across the screen,
hauntingly young, unbowed,
not yet absurd, not yet insane,
Antonin Artaud in a bit part:
the 'good' priest,
the one who declaims
'You are persecuting a saint!'
but does not offer
to die beside her.

And how is any of this
different today,
except now in color, and talky –
this prurient close
examination of pain,
fanaticism, terror?

Though the judges dress
like World War I British
soldiers in tin helmets
and Sam Browne belts,
though the music exactly
matches the mouthed words,
though Jeanne's
enormous wounded-doe's eyes
roll up or shut down
in hope, in anguish,
though Renée Falconetti,
who plays this part, was merely
a comic-stage actress
and never shows up on celluloid again,

though Artaud
tonsured for the set
walks the streets of Paris
in costume in 1928

and is mocked by urchins
and is peppered with catcalls,
what does it profit us?

Artaud will die in the madhouse
in terror for his immortal soul,
Falconetti will drop out of sight,
an émigrée in the Argentine,
we few will finish the wine
and skulk out on this spring night
together, unsafe on Capitol Hill.

Maxine Kumin*

The Truly Great

I think continually of those who were truly great.
Who, from the womb, remembered the soul's history
Through corridors of light, where the hours are suns,
Endless and singing. Whose lovely ambition
Was that their lips, still touched with fire,
Should tell of the Spirit, clothed from head to foot in song.
And who hoarded from the Spring branches
The desires falling across their bodies like blossoms.

What is precious, is never to forget
The essential delight of the blood drawn from ageless springs
Breaking through rocks in worlds before our earth.
Never to deny its pleasure in the morning simple light
Nor its grave evening demand for love.
Never to allow gradually the traffic to smother
With noise and fog, the flowering of the spirit.

Near the snow, near the sun, in the highest fields,
See how these names are fêted by the waving grass
And by the streamers of white cloud
And whispers of wind in the listening sky.

The names of those who in their lives fought for life,
Who wore at their hearts the fire's centre.
Born of the sun, they travelled a short while toward the sun
And left the vivid air signed with their honour.

Stephen Spender*

A Song in Subtitles

The timeless shadow, infinite of reach,
Declines in time from silence into speech.

You, idol of our finite time and place,
Who spoke me, accent wholly without grace,

My common need and its specific steps,
Repeat them still, but only move your lips;

And all your motions, gauche or overtrained,
I have remembered. I have freed, restrained.

Such eloquence as they have now is mine.
It is the art these actors, grown pure line,

Attain through being mute; and their myth, you,
So much more pre-existent now, seem too;

Until the simple gesture (more is less)
Brings back the other side of consciousness;

And they and we, in silence beyond sound,
Re-enter what is there, or is not found.

Turner Cassity

Talkies

Already there is gossip in Hollywood
About something new. Even the stars will need tests.

In the beginning was the caption,
Ringlets, a balletic flow of knees;

Crowds opened their mouths, then closed them.
Now some will never be heard of again

If between camera-loving, soundless lips
Is a foreign accent, or that timbre of voice which means

The microphone doesn't like you.
Friends swell into enormous heart-throbs:

Their voices are good. 'Retraining?
Let me get you another drink.'

At the neat wrought-iron table,
Legs crossed, she stares at the studio,

A hangar, a camp, a silo. Work
Means something else now, something other

Than what she set her heart on, black and white silk, panache.
With a longer lifespan she might become

A nostalgia executive, a Last of the, a rediscovery.
But the dates are wrong; leaving her speechless

At this technology crackling over California
Eagerly, far out of sight.

Robert Crawford*

NOTES

(Bracketed numbers at the end of each note give the page number of the poem concerned.)

'The Toyman' (Dobson). The device featured in the poem is the thaumatrope, one of the numerous persistence-of-vision toys (others include the praxinoscope and the zoetrope) that preceded the cinema. The first reference cited by the OED is 1827 and the name derives from the Greek words for 'wonder' and 'turning'. (29)

'Still Life' (Hazard). Fred Ott, a mechanic in Thomas Alva Edison's workshop, and by all accounts the firm's resident jester, appeared in numerous experimental Edison films and has thus been claimed as the cinema's first actor. His most memorable appearance is in a comic sketch, a few seconds long, made in 1893 for showing on the kinetoscope, in which an office boy uses pepper to make his boss sneeze. Directed by William Kennedy Laurie Dickson in Edison's 'Black Maria' studio in New Jersey, this brief film is known variously as *Fred Ott's Sneeze* or *Monkeyshines* and features Ott in cinema's first close-up. (30)

'Epitaph for John Bunny' (Lindsay). The Brooklyn-born Bunny (1863–1915) worked in vaudeville and the theatre before entering the cinema in 1910 with Vitagraph, one of America's earliest production companies. The immensely fat performer became the first comedy star of the US cinema and appeared in over 200 films (including a version of *Pickwick Papers* shot in England). His death at the height of his fame occurred as Fatty Arbuckle and Charlie Chaplin were emerging on the movie scene. (31)

'To Mr Mack Sennett' (Bishop). The self-styled 'King of Comedy', Canadian-born Mack Sennett (1880–1960) entered movies as an actor with D. W. Griffith's company and in 1912 started his own Keystone company which was soon to move to California and become Hollywood's most prolific comedy factory. His stars at various times included most of the great comedians of the silent era – Chaplin, Harold Lloyd, Chester Conklin, Harry Langdon, Ben Turpin, the Keystone Kops – as well as such beauties as Mabel Normand and Gloria Swanson. He failed to come to terms with talking pictures and the big studio system. (32)

'Mae Marsh, Motion Picture Actress' (Lindsay). Born in New Mexico, the convent-educated Marsh (1895–1968) was spotted by D. W. Griffith when at the age of fifteen she visited her actress sister, Marguerite, on the set of one of his pictures. She subsequently became a star of his stock company. Her best-known appearances are in Griffith films as 'the Little Sister' in *Birth of a Nation* and as the wife of the workman condemned to death in the modern episode of *Intolerance*. In the sound era she became a character actress and after World War Two had small roles in four John Ford movies. (33)

'Elegy on the Heroine of Childhood' (Watkins). The Montana-born circus rider and itinerant actress Pearl White (1889–1938) became one of the earliest movie stars, appearing in adventure yarns, Westerns and, above all, cliff-hanging serials, beginning in 1914 with the epoch-making *The Perils of Pauline*. She wrote her autobiography in 1919 and retired to France in 1923. (34)

'Ode to Felix' (Brownjohn). Felix the Cat was the first important cartoon character of the American cinema. Created by the Australian-born animator Pat Sullivan (1887–1933), Felix began life in a newspaper strip before reaching the screen in 1914. Pat Sullivan Jr ran a company called Felix the Cat Creations that brought Felix to television. (35)

'The Vampfollowers' (Sherwood). Sherwood's poem, one of a series on figures in contemporary silent movies, is a parody of Kipling's 'The Vampire', the inspiration for the influential Theda Bara movie *A Fool There Was* (1915). (40)

'Caligari by Dreamlight' (Chappell). *The Cabinet of Dr Caligari* (1919) is the seminal movie of German cinematic expressionism. Directed by Robert Wiene, it made Conrad Veidt a star. The story of a sleepwalking killer controlled by a fairground owner turns out to be the dream of a madman in an asylum. (42)

'Dream Song 222' (Berryman). The great silent comedian Roscoe 'Fatty' Arbuckle (1887–1933) was at the height of his fame when in 1921 he threw an orgiastic party at a San Francisco hotel during which a starlet called Virginia Rappe died of a ruptured bladder. A censorious press, out to get at the movie industry through Arbuckle, played up various dubious details of an assault upon her by the 320-pound star involving a bottle, ice and his vast weight. Charged with manslaughter, he was acquitted at a third trial following two hung juries. His career was destroyed and the affair and its apocrypha entered the mythology of Hollywood scandal. (43)

'Chaplinesque' (Crane). By no means the first verse tribute to Charlie Chaplin (1889–1977) – on the Western Front during the Great War soldiers were singing the parodic 'The Moon Shines Bright On Charlie Chaplin' – but by general consent it is the first of real quality in English. The poem was written in 1921 shortly after Hart Crane had seen *The Kid*. (44)

'Buster Keaton & the Cops' (Keithley). Christened Joseph Francis, the son of itinerant vaudeville performers, Buster Keaton (1895–1966) was supposedly given his nickname by the escapologist Harry Houdini in recognition of the way he survived a fall downstairs as an infant in a theatrical lodging house. Alongside Chaplin and Harold Lloyd, he was one of the three greatest American comedians of the silent era. Unlike them he was careless with his rapidly acquired wealth.

Keaton's career did not survive the coming of sound, though he lived to enjoy the beginning of his rehabilitation. (45)

'In the Days of Rin Tin Tin' (Hoffman). The first great canine star, Rin Tin Tin was a German Shepherd born in Germany in 1916 and brought to America by a member of the American Expeditionary Force, Captain Lee Duncan, who found him in a trench on the Western Front. Until his death in 1932 he took the biscuit as a crucial breadwinner at Warner Brothers, their biggest attraction until the coming of sound. Writing scripts for Rin Tin Tin adventures was among the first major assignments of Darryl F. Zanuck, the future creator of 20th Century-Fox. (47)

'The Bright Reel Theatre' (Fuller). In this popular Leningrad cinema, the teenage Dmitri Shostakovich (1906–75) eked out a living in 1924 as a pianist while writing his First Symphony. He is said to have been fired for laughing too much at American comedies and forgetting to provide the accompanying music; he claimed to have resigned and sued the manager for non-payment of wages. He later wrote scores for several major films, including *The New Babylon* (1929), two parts of Donskoi's *Gorki Trilogy, Hamlet* (1964) and *King Lear* (1971). Freud saw his first movie in late August 1909 in New York on his first visit to the United States. He was accompanied by A. A. Brill, Ernest Jones and Sandor Ferenczi. According to Jones's biography it was 'one of the primitive films of those days with plenty of wild chasing. Ferenczi in his boyish way was very excited by it, but Freud was only quietly amused.' (48)

'Naaman's Song' (Kipling). Following a practice established early in the century, Rudyard Kipling wrote this powerful, obscure poem in the 1920s to accompany and comment on his discursive shaggy-dog story 'Aunt Ellen', published in 1932 in his final collection, *Limits and Renewals*. The story concerns a bizarre motor-car journey from Yorkshire to London of an unnamed narrator and his military friend, Colonel Brankes Lettcombe, OBE, 'whose mission, in peace, was the regeneration of our native cinema industry'. We learn that Lettcombe had 'returned lately from a place called Hollywood, and he told of energies unparalleled, and inventions beyond our imaginings, controlled by super-men who, having no racial prepossessions, could satisfy the "mass-appetence" of all the races who attend "Sinnymus".' Colonel Lettcombe has a grandiose scheme 'in conjunction with Hollywood' to create a British film industry to make historical and biblical epics, though he had rejected the narrator's suggestion to build 'vast studios at the top of Helvellyn; with marine annexes on the Wash and Holy Island'. This story was probably inspired by Kipling's encounter in 1926 with S. G. (later Sir Stephen) Talents, secretary to the Empire Marketing Board. Kipling pressed on Talents the desirability of producing propaganda films and recommended as producer Major Walter Creighton, who'd worked in the theatre with Sir Herbert Tree and C. B. Cochran. Creighton and Kipling developed a script that was abandoned. Subsequently Creighton studied the movie business and in 1929 he brought in John Grierson to direct *Drifters*, the first major British documentary.

It could therefore be said that Kipling played a crucial part in founding the British documentary film movement.

The poem's subject matter is the production of large-scale biblical epics in Hollywood (Kipling was invited to work in the movie industry and had visited the film colony). The Israelites are clearly both the biblical tribe and the Jewish film-makers who created Hollywood. The Old Testament Naaman of the title is the Syrian general (2 Kings, 5) who suffered from leprosy and after somewhat reluctantly seeking the advice of the Israelite enemy was advised by the prophet Elisha to bathe in the River Jordan. This led to a cure and he became a worshipper of Yahweh while retaining a formal attachment to his national temples. (48)

'At a Private Showing in 1982' (Kumin). *The Passion of Joan of Arc*, made in France in 1927 by the great Danish director Carl Theodor Dreyer (1889–1968) is one of the unimpeachable classics of world cinema. In her only film performance, the Corsican-born actress Renée Falconetti (1893–1946) attained immortality as Joan. As an attendant priest, the poet and literary theorist Antonin Artaud put on record for ever an image of himself at his most appealing and cruelly agonizing. Dreyer's gifted Polish-born cinematographer, Rudolph Maté (1898–1964) went on to become a busy Hollywood cameraman and director. (49)

'The Truly Great' (Spender). Sir Stephen Spender wrote this, probably his single most famous poem, in 1930, when he was 21. In a letter to the editors he has explained that in the first stanza he was thinking about traditional artists of genius and the souls of such artists, especially Beethoven and his late quartets. In the second stanza he moved on from spirituality to the body, celebrating the fiction of D. H. Lawrence. 'The third stanza is revolutionary,' he writes. 'The images are here drawn from black-and-white Russian movies – Eisenstein etc.'

Revisiting 'The Truly Great' in this light, we are reminded of a numinous passage in *World Within World*, Sir Stephen's 1951 autobiography. Looking back to the time he spent in Germany in the late 1920s, when Christopher Isherwood was the resident expert on Weimar society, Spender's sceptical Oxford friend W. H. Auden dropped in from the West and Isherwood's doctrinaire Cambridge Communist chum, Edward Upward, passed through on his way home from the Soviet paradise, Spender recalled:

Whenever we could, we went to see those Russian films which were shown often in Berlin at this period: *Earth*, *The General Line*, *The Mother*, *Potemkin*, *Ten Days that Shook the World*, *The Way into Life*, etc. These films, which form a curiously isolated episode in the aesthetic history of this century, excited us because they had the modernism, the poetic sensibility, the satire, the visual beauty, all those qualities we found most exciting in other forms of modern art, but they also conveyed a message of hope like an answer to *The Waste Land*. They extolled a heroic attitude which had not yet become officialized; in this they foreshadowed the defiant individualism of the Spanish Republicans. We used to go long journeys to little cinemas in the outer suburbs of Berlin, and there among the grimy tenements we saw the images of the New Life of workers building with machine tools and tractors their socially just world under the shadows of baroque statues reflected in ruffled waters of Leningrad, or against waving, shadow-pencilled plains of corn. (51)

'Talkies' (Crawford). Sound came to Hollywood in 1927, with Warner Brothers' *The Jazz Singer*. There were numerous earlier attempts to introduce the talking picture and the reigning movie moguls believed that two seemingly different arts – the subtle, silent cinema and the crude talkie – could permanently coexist. Crawford's poem reflects various anxieties of the transition. (52)

II

Hollywood

Landscape

On a mountain-side the real estate agents
Put up signs marketing the city lots to be sold there.
A man whose father and mother were Irish
Ran a goat farm half-way down the mountain;
He drove a covered wagon years ago,
Understood how to handle a rifle,
Shot grouse, buffalo, Indians, in a single year,
And now was raising goats around a shanty.
Down at the foot of the mountain
Two Japanese families had flower farms.
A man and a woman were in rows of sweet peas
Picking the pink and white flowers
To put in baskets and take to the Los Angeles market.
They were clean as what they handled
There in the morning sun, the big people and baby-faces.
Across the road high on another mountain
Stood a house saying, 'I am it', a commanding house.
There was the home of a motion picture director
Famous for lavish doll house interiors,
Clothes ransacked from the latest designs for women
In the combats of 'male against female'.
The mountain, the scenery, the layout of the landscape,
And the peace of the morning sun as it happened,
The miles of houses pocketed in the valley beyond –
It was all worth looking at, worth wondering about,
How long it might last, how young it might be.

Carl Sandburg*

The Lost World

I CHILDREN'S ARMS

On my way home I pass a cameraman
On a platform on the bumper of a car
Inside which, rolling and plunging, a comedian
Is working; on one white lot I see a star
Stumble to her igloo through the howling gale
Of the wind machines. On Melrose a dinosaur
And pterodactyl, with their immense pale
Papier-mâché smiles, look over the fence
Of *The Lost World*.

                Whispering to myself the tale
These shout – done with my schoolwork, I commence
My real life: my arsenal, my workshop
Opens, and in impotent omnipotence
I put on the helmet and the breastplate Pop
Cut out and soldered for me. Here is the shield
I sawed from beaver board and painted; here on top
The bow that only Odysseus can wield
And eleven vermilion-ringed, goose-feathered arrows.
(The twelfth was broken on the battlefield
When, searching among snap beans and potatoes,
I stepped on it.) Some dry weeds, a dead cane
Are my spears. The knife on the bureau's
My throwing-knife; the small unpainted biplane
Without wheels – that so often, helped by human hands,
Has taken off from, landed on, the counterpane –
Is my Spad.

          O dead list, that misunderstands
And laughs at and lies about the new live wild
Loves it lists! that sets upright, in the sands
Of age in which nothing grows, where all our friends are old,
A few dried leaves marked THIS IS THE GREENWOOD –
O arms that arm, for a child's wars, the child!

And yet they are good, if anything is good,
Against his enemies . . . Across the seas
At the bottom of the world, where Childhood

Sits on its desert island with Achilles
And Pitamakan, the White Blackfoot:
In the black auditorium, my heart at ease,
I watch the furred castaways (the seniors put
A play on every spring) tame their wild beasts,
Erect their tree house. Chatting over their fruit,
Their coconuts, they relish their stately feasts.
The family's servant, their magnanimous
Master now, rules them by right. Nature's priests,
They worship at Nature's altar; when with decorous
Affection the Admirable Crichton
Kisses a girl like a big Wendy, all of us
Squirm or sit up in our seats . . . Undone
When an English sail is sighted, the prisoners
Escape from their Eden to the world: the real one
Where servants are servants, masters masters,
And no one's magnanimous. The lights go on
And we go off, robbed of our fruit, our furs –
The island that the children ran is gone.

The island sang to me: *Believe! Believe!*
And didn't I know a lady with a lion?
Each evening, as the sun sank, didn't I grieve
To leave *my* tree house for reality?
There was nothing there for me to disbelieve.
At peace among my weapons, I sit in my tree
And feel: *Friday night, then Saturday, then Sunday!*

I'm dreaming of a wolf, as Mama wakes me,
And a tall girl who is – outside it's gray,
I can't remember, I jump up and dress.
We eat in the lighted kitchen. And what is play
For me, for them is habit. Happiness
Is a quiet presence, breathless and familiar:
My grandfather and I sit there in oneness
As the Sunset bus, lit by the lavender
And rose of sunrise, takes us to the dark
Echoing cavern where Pop, a worker,
Works for our living. As he rules a mark,
A short square pencil in his short square hand,
On a great sheet of copper, I make some remark

He doesn't hear. In that hard maze – in that land
That grown men live in – in the world of work,
He measures, shears, solders; and I stand
Empty-handed, watching him. I wander into the murk
The naked light bulbs pierce: the workmen, making something,
Say something to the boy in his white shirt. I jerk
As the sparks fly at me. The man hammering
as acid hisses, and the solder turns to silver,
Seems to me a dwarf hammering out the Ring
In the world under the world. The hours blur;
Bored and not bored, I bend things out of lead.
I wash my smudged hands, as my grandfather
Washes his black ones, with their gritty soap: ahead,
Past their time clock, their pay window, is the blue
And gold and white of noon. The sooty thread
Up which the laborers feel their way into
Their wives and houses, is money; the fact of life,
The secret the grown-ups share, is what to do
To make money. The husband Adam, Eve his wife
Have learned how not to have to do without
Till Santa Claus brings them their Boy Scout knife –
Nor do they find things in dreams, carry a paper route,
Sell Christmas seals . . .
                              Starting *his* Saturday, his Sunday,
Pop tells me what I love to hear about,
His boyhood in Shelbyville. I play
What he plays, hunt what he hunts, remember
What he remembers: it seems to me I could stay
In that dark forest, lit by one fading ember
Of his campfire, forever . . . But we're home.
I run in love to each familiar member
Of this little state, clustered about the Dome
Of St Nicholas – this city in which my rabbit
Depends on me, and I on everyone – this first Rome
Of childhood, so absolute in every habit
That when we hear the world our jailor say:
'Tell me, art thou a Roman?' the time we inhabit
Drops from our shoulders, and we answer: 'Yea.
I stand at Caesar's judgment seat, I appeal
Unto Caesar.'

I wash my hands, Pop gives his pay
Envelope to Mama; we sit down to our meal.
The phone rings: Mrs Mercer wonders if I'd care
To go to the library. That would be ideal,
I say when Mama lets me. I comb my hair
And find the four books I have out: *The Food
Of the Gods* was best. Liking that world where
The children eat, and grow giant and good,
I swear as I've often sworn: '*I'll* never forget
What it's like, when *I've* grown up.' A prelude
By Chopin, hammered note by note, like alphabet
Blocks, comes from next door. It's played with real feeling,
The feeling of being indoors practicing. 'And yet
It's not as if –' a gray electric, stealing
To the curb on silent wheels, has come; and I
See on the back seat (sight more appealing
Than any human sight!) my own friend Lucky,
Half wolf, half police-dog. And he can play the piano –
Play that he does, that is – and jump so high
For a ball that he turns a somersault. 'Hello,'
I say to the lady, and hug Lucky . . . In my
Talk with the world, in which it tells me what I know
And I tell it, 'I know –' how strange that I
Know nothing, and yet it tells me what I know! –
I appreciate the animals, who stand by
Purring. Or else they sit and pant. It's so –
So *agreeable*. If only people purred and panted!
So, now, Lucky and I sit in our row,
Mrs Mercer in hers. I take for granted
The tiller by which she steers, the yellow roses
In the bud vases, the whole enchanted
Drawing room of our progress. The glass encloses
As glass does, a womanish and childish
And doggish universe. We press our noses
To the glass and wish: the angel- and devilfish
Floating by on Vine, on Sunset, shut their eyes
And press their noses to their glass and wish.

II A NIGHT WITH LIONS

When I was twelve we'd visit my aunt's friend
Who owned a lion, the Metro-Goldwyn-Mayer
Lion. I'd play with him, and he'd pretend
To play with me. I was the real player
But he'd trot back and forth inside his cage
Till he got bored. I put Tawny in the prayer
I didn't believe in, not at my age,
But said still; just as I did everything in fours
And gave to Something, on the average,
One cookie out of three. And by my quartz, my ores,
My wood with the bark on it, from the Petrified
Forest, I put his dewclaw . . .
                              Now the lion roars
His slow comfortable roars; I lie beside
My young, tall, brown aunt, out there in the past
Or future, and I sleepily confide
My dream-discovery: my breath comes fast
Whenever I see someone with your skin,
Hear someone with your voice. The lion's steadfast
Roar goes on in the darkness. I have been
Asleep a while when I remember: you
Are – you, and Tawny was the lion in –
In *Tarzan*. In *Tarzan!* Just as we used to,
I talk to you, you talk to me or pretend
To talk to me as grown-up people do,
Of *Jurgen* and Rupert Hughes, till in the end
I think as a child thinks: 'You're my real friend.'

III A STREET OFF SUNSET

Sometimes as I drive by the factory
That manufactures, after so long, Vicks
VapoRub Ointment, there rises over me
A eucalyptus tree. I feel its stair-sticks
Impressed on my palms, my insteps, as I climb
To my tree house. The gray leaves make me mix
My coughing chest, anointed at bedtime,
With the smell of the sap trickling from the tan
Trunk, where the nails go in.

My lifetime
Got rid of, I sit in a dark blue sedan
Beside my great-grandmother, in Hollywood.
We pass a windmill, a pink sphinx, an Allbran
Billboard; thinking of Salâmmbo, Robin Hood,
The old prospector with his flapjack in the air,
I sit with my hands folded: I am good.

That night as I lie crossways in an armchair
Reading *Amazing Stories* (just as, long before,
I'd lie by my rich uncle's polar bear
On his domed library's reflecting floor
In the last year of the first World War, and see
A poor two-seater being attacked by four
Triplanes, on the cover of the *Literary
Digest*, and a Camel coming to its aid;
I'd feel the bear's fur warm and rough against me,
The colors of the afternoon would fade,
I'd reach into the bear's mouth and hold tight
To its front tooth and think, 'I'm not afraid')
There off Sunset, in the lamplit starlight,
A scientist is getting ready to destroy
The world. 'It's time for you to say good night,'
Mama tells me; I go on in breathless joy.
'Remember, tomorrow is a school day,'
Mama tells me; I go on in breathless joy.

At last I go to Mama in her gray
Silk, to Pop, to Dandeen in her black
Silk. I put my arms around them, they
Put their arms around me. Then I go back
To my bedroom; I read as I undress.
The scientist is ready to attack.
Mama calls, 'Is your light out?' I call back, 'Yes,'
And turn the light out. Forced out of life into
Bed, for a moment I lie comfortless
In the blank darkness; then as I always do,
I put on the earphones of the crystal set –
Each bed has its earphones – and the uneasy tissue
Of their far-off star-sound, of the blue-violet
Of space, surrounds the sweet voice from the Tabernacle

Of the Four-Square Gospel. A vague marionette,
Tall, auburn, holds her arms out, to unshackle
The bonds of sin, of sleep – as, next instant, the sun
Holds its arms out through the fig, the lemon tree,
In the back yard the clucking hens all cackle
As Mama brings their chicken feed. I see
My magazine. My magazine! Dressing for school,
I read how the good world wins its victory
Over that bad man. Books; book strap; jump the footstool
You made in Manual Training . . . Then we three
Sit down, and one says grace; and then, by rule,
By that habit that moves the stars, some coffee –
One spoonful – is poured out into my milk
And the milk, transubstantiated, is coffee.
And Mama's weekday wash-dress, Dandeen's soft black silk
Are ways that habit itself makes holy
Just as, on Sunday mornings, Wednesday nights, His will
Comes in their ways – of Church, of Prayer Meeting – to set free
The spirit from the flesh it questions.
                                                              So,
So unquestioned, my own habit moves me
To and through and from school, like a domino,
Till, home, I wake to find that I am playing
Dominoes with Dandeen. Her old face is slow
In pleasure, slow in doubt, as she sits weighing
Strategies: patient, equable, and humble,
She hears what this last child of hers is saying
In pride or bewilderment; and she will grumble
Like a child or animal when, indifferent
To the reasons of my better self, I mumble:
'I'd better stop now – the rabbit . . .'
                                                      I relent
And play her one more game. It *is* miraculous
To have a great-grandmother: I feel different
From others as, between moves, we discuss
The War Between the States. The cheerful troops
Ride up to our farmhouse, steal from us
The spoons, the horses – when their captain stoops
To Dandeen and puts Dandeen on his horse,
She cries . . . As I run by the chicken coops

[68]

With lettuce for my rabbit, real remorse
Hurts me, here, now: the little girl is crying
Because I didn't write. Because –
                                    of course,
I *was* a child, I missed them so. But justifying
Hurts too: if only I could play you one more game,
See you all one more time! I think of you dying
Forgiving me – or not, it is all the same
To the forgiven . . . My rabbit's glad to see me;
He scrambles to me, gives me little tame
Bites before he eats the lettuce. His furry
Long warm soft floppy ears, his crinkling nose
Are reassuring to a child. They guarantee,
As so much here does, that the child knows
Who takes care of him, whom he takes care of.

Mama comes out and takes in the clothes
From the clothesline. She looks with righteous love
At all of us, her spare face half a girl's.
She enters a chicken coop, and the hens shove
And flap and squawk, in fear; the whole flock whirls
Into the farthest corner. She chooses one,
Comes out, and wrings its neck. The body hurls
Itself out – lunging, reeling, it begins to run
Away from Something, to fly away from Something
In great flopping circles. Mama stands like a nun
In the center of each awful, anguished ring.
The thudding and scrambling go on, go on – then they fade,
I open my eyes, it's over . . . Could such a thing
Happen to anything? It could to a rabbit, I'm afraid;
It could to –
                'Mama, you won't kill Reddy ever,
You won't ever, will you?' The farm woman tries to persuade
The little boy, her grandson, that she'd never
Kill the boy's rabbit, never even think of it.
He would like to believe her . . . And whenever
I see her, there in that dark infinite,
Standing like Judith, with the hen's head in her hand,
I explain it away, in vain – a hypocrite,
Like all who love.

Into the blue wonderland
Of Hollywood, the sun sinks, past the eucalyptus,
The sphinx, the windmill, and I watch and read and
Hold my story tight. And when the bus
Stops at the corner and Pop – Pop! – steps down
And I run out to meet him, a blurred nimbus,
Half-red, half-gold, enchants his sober brown
Face, his stooped shoulders, into the All-Father's.
He tells me about the work he's done downtown,
We sit there on the steps. My universe
Mended almost, I tell him about the scientist. I say,
'He couldn't really, could he, Pop?' My comforter's
Eyes light up, and he laughs. 'No, that's just play,
Just make-believe,' he says. The sky is gray,
We sit there, at the end of our good day.

Randall Jarrell

Driving Around Through 1922

For King Vidor

Sundays the dead come struggling
up through old mud flows of 1922
cinematography: the eyes and bulk of Roscoe
Arbuckle resting in a can in Beverly Hills
his unreleased face stored in a dusty vault.

Houses shift to houses then to houses
(star's residence to brothel to rest home
on Adams Blvd.)
A boat and Buster Keaton go
in and out the window projected by a 1922
projector.
It is Mabel Normand's birthday.
I have the cake set out with candles
under Aspen branch with the best champagne.
I have her picture on a wall

owned by Ben Turpin
who has lost his name next to her
on the wall, crossed eye watching shadows
build beneath the piano.

It is Mabel Normand's birthday at William
Desmond Taylor's grave and on the lawn at Pickfair,
In Chaplin's Switzerland, in the bedroom
of Sam Goldwyn. I cut the cake for Bessie Love,
for Mae Marsh, Mae Murray,
for Rod La Rocque and Vilma Banky,
for the guys who murdered Wallace Reid.
I eat for them. Miss Banky speaks the names
in a faded Swedish
lace. Up the hill is Pickfair
walled in with Wallace Stevens trees;
it looks down on both sides
of the day.

Near Sunset is the place Fatty
holed up in after his victory
(one of those LA birthdaycake apartments –
white cream balconies
phony Moorish arches.)

I have a champagne on the Strip
looking down at Fatty. I order one all around:
for the whole gang: for Pola Negri and Charles Ray,
for Clara Bow and Al St John.
Here's to you and you and you.
It's Mabel Normand's birthday.

                                        Ben Pleasants*

'death is more than'

death is more than
certain a hundred these
sounds crowds odours it

is in a hurry
beyond that any this
taxi smile or angle we do

not sell and buy
things so necessary as
is death and unlike shirts
neckties trousers
we cannot wear it out

no sir which is why
granted who discovered
America ether the movies
may claim general importance

to me to you nothing is
what particularly
matters hence in a

little sunlight and less
moonlight ourselves against the worms

hate laugh shimmy

e. e. cummings

The Playwright in Paradise

A Legend of the Beverly Hills

What shining phantom folds its wings before us?
  What apparition, smiling yet remote?
Is this – so portly yet so lightly porous –
  The old friend who went West and never wrote?
That somber prince of wits, oppressed by Evil,
  Who made the rafters ring with insolent patter,
The floors quake with temblores of upheaval,
  The windows rattle to the tumbrils' clatter?
The same, but born anew and better dressed;
  He has outsoared the shadow of our night;

We cannot clasp again the hand we pressed;
   Our anxious tasks are senseless in his sight;
We cannot speak to him.

                Yet we must listen.
   'Beyond the mountains lies the sea,' he breathes,
'Where billows, blue and brineless, glide and glisten –
   And there we dance in bougainvillea wreaths,
Speeding the golden day with golden shoes;
   Or idle in an innocent collapse,
With music and the lucent orange juice,
   While avocadoes drop into our laps.
We talk of glory – who glows brightest, least;
   And tell our gains, in decimals most dear
– And yet our riches may not reach the East,
   But fade like fairy gold at the frontier.

'We know that what we make is fair and good –
   From furrowed thought and sternest effort wrung.
– And yet to you who are not of our blood,
   Our very language seems a goblin tongue;
Our passions make you sleep or make you sick;
   Our characters are cookies cut from dough;
Our cunning plots, pure theorems of technique,
   Look all alike, and work you only woe.
Blind lead to you our glazing diamond prisms:
   A perfect pratfall[1] delicately placed;
A weenie[2] won through countless cataclysms;
   A dash of glamorous French muff[3] made chaste;
All history galloped as a gallant twosome,
   Designed with daring gag[4] and dainty drehdel,[5]
With many a big take,[6] grand oh,[7] high gruesome:[8]
   A king in mufti and a cottage mädel!
To see the life of music as a crooner
   Who loves a queen of song and doubts his future,
Dismayed by Continental goona-goona,[9]
   But rescued by his native ouchimagoocha![10]
To see the principles of Truth and Right
   Embodied in Paul Muni with a beard;
The toiling masses and their touching plight,
   Paul Muni with his chin and cheekbones smeared!

'You mock our paradoxes – you are rash!
   Our blessed dogmas make us free, though fettered –
Great Communists who only work for cash;
   Great stylists spelling 'cat' for the unlettered;
These and the great directors, Titans tenser
   Than straining whippers, dreamers of bold scope –
Submissive to a medieval censor
   A Mr Breen commended by the Pope.

'– And now the supervisor calls,' he cried.
   'I must away!'

        He left us in a breath;
And that bright specter seemed to turn a dried
   Cadaver in the golden air of death.

                Edmund Wilson*

---

1 *Pratfall*: full-length cropper, theoretically on the rear. Groucho Marx and his blonde topple and crash on the dance-floor.

2 *Weenie: dénouement*. The Girl has sworn she will marry a Navy man; the Boy has been deprived of his commission for lovable insubordination. He retrieves it through an amazing feat of bravery and makes it possible for her to keep her vow.

3 *Muff*: the feminine element. An example of the achievement mentioned is the sequence in which Danielle Darrieux and Douglas Fairbanks, Jr, spend a night in a hunting lodge together without offending the Legion of Decency.

4 *Gag*: a joke, a comic device, usually acted out. The Bengal Lancer plays his flute, and a cobra comes out from under the bed and sways in rhythm to the music, thereby causing much mirth in the Mess.

5 *Drehdel* (from the German *drehen*): an unexpected twist to a plot. Edward G. Robinson instructs his henchman to give the hero some knock-out drops; but, to the surprise of the audience, the admirable young man continues to fight Robinson fiercely. The accomplice has gone over to the hero's side.

6 *Big take*: strong emotional response to a situation. The Frankenstein monster sees that his buddy has been killed and goes mad with grief and rage. He *takes it big*.

7 *Grand oh*: extreme surprise. Maurice Chevalier is kissing the French maid when his wife comes into the room. They turn around and see her.

8 *High gruesome*: hair-raising drop from a great height. Harold Lloyd falls off the roof of an office building and only saves himself by grabbing the flagpole.

9 *Goona-goona*: erotic carryings-on. Derived from a picture about the love life of the brassièreless inhabitants of Bali.

10 *Ouchimagoocha*: Spanish or Mexican love-making, with hot-blooded exclamations.

Hollywood

I am the fairy-tale, the lovely lie, the brighter-than-truth
The mirror of transformation, the face of youth
Answering the eye of age with 'I
Am You, and cloudier mirrors lie!'

I am Olympus with the last mist rolled away:
Gods-in-your-image moving in a brighter day.
Watch Venus Anadyomene: she will whitely rise
From seas of arc-lights; these are moons that were her eyes
And sun that was her hair: for this is She,
Helen and Beatrice, Laura, La Belle Dame Sans Merci!

                                          A. S. J. Tessimond

Hollywood

Farthest from any war, unique in time
Like Athens or Baghdad, this city lies
Between dry purple mountains and the sea.
The air is clear and famous, every day
Bright as a postcard, bringing bungalows
     And sights. The broad nights advertise
For love and music and astronomy.

Heart of a continent, the hearts converge
On open boulevards where palms are nursed
With flare-pots like a grove, on villa roads
Where castles cultivated like a style
Breed fabulous metaphors in foreign stone,
     And on enormous movie lots
Where history repeats its vivid blunders.

Alice and Cinderella are most real.
Here may the tourist, quite sincere at last,
Rest from his dream of travels. All is new,
No ruins claim his awe, and permanence,

Despised like customs, fails at every turn.
  Here where the eccentric thrives,
Laughter and love are leading industries.

Luck is another. Here the body-guard,
The parasite, the scholar are well paid,
The quack erects his alabaster office,
The moron and the genius are enshrined,
And the mystic makes a fortune quietly;
  Here all superlatives come true
And beauty is marketed like a basic food.

O can we understand it? Is it ours,
A crude whim of a beginning people,
A private orgy in a secluded spot?
Or alien like the word *harem*, or true
Like hideous Pittsburgh or depraved Atlanta?
  Is adolescence just as vile
As this its architecture and its talk?

Or are they parvenus, like boys and girls?
Or ours and happy, cleverest of all?
Yes. Yes. Though glamorous to the ignorant
This is the simplest city, a new school.
What is more nearly ours? If soul can mean
  The civilization of the brain,
This is a soul, a possibly proud Florence.

                                   Karl Shapiro

Movies for the Troops

I

In Hollywood the pale white stars
Slump (drunk and jeweled) in Milk Bars,
Or tour the palm-lined avenues
In gently rocking open cars.

II

The burly boys off to the wars
To die (with mention in the news)
Accept these images that fuse,
And clap their hands, and thank their stars.

William Jay Smith*

Hollywood Jabberwocky

'Twas ciros, and the cinelords
Were lollyparsing with their babes:
All goldwyns were acadawards
But demille rules the nabes.

'Beware the Jarthurank, my lad!
The lion's claw, the eagle's wing!
And when U-I his pix, be glad
That DOS dos everything!'

He took his johnston code in hand:
Long time the ranksome foe he sought —
So reste he by the schary tree,
And stood awhile in thought.

And as in quota-quotes he stood,
The Jarthurank, of happy breed,
Came boulting through the korda wood
And caroled on his reed!

For sin! For shame! On cleavaged dame
The censor shears went flicker-flack!
He scarred the Bard, and coward marred
Went gallupolling back.

'And hast though haysed the Jarthurank?
Come to my arms, my breenish boy!
O date and day! Elate! LA!'
He xenophobed with joy.

[77]

'Twas ciros, and the cinelords
Were lollyparsing with their babes:
All goldwyns were acadawards
But demille ruled the nabes.

I. A. L. Diamond*

Daffy Duck in Hollywood

Something strange is creeping across me.
La Celestina has only to warble the first few bars
Of 'I Thought about You' or something mellow from
Amadigi di Gaula for everything – a mint-condition can
Of Rumford's Baking Powder, a celluloid earring, Speedy
Gonzales, the latest from Helen Topping Miller's fertile
Escritoire, a sheaf of suggestive pix on greige, deckle-edged
Stock – to come clattering through the rainbow trellis
Where Pistachio Avenue rams the 2300 block of Highland
Fling Terrace. He promised he'd get me out of this one,
That mean old cartoonist, but just look what he's
Done to me now! I scarce dare approach me mug's attenuated
Reflection in yon hubcap, so jaundiced, so déconfit
Are its lineaments – fun, no doubt, for some quack phrenologist's
Fern-clogged waiting room, but hardly what you'd call
Companionable. But everything is getting choked to the point of
Silence. Just now a magnetic storm hung in the swatch of sky
Over the Fudds' garage, reducing it – drastically –
To the aura of a plumbago-blue log cabin on
A Gadsden Purchase commemorative cover. Suddenly all is
Loathing. I don't want to go back inside any more. You meet
Enough vague people on this emerald traffic-island – no,
Not people, comings and goings, more: mutterings, splatterings,
The bizarrely but effectively equipped infantries of happy-go-nutty
Vegetal jacqueries, plumed, pointed at the little
White cardboard castle over the mill run. 'Up
The lazy river, how happy we could be?'
How will it end? That geranium glow

[78]

Over Anaheim's had the riot act read to it by the
Etna-size firecracker that exploded last minute into
A *carte du Tendre* in whose lower right-hand corner
(Hard by the jock-itch sand-trap that skirts
The asparagus patch of algolagnic *nuits blanches*) Amadis
Is cozening the Princesse de Clèves into a midnight micturition spree
On the Tamigi with the Wallets (Walt, Blossom, and little
Skeezix) on a lamé barge 'borrowed' from Ollie
Of the Movies' dread mistress of the robes. Wait!
I have an announcement! This wide, tepidly meandering,
Civilized Lethe (one can barely make out the maypoles
And *châlets de nécessité* on its sedgy shore) leads to Tophet, that
Landfill-haunted, not-so-residential resort from which
Some travellers return! This whole moment is the groin
Of a borborygmic giant who even now
Is rolling over on us in his sleep. Farewell bocages,
Tanneries, water-meadows. The allegory comes unsnarled
Too soon; a shower of pecky acajou harpoons is
About all there is to be noted between tornadoes. I have
Only my intermittent life in your thoughts to live
Which is like thinking in another language. Everything
Depends on whether somebody reminds you of me.
That this is a fabulation, and that those 'other times'
Are in fact the silences of the soul, picked out in
Diamonds on stygian velvet, matters less than it should.
Prodigies of timing may be arranged to convince them
We live in one dimension, they in ours. While I
Abroad through all the coasts of dark destruction seek
Deliverance for us all, think in that language: its
Grammar, though tortured, offers pavilions
At each new parting of the ways. Pastel
Ambulances scoop up the quick and hie them to hospitals.
'It's all bits and pieces, spangles, patches, really; nothing
Stands alone. What happened to creative evolution?'
Sighed Aglavaine. Then to her Sélysette: 'If his
Achievement is only to end up less boring than the others,
What's keeping us here? Why not leave at once?
I have to stay here while they sit in there,
Laugh, drink, have fine time. In my day
One lay under the tough green leaves,

Pretending not to notice how they bled into
The sky's aqua, the wafted-away no-color of regions supposed
Not to concern us. And so we too
Came where the others came: nights of physical endurance,
Or if, by day, our behavior was anarchically
Correct, at least by New Brutalism standards, all then
Grew taciturn by previous agreement. We were spirited
Away *en bateau*, under cover of fudge dark.
It's not the incomplete importunes, but the spookiness
Of the finished product. True, to ask less were folly, yet
If he is the result of himself, how much the better
For him we ought to be! And how little, finally,
We take this into account! Is the puckered garance satin
Of a case that once held a brace of dueling pistols our
Only acknowledging of that color? I like not this,
Methinks, yet this disappointing sequel to ourselves
Has been applauded in London and St Petersburg. Somewhere
Ravens pray for us.'
                    The storm finished brewing. And thus
She questioned all who came in at the great gate, but none
She found who ever heard of Amadis,
Nor of stern Aureng-Zebe, his first love. Some
There were to whom this mattered not a jot: since all
By definition is completeness (so
In utter darkness they reasoned), why not
Accept it as it pleases to reveal itself? As when
Low skyscrapers from lower-hanging clouds reveal
A turret there, an art-deco escarpment here, and last perhaps
The pattern that may carry the sense, but
Stays hidden in the mysteries of pagination.
Not what we see but how we see it matters; all's
Alike, the same, and we greet him who announces
The change as we would greet the change itself.
All life is but a figment; conversely, the tiny
Tome that slips from your hand is not perhaps the
Missing link in this invisible picnic whose leverage
Shrouds our sense of it. Therefore bivouac we
On this great, blond highway, unimpeded by
Veiled scruples, worn conundrums. Morning is
Impermanent. Grab sex things, swing up

Over the horizon like a boy
On a fishing expedition. No one really knows
Or cares whether this is the whole of which parts
Were vouchsafed – once – but to be ambling on's
The tradition more than the safekeeping of it. This mulch for
Play keeps them interested and busy while the big,
Vaguer stuff can decide what it wants – what maps, what
Model cities, how much waste space. Life, our
Life anyway, is between. We don't mind
Or notice any more that the sky *is* green, a parrot
One, but have our earnest where it chances on us,
Disingenuous, intrigued, inviting more,
Always invoking the echo, a summer's day.

John Ashbery*

The Faceless One

I am Hollywood. The Movies. The Faceless One with ten thousand faces.
I am all Ages, all Bloods, all Sexes . . . I am the Three Graces.
'Three!' shrieks Glockbauer, the Producer. 'Make it Thirty!'
I am all Beauty . . . Venus, Eve, Ishtar, Kwanyin and Dirty Gertie.
I am the Great Hermaphrodite . . . Male, Female and Neuter.
I am Lover and Beloved, Romeo and Juliet, The Sought and the Suitor.
My Silver-Screen Mirror reflects the Spirit, the Flesh and the Devil.
I am Universal Water, seeking . . . and finding . . . *your* level.
I am the Tempting Mouth, the Luscious Curve, the Eloquent Eyebrow.
I speak all tongues, all idioms, the Lowbrow, Nobrow and Highbrow.
I am the Emotional Automat . . . for your dollar, dime or nickel
I dish out Caviar, Gefultefish, Hamburger . . . with or without pickle.
I am Virtue in Rags, Sin in Sequins, Love in a Bustle,
Garbo, Gable, Grable, Bergman, Crawford . . . and Jane Russell.
(Change the names with the years . . . the types are eternal.)
I am What-You-See-In-Me . . . Love, Sacred, Profane or Infernal.
I am Boy-Meets-Girl, Fata Morgana, Horatio Alger, the Happy Ending.
I am Symbol of Fur-Lined Bathtubs and Prodigal Spending.
I am Prodigal Son, the Fatted Calf, The Golden Calf, Cain and Abel.

Speaking of Calves, I'm more Leg Conscious than a Centipede or a Table.
I am Music of the Spheres, Ave Maria and the Siren's Song.
I am the Song of Bernadette . . . and She Done Him Wrong.
I am Heloise and Abelard, Frankie and Johnnie, Bill and Min,
Broken Blossoms, Birth of a Nation, What Price Glory and Elinor Glyn.
I am Over The Hill To The Poorhouse and Brewster's Millions,
I am Low-down Hoe-downs, Polkas, Kootches and Court Cotillions,
I am Vicarious Passion for Dreamers and Frustrated Females.
I am Yum-Yum, Pin-Up Girl, Pictured Itch for Sex-Hungry He-males.
I am News Reel, Time Marching On, The Candid and Candied Camera.
I am Life in the Raw, the Great Strip Tease, The Revealer and the
  Glamourer.
I think in Capital Letters, Superlatives, Super-Colossals,
I am Mother of Novelties and Reviver of Joe Miller's Fossils.
I am the Great Weep, Libido, The Belly Laugh, Snicker and Chuckle.
I am the Tragic Buffoon . . . the ghost of Fatty Arbuckle.
The Chaplin-Who-Was, Mary Pickford's Curls, Shirley Temple's
  Dimples,
Moron's Delight, Substitute for Thought, an Adolescent's Pimples.
I am a Cowboy who doesn't know which end of a Horse is
Which end of a Horse. I am an Orgy in Five Reels and Courses.
I am the Grand Chameleon, mimicking Life in Technicolor,
Merton of the Movies, Topsy and Eva, Uncle Tom, Lillith and Maud
  Muller.
I am Gloria Glamour, Harry Chest, Maurice Musclebound, Cutie Cuticle.
I am the Great Cathartic . . . Emotional, not Pharmaceutical.
I can be Joan the Woman, Mary the Mother, the Repentant Magdalene,
The Drab, the Indestructible Virgin, Empress, Burlesque Queen,
I am the Vociferous Duck, Krazy Kat, a Slap-Happy Mouse,
I am What Makes Sammy Run, A Genius, a Hero . . . a Louse.
I am the Leer, the Burning Glance, the Lips A-Tremble With Passion.
The Gay Nineties, Gone With the Wind . . . and the Last Screech of
  Fashion.
I am a Kick in the Pants, Pie in the Face, Prat Fall, the Amplified Belch.
I speak Chinese, Esquimo, English, American, Brooklynese, Okie and
  Welch.
My Featureless Face wears the Grief of Niobe, the Mask of Medusa.
I am the Goal for Youth from the Ultimate Pole to Azusa.
I am the Horror of Dracula, Sweat of Jean Valjean, Blood of a Martyr,
Zaza, Billy the Kid, Little Lord Fauntleroy, Pollyanna, A Tartar.

Aladdin's Lamp, The Magic Carpet, the Wishing Ring, the Maze of
  Mystery.
I record Today, predict Tomorrow and rewrite the Script of History.
I am Prince Charming, Hamlet as John Barrymore, I am Norma Shearer.
I am What-The-Public-Wants, I am Yourselves, seen in your Docile
  Mirror.
I am Truth, Hokum, Trash, Kindly Light. I am What-You-Wish-Me.
Intellectuals Scorn Me, People Adore Me, Columnists Dish Me.
I wear the Masks that You Fashion. Love Me. Damn Me. Flout Me.
I am Hollywood . . . Fabulous Follywood. What would you do without
  me?

Don Blanding*

This is Merely Part of the Studio Tour

On Stage Seven we are shooting an historical epic,
And today we are taking angle shots of the Four Horsemen,
Who are somewhere in the background of every scene,
Four fine old actors hired through Central Casting,
Only one has grown fat, the others are very lean.

The stars of the picture are scattered about the set:
That one with the pout is the villain, this one dies in Reel Four,
That girl is fine in portrayals of outraged honour.
No one is ever sure whom she plays, and yet at her appearance
The audience cheers, and critics heap praise upon her.

The Assistant Directors have finished their shouts of 'Quiet!'
The stand-ins have ended their work beneath the Kliegs,
Now all is ready, and this is the actual take.
Microphones hang from their booms in the best positions
To pick up the thunderous noises the horsemen make.

They are riding a treadmill through manufactured smoke.
It will, on the screen, be a terrifying prospect,
Not recommended for children. Their mothers will protest,
Saying it makes them sweat or scream from their pillows,
Or somehow disturbs their innocent, silly rest.

O, watch those four old character actors, hired
Through Central Casting, one of them fat, three lean.
They perform as though they all were quite inspired,
And yet they all have moved across the screen
For longer than I can remember. They must be very tired.

                                        Harry Brown

To the Film Industry in Crisis

Not you, lean quarterlies and swarthy periodicals
with your studious incursions toward the pomposity of ants,
nor you, experimental theatre in which Emotive Fruition
is wedding Poetic Insight perpetually, nor you,
promenading Grand Opera, obvious as an ear (though you
are close to my heart), but you, Motion Picture Industry,
it's you I love!

In time of crisis, we must all decide again and again whom we love.
And give credit where it's due: not to my starched nurse, who taught me
how to be bad and not bad rather than good (and has lately availed
herself of this information), not to the Catholic Church
which is at best an oversolemn introduction to cosmic entertainment,
not to the American Legion, which hates everybody, but to you,
glorious Silver Screen, tragic Technicolor, amorous Cinemascope,
stretching Vistavision and startling Stereophonic Sound, with all
your heavenly dimensions and reverberations and iconoclasms! To
Richard Barthelmess as the 'tol'able' boy barefoot and in pants,
Jeanette MacDonald of the flaming hair and lips and long, long neck,
Sue Carroll as she sits for eternity on the damaged fender of a car
and smiles, Ginger Rogers with her pageboy bob like a sausage
on her shuffling shoulders, peach-melba-voiced Fred Astaire of the feet,
Eric von Stroheim, the seducer of mountain-climbers' gasping spouses,
the Tarzans, each and every one of you (I cannot bring myself to prefer
Johnny Weissmuller to Lex Barker, I cannot!), Mae West in a furry sled,
her bordello radiance and bland remarks, Rudolph Valentino of the
     moon,
its crushing passions, and moonlike, too, the gentle Norma Shearer,

Miriam Hopkins dropping her champagne glass off Joel McCrea's yacht
and crying into the dappled sea, Clark Gable rescuing Gene Tierney
from Russia and Allan Jones rescuing Kitty Carlisle from Harpo Marx,
Cornel Wilde coughing blood on the piano keys while Merle Oberon
    berates,
Marilyn Monroe in her little spike heels reeling through Niagara Falls,
Joseph Cotten puzzling and Orson Welles puzzled and Dolores del Rio
eating orchids for lunch and breaking mirrors, Gloria Swanson reclining,
and Jean Harlow reclining and wiggling, and Alice Faye reclining
and wiggling and singing, Myrna Loy being calm and wise, William
    Powell
in his stunning urbanity, Elizabeth Taylor blossoming, yes, to you

and to all you others, the great, the near-great, the featured, the extras
who pass quickly and return in dreams saying your one or two lines,
my love!
Long may you illumine space with your marvellous appearances, delays
and enunciations, and may the money of the world glitteringly cover you
as you rest after a long day under the klieg lights with your faces
in packs for our edification, the way the clouds come often at night
but the heavens operate on the star system. It is a divine precedent
you perpetuate! Roll on, reels of celluloid, as the great earth rolls on!

                                                    Frank O'Hara*

The Big Sleep

    tough as Marlowe sassing Eddie Mars
    hombres flushed out of gold field
    city of renegades
            four flushers
            on the make
    'wanna be in movies?'
    'wanna buy a duck?'
    Lasky's Barn   the 20th century starting to explode
    the Pueblo's 11 families   from sleepy Sonora and Sinaloa
    of rancheros   Don Vincente Lugo and Pio Pico
    out of the Valley his brother Andres

                        [85]

Sepulveda down in San Pedro
de la Guerra out in Santa Barbara
this land spilled over
tracts back to back   Olvera St to anywhere
on top of mountains and too steep ridges
Van Nuys   Lankershim   Otis   Chandler
making bucks off the newcomers
drive out to buy a lot
'make the San Fernando Valley your home'
Oranges and sun from the Tournament of Roses
draw us west   gold in the eyes
bigger than life   on the super screen
the reality behind the set: a few studs
colored lights   and glittering cut glass baubles
'You looked good!   Awful good!   I didn't
know they made them that good any more'
This LA facade now propped and grounded
smogged   face-lifted and greying
    'What's wrong with you?'
    'Nothing you can't fix!'
What Bogie tells Bacall
We say to LA
        this 200th year of a day.

Paul Sawyer*

A Descent from San Simeon

Marion, device and balustrade
Emblazon and protect, seclude and shade;

And if the artist's shield, the builder's lime,
Alike go down before the siege of time,

We precede them – in our Packard twelves
No little of the juggernaut ourselves.

In sacrifice to my departing car
Swarm left and right the purchases we are:

[86]

Displaced sarcophagi, the forty maids,
The zebras who are equine colonnades.

Underneath your wheels, another we,
More abstract, reach the presence they will be

That have, eternal love, the empty cool
By Roman columns and the level pool;

While who desert them, sick with mortal ills,
Conclude full circle. Let these yellow hills

Consign them. You to a stammered discontent,
I to silence, then to Millicent.

Turner Cassity*

Patriotic Ode on the Fourteenth Anniversary of the Persecution of Charlie Chaplin

Come on out of there with your hands up, Chaplin,
In your Sitting Bull suit, with your amazing new Presto Lighter.
We caught you. We found your fingerprints on the World's Fair.
Give us back the money and start over as a cowboy.
Come on, Chaplin, we mean business.

Bob Kaufman*

Hollywood and Vine

Flotsam and jetsam . . .
Hollywood gets 'em.

Don Blanding

Notes for a Documentary in Search of a Sponsor

. . . A land partly Disney and partly Krafft-Ebing,
With slithy toves gimbling and mome raths outgrabing.
The junior-high nymphets, the grim Golden Agers,
The motorbike black-leather-jacket rampagers,
The surfers who spring from their boards to the airwaves
On Beatlesome discs to emit *mal de mer* waves,
The adenoid groups with their flaming hot rods,
And the addlepate dupes with their multiple gods,
The pitchmen who peddle from neon-lit rostrums
Their political, medical, spiritual nostrums,
The perennial crop of lush Aimée Semples,
The swamis, the psychics, the shrines and the temples,
The prophets in sandals who prey as they preach,
And the gilded narcissists who haunt Muscle Beach.
Then there's kind of a Klan, but in much higher brackets,
Who meet not in sheets, but pongee dinner jackets.
Kissin'-cousins are they to the genuine Klan,
Whose devotion to God leads to hatred of man.
On each dedicate heart when in conclave they sit
'*De mortuis nil nisi bonum*' is writ,
In translation which proves to their great satisfaction
That the only good Nisei is one killed in action.
They cherish the noble conquistadors' fame
And pronounce like Castilians each Spanish place name;
For tradition and status there isn't a doubt
That the Spanish are in – and the Mexicans out.
Oh, the anile John Birches, the smooth pseudo-Britons,
The tosspots, the sexpots, the purring sexkittens,
The plush poinsettia acres of acres
Of toddlers in training to be Carroll Bakers,
The moviedom moguls whose Rolls-wise luxuriance
Computer-wise proves that there's profit in prurience
As each tawdry sex-epic reveals that there's no biz,
No, no biz, by Allah, as low biz as show biz.
They bejewel the mountains from foothill to crown
With palazzos that either burn up or slide down.
On TV they expose their delusion unclad

That we all are, like Hollywood, Hollywood-mad.
With the same inside jokes they persistently plague us,
The same jocular hints about boozing and Vegas,
The same jolly feuds 'twixt the same individuals,
The same shameless plugs for each other's residuals,
So when tournament golf turns up on your screen
Only once in a while are the pros to be seen;
With the keen X-ray eye of a high-class embalmer
You must look through Phil Harris to find Arnold Palmer.
There's the thrice-married lamb and the thrice-divorced tup
Who 'neath sunlight and spotlight grow old, but not up,
And coyly elope when new urges inflate them,
Escaping from Zanuck knows who would frustrate them,
All living it up, but when they are through,
Behold Forest Lawn — they can die it up, too . . .

Ogden Nash

century city

¡shazam!
cried the prop mistress
on
the back lot at
20th
and while
phthisic set designers
took a nap
between takes
fenestrated hostess cakes
rose skywards
bordered with
alcoa wrap

now
down
the avenue of the stars
corporate studs

[89]

ride
magic reams of negotiable
paper
while
shopgirls-on-the-mall
mount a wall
of
endless charge plates
                          marking time for
happy hours
at
the century house
and
on a clear day
futuristic city planners
scan
a far horizon
for
visionary sites
already coruscating
with
triple-net
logarhithmic
projections

Mark St George*

Moguls and Monks

A dollar-green Cadillac limousine
pulls from the gate at Paramount
and turns down Melrose.
The mogul passenger leans his bald head
back on his head rest and smiles,
his face a mass of pure contentment

as two Buddhist monks bow by,
waiting at the corner for the light to change
so they can bow across Gower.
Though they don't
see each other, I am them both
as I turn up Highland, cruising
in the twelve spiritual
directions, with the
thirteen calls for cash.

But last night I met someone who was fine.

Fates, be kind.

Lewis Mac Adams

Michaelmas in Hollywood

It is Michaelmas in Hollywood
Time to get a tattoo
To visit a bookstore, if only for the readers
Un-coyly cruising between the bookshelf aisles.
My dreams are so vivid, these days,
Forks, with blood on them,
Cities carpeted in steamy clouds of dried ice fogs,
Circling LAX for a landing,
I see two race tracks,
Hollywood Park, neat and perfect, and
A sloppy oval of a track,
That must be used for practice.
I am abandoning my practice tracks,
In order to run on the best turf.
Testing my caliber
on the blue ribbon sweepstakes.
Hexagrams say decorum will be of aid
In dealing with wild, intractable people.
Winter, on Hollywood Boulevard,
Neon blending with the light of auto headlights
Shine towards the candlepowered beams,

already on the scene
Crackling on the pickup beds
Red wreaths spray-painted with silver snow.
I sit on a cinder block parking lot wall,
Waiting in line
For the flicks at Grauman's Chinese Theater
Funky new wave punks run
Combs through their rainbow hair
Tinsel has invaded the hairdressers.
Ticket   holders   line
containing   lovers   nuzzling
each   other,
Bikers, squaring their shoulders,
Fingering their tickets,
An hour long wait, filled in
With steaming, handheld burritos
Casual reading of the brass letters
On the pink stone starry sidewalk.
Names in the cracks of unknown mothers' backs.
Leading to the long sit
Alone on the velveteen seats
Watching reflections of stars.

Israel Halpern

L.A.

Lo, at its center one can find oneself
atop a paved and windy hill, with weeds
taller than men on one side and on the other
a freeway thundering a canyon's depth below.
New buildings in all mirror-styles of blankness
are being assembled by darkish people while
the tan-bricked business blocks that Harold Lloyd
teetered upon crouch low, in shade, turned slum.

The lone pedestrian stares, scooped at by space.
The palms are isolate, like psychopaths.

Conquistadorial fevers reminisce
in the adobe band of smog across the sky,
its bell of blue a promise that lured too many
to this waste of angels, of ever-widening gaps.

John Updike

Flying Down to Rio

A Ballad of Beverly Hills

Big mouth of the horn of plenty
horny   horny Hollywood
Food   flesh   fashion *cognoscenti*
grudge the midge her mite of blood

Fat bugs fry and small gnats ping
against *Insectecutor* bars
so no slight unsightly sting
blemishes the flesh of stars

Don't adjust the skew-whiff Manet
you'll touch off the thief device
monitored each nook and cranny
of this closed circuit paradise

but tonight she's feeling spooky
plucking plasmic plectra strike her
nervestrings like a bop bazouki
boogie-woogie balalaika

Divinely draped in 3rd World 'folk art'
(Locations where the labour's cheap!)
unaware she'll soon join Bogart
big C first and then big sleep

Brown tits $\frac{7}{8}$ on show'll
scotch the lies they're not her own
Death's the only gigolo 'll
rumble that they're silicone

[93]

Death   the riveting romancer
in sheerest X-ray underwear
nimble-footed fancy dancer
bonier than Fred Astaire

Girning atcha *gotcha gotcha*
(on his dance card once you're born)
cold carioca or chill cha-cha
charnelwise to Forest Lawn

Or choker sheikh whose robes hang loose
O worse than loss of honour fate!
His kisser sags from black burnous
your veils are blue barbiturate

Freeway skiddy with crashed star's gore
(fastlivingwecanshow'em!)
the jelling jugular 'll pour
at least a jeroboam . . .

Places that you once changed planes at
or hardened second units shot
this afterlife eternal flat
horizonless back lot

places   faces from your worst dream
say   starvelings of Recife
who made your slimmer's body seem
embarrassingly beefy

On such locations old at twenty
boys grub green crabs from grey mud –
big mouth of the horn of plenty
horny   horny Hollywood.

Tony Harrison

Lines Written in Dejection

The baby-faced executive
has only so much time to give

The VPs file in through the door
your current script is on the floor

a tasteful parquet, newly done
to signify the Brits have come

they ask why it's not like your last
you tell them that emotion's past

they say your forte seems to be
film noir and not filmed comedy

I thought I'd try my hand at farce
you mumble, thinking what these ass-

holes need to hear is repartee
so try a line or two to see

how it goes down and when it dies
you hit them with some other ploys

it's visual so that all the laughs
come out of what you'll photograph

the bed that falls down through the floor
that's not been seen on screen before

the bus that rises from the bog
means more than all the dialogue

a deft amalgam of what's best
in *Quiet Man* and *Ghost Goes West*

The classic form, the current theme
the surreal logic of a dream

then seeing their attention wane
you try another tack again

the gore, the blood, the sex, the crack
the fun is necrophiliac

they smile politely, not too much
promise that they'll be in touch

we'd love to work with you someday
if not on this we'll find a way

I like your suit, what's your hotel?
you hear the elevator bell

you swing your budget rent-a-car
left on Santa Monica

you crash a light, then hit a kerb
and scream a solitary verb

the bimbo in the left hand lane
screams it back at you again

your driving's bad, your script's a mess
your credit card is creditless

you're melting slowly in the haze
that typifies Los Angeles

you threaten to, if things get worse
go back to writing awful verse

you only ever said you'd come
so postcards might impress your mum

so buy one while the going's good
your loving son in Hollywood

Neil Jordan*

NOTES

'Landscape' (Sandburg). The poem was inspired by a visit that Sandburg made to Los Angeles in 1923. (61)

'Driving Around Through 1922' (Pleasants). Mabel Normand (1894–1930), a comic star at Biograph and Keystone and a Chaplin leading lady, never recovered from the bad publicity surrounding the murder (still officially unsolved) of the director William Desmond Taylor in 1922. King Vidor (1894–1982) spent some time in 1967 reinvestigating the murder but was unable to finance a film based on his discoveries. An account of Vidor's obsession can be found in *A Cast of Killers* by Sidney Kirkpatrick (1986). (70)

'The Playwight in Paradise' (Wilson). Edmund Wilson, arguably America's greatest man-of-letters of the twentieth century, was fascinated and appalled by California and Hollywood. Several of his friends and protégés had been lured away from the literary life by the movie colony, most notably his Princeton contemporary, F. Scott Fitzgerald. Wilson edited Fitzgerald's unfinished Hollywood novel *The Last Tycoon*. This poem was written as a preface to Wilson's 1941 monograph *The Boys in the Back Room*, a seminal study of West Coast writers in touch with and influenced by Hollywood, published by a small Californian press that went bust shortly after the book appeared. A revised version of the text was subsumed into Wilson's 'Literary Chronicle of the Forties', *Classics and Commercials* (1950); the poem was removed from its context and published in his collection of verse, *Wilson's Night Thoughts*. The literary critic Leslie Fiedler drew on the opening lines of Wilson's poem for his devastating essay 'What Shining Phantom: Writers and the Movies' (*Man and the Movies*, edited by W. R. Robinson, Baton Rouge, Louisiana, 1967). (72)

'Movies for the Troops' (Smith). During World War Two the movie colony put out the red carpet for servicemen passing through Los Angeles, as demonstrated in such star-studded morale-boosting productions as *Star Spangled Rhythm* (1942) and *Hollywood Canteen* (1944). William Jay Smith was there as a soldier to observe it in this contemporary poem. (76)

'Hollywood Jabberwocky' (Diamond). 'Izzy' Diamond came to Hollywood after graduating from Columbia in the 1940s to work as a screenwriter and collaborated with Billy Wilder from 1956 to 1981. His 'Hollywood Jabberwocky' was written for the professional journal *The Screenwriter* shortly after World War Two when the British miller and movie mogul J. Arthur Rank (1888–1972) was taking on Hollywood. The dominant figure in British production and exhibition, Rank briefly made inroads into the American market through his financial interest in and distribution deal with the Universal-International studio. At the same time some of his films, through the low-cut dresses worn by the heroines of Gainsborough Studio costume productions, ran into trouble with American censors and special versions were shot for US distribution. In Diamond's Lewis Carroll pastiche there are references to Ciro's (fashionable Hollywood night-club); studio heads (in *Time* parlance 'cinelords'); Hearst columnist Louella Parsons ('lollyparsing'); Sam Goldwyn; Cecil B. DeMille; suburban cinemas (called 'nabes' in *Variety*); the short-lived Eagle-Lion studio (with which Rank was associated); Universal-International (U-I); producer David O. Selznick (known as DOS); the Johnston Code of official industrial censorship (formerly the Hays Office Code, named for Will H. Hays's successor as President of the Motion Picture Association of America, Eric Johnston); Dore Schary, head of production at RKO and later MGM; Noël Coward's *This Happy Breed*; the Boulting Brothers; British movie tycoon Alexander Korda; Carol Reed; Gallup Polls; Joseph Breen (chief censor as enforcer of the Johnston Office Code). (77)

'Daffy Duck in Hollywood' (Ashbery). The wise-cracking, wise-quacking Daffy Duck, Warner Brothers' answer to Disney's web-footed Donald Duck, was created in 1937 by Tex Avery and his team of animators, and developed as a character by Bob Clampett. Whereas Disney's Donald was an exasperated middle-American type, Daffy became a rebarbative, sometimes truly malevolent figure in half a century of cartoons for the cinema and television. Daffy and Donald appeared together for the first and only time as a nightclub act in the great 1988 Robert Zemeckis film *Who Framed Roger Rabbit?* (78)

'The Faceless One' (Blanding). The references in this poem are far wider than those in Diamond's 'Jabberwocky', ranging as they do from Jean Valjean, hero of the various movie versions of *Les Misérables*, to *What Makes Sammy Run?*, Budd Schulberg's devastating novel about Hollywood. But they're less compacted and encoded. (81)

'To the Film Industry in Crisis' (O'Hara). This is the most frequently anthologized poem about the cinema by a poet peculiarly responsive to the movies, the visual arts (he worked at the Museum of Modern Art) and popular culture. The references in this poem come too thick and fast to annotate, but they are unerringly accurate, on screen and off: Erich von Stroheim, Ginger Rogers and Fred Astaire, Jeanette MacDonald, a couple of Tarzans, the Marx Brothers at the opera, Monroe in *Niagara*, the *Thin Man* movies, and so on. One might perhaps note Richard Barthelmess (1895–1963) as the handsome silent star of Griffith's *Broken Blossoms* (1919) and *Way Down East* (1920) and Henry King's *Tol'able David* (1921). His best talking role was in Howard Hawks's *Only Angels Have Wings* (1939). Sue Carol (1907–82), misspelled by O'Hara as Carroll, was the Chicago socialite, minor star and second wife (her fourth husband) of Alan Ladd. (84)

'The Big Sleep' (Sawyer). Raymond Chandler played a major role in creating a mythic Southern California and this poem conflates the historical and legendary Los Angeles and Hollywood by way of the 1945 film version of Chandler's *The Big Sleep*. 'Lasky's Barn' was Hollywood's first studio, where DeMille shot *The Squaw Man* for Famous Players–Lasky, the future Paramount company. The names in line 17 are of property developers who became the city's fabulously rich founding families. (85)

'A Descent from San Simeon' (Cassity). San Simeon was the press tycoon William Randolph Hearst's palatial mansion on the Californian coast north of Los Angeles, the model for Xanadu in Orson Welles's *Citizen Kane* (1941). It was ruled over by Hearst's longtime mistress, the movie star Marion Davies (1897–1961), noted for her attractive stammer. Hearst's estranged wife Millicent spent most of her time on the East Coast and inherited her husband's estate. (86)

'Patriotic Ode on the Fourteenth Anniversary of the Persecution of Charlie Chaplin' (Kaufman). Chaplin, the greatest movie star of all time, was the subject, or victim, of official and unofficial investigations, of moral opprobrium and unfocused professional jealousy over several decades. His refusal to become an American citizen, his rejection of the Hollywood studio system, his espousal of radical causes, his blatant sexuality, his 'premature antifascism' with *The Great Dictator*, his World War Two dedication to the opening up of a Second Front, made him a target for vindictive local pressure groups and federal agencies. Among the baseless charges were that he was a Communist and that he was a tax delinquent. In 1952 he made his final Hollywood movie, *Limelight*, and in the autumn of that year en route to the London première, he was informed in mid-Atlantic that the US attorney-general had withdrawn his residency permit and would refuse him a re-entry visa unless he submitted to special interrogation. He subsequently settled in Switzerland and made two films in Britain. In 1972 Chaplin returned to Los Angeles to receive an Honorary Academy Award. (87)

'century city' (St George). In 1961, haemorrhaging from the escalating costs of *Cleopatra*, the 20th Century-Fox company sold off a large section of their exotic backlot at Pico Boulevard and Beverly Glen Boulevard for a gigantic complex of offices, shops, apartment houses, a theatre and hotels known as Century City. This gleaming, futuristic area, all shining steel and reflecting glass, became itself a much-used location for glossy comedies and such fantasies as the 1972 *Conquest of the Planet of the Apes*. (89)

'Lines Written in Dejection' (Jordan). In the late 1980s, following his success in Britain with *Angel*, *The Company of Wolves* and *Mona Lisa*, Neil Jordan went to Los Angeles to raise money for *High Spirits* (1988), a comedy set in a haunted Irish castle featuring Peter O'Toole, several Hollywood stars and an

Irish supporting cast. It was not a box-office success. Nor was his American movie *We're No Angels* (1989). He returned to Europe and made two admirable films, *The Miracle* and *The Crying Game*. The latter was nominated for five Academy Awards and in the event brought Jordan an Oscar for the best original screenplay of 1992. (95)

III

Movie Houses and Moviegoing

Gift of a Magic Lantern to Plato

1   CRANIUM

convoluted body beneath the domed bone
the silence prickles with living light
white flashes spark between moist filaments
like the failed communication of stars
separated by hollow shadow
the lids roll open   whiteness fading to a red swirl
the stunned ache   the contraction to a jellied globe
the widening   the penetration
the wet sparks leaping to a pattern
solitary darknesses move together
to share this pain   this power   this light
hesitantly one finger is raised
to touch an alien eye in the salt of recognition

2   CAVE

Dark arch of smudged stone overhead
animal grunts and shufflings in the near blackness
stale food and foetid stains underfoot
salt smell of slick touchings   of fear   of excitement
Then the lighter dark falling
onto the wall   the brute gasp
of astonishment as the bones reassemble
the dead branch blossoms
the stone cracks to reveal the blood jelly within
The muscle cringes at the power   the encantation
of warm figures   movings across cold stone
Touch them: deception   horror   the longing
to dive into the light from which these figures fall
The brute hand paws at the flame.

3   CINEMA

Light crystallized by electricity flashes
from lenses to screen, becoming

a body, a building, a broken branch.
The hollow bones of the cranium
knit together again, more real than ever before.
The hands fly together again and again
as though to make darkness and light
solidify between them forever.

Jack W. Thomas

The Movie

The old picture plays
Lights across the screen.
Overhead, the beam
From the thoughtful booth
Flickers in a kind
Of code that only
The screen can read out.

Lights like memories
Flicker on the screen
Of your deep gazing.
My eyes and my hand
Are like some part of
The surrounding dark.

John Hollander

An Image of Leda

The cinema is cruel
like a miracle. We
sit in the darkened
room asking nothing
of the empty white

space but that it
remain pure. And
suddenly despite us
it blackens. Not by
the hand that holds
the pen. There is
no message. We our-
selves appear naked
on the river bank
spread-eagled while
the machine wings
nearer. We scream
chatter prance and
wash our hair! Is
it our prayer or
wish that this
occur? Oh what is
this light that
holds us fast? Our
limbs quicken even
to disgrace under
this white eye as
if there were real
pleasure in loving
a shadow and caress-
ing a disguise!

Frank O'Hara

Mrs Myrtle Tate, Movie Projectionist

Mrs Myrtle Tate, movie projectionist
died Wednesday in San Francisco.
  She was 66, retired.

We must remember again the absolute
excitement of the moon and think lyrically
  about her death.

It is very important for our Twentieth Century
souls because she was 'one of the few women
  who worked as a movie projectionist.'

Oh, honor this mothersisterbride
of magic lanterns with an endless waterfall of
  visions.

Richard Brautigan

Poem for a Cinema Organist

Fifteen years ago you sank
in glorious bars of purple light,
your silver hair
a landmark where
an era disappeared from sight.

Now, as unpredictably,
you surface here, inside a school,
to intercede
in sloppy tweeds
for all things bright and beautiful.

Metronomic fingers wag
around the old harmonium –
when pleasure's gone
God's antiphon
is what the prodigal becomes.

God be praised, at your first touch
usherettes tap-dance down the aisles,
improving quatrains
melt to profane
Savoy arpeggios, wicked style.

Sparkling syncopations guard
the faith you've kept while growing older –
while angels hum

the rainbow comes
to curve its colours at your shoulder.

Lawrence Sail

Newsreel

Enter the dream-house, brothers and sisters, leaving
Your debts asleep, your history at the door:
This is the home for heroes, and this loving
Darkness a fur you can afford.

Fish in their tank electrically heated
Nose without envy the glass wall: for them
Clerk, spy, nurse, killer, prince, the great and the defeated,
Move in a mute day-dream.

Bathed in this common source, you gape incurious
At what your active hours have willed –
Sleep-walking on that silver wall, the furious
Sick shapes and pregnant fancies of your world.

There is the mayor opening the oyster season:
A society wedding: the autumn hats look swell:
An old crocks' race, and a politician
In fishing-waders to prove that all is well.

Oh, look at the warplanes! Screaming hysteric treble
In the long power-dive, like gannets they fall steep.
But what are they to trouble –
These silver shadows to trouble your watery, womb-deep sleep?

See the big guns, rising, groping, erected
To plant death in your world's soft womb.
Fire-bud, smoke-blossom, iron seed projected –
Are these exotics? They will grow nearer home:

Grow nearer home – and out of the dream-house stumbling
One night into a strangling air and the flung

Rags of children and thunder of stone niagaras tumbling,
You'll know you slept too long.

                                                    C. Day Lewis

Chicks at the Flicks

An investigation into children's reactions to films, conducted for the Carnegie United Kingdom Trust by Miss Mary Field, showed that children in Camden Town 'do not bat an eyelid' at scenes of violence which distress those of Chippenham, Wilts.

With children reared at Chippenham
  The mildest plots go down,
But pictures with a zip in 'em
  Are 'musts' at Camden Town —
With sawn-off shotgun rippin' 'em
  The villain wins renown,
And films that make a nipper numb
From nervousness at Chippenham
Have not a hope of grippin' 'em
  In callous Camden Town.

With feud and frontier trouble you
  Their little minds can cram
In London's tough N.W.,
  But not in Chippenham!

Assassins, growing ranc'rous,
  Plunge daggers to their hilts.
'Hooray!' cries young St Pancras.
  'Horrific!' cries young Wilts.

From Warminster to Pewsey,
  From Salisbury to Seend,
The Wiltshire child is choosey,
  Reflective, and refeened.

His coins you can't inveigle
  With violence and crime.

It's nice Miss Anna Neagle
  Who gets him every time.

Jean Simmons is an asset,
  And Bambi packs them in,
But at Oare and Wootton Bassett
  The fledglings flinch from Flynn.

And youngsters of all sizes
  Deplore the lust to kill
At Amesbury, Devizes,
  And Longbridge Deverill.

O'Rourke – aggressive Mountie,
  Who always gets his man –
In Wiltshire's tranquil county
  Oft jars the junior fan.

The little chap will have no part
  Of pictures grim or gory,
And, with his hand upon his heart,
  Requests Love's Old Sweet Story.

In Camden Town, how flimsy
  Such fripperies appear!
Romance is out, and whimsy
  Rejected with a jeer.

For kindergarten Cockneys love
  To see the Rule of Law
Obstructed by a loaded glove
  A-socking of a jaw.

When suitor raps with pebbles
  His dear one's window pane
They raise their childish trebles
  In deafening disdain,

And stars enacting, chin to chin,
  The final close-up kiss,
Are mocked by every moppet in
  The north Metropolis.

Ye Ranks and Balcons, hearken well!
  One cinematic code

Inspires the young from Clerkenwell
   To Caledonian Road.

'Tis this: That sentiment is tosh.
   They dearly dote on blood,
The music of a well-aimed cosh,
   The sweetly sickening thud.

The bairns of Barnsbury boldly state
   They want their drama stark,
And tales of torture titillate
   The tots of Tufnell Park.

While cherub-like at Chippenham
   The children settle down
To films with ne'er a slip in 'em
   That prompts a parent's frown,
On London screens they're strippin' 'em
   Of wallet, gem and gown,
And wallopin' and whippin' 'em,
Which chills the child of Chippenham,
But hark at 'em hip-hippin' 'em –
   The kids of Camden Town!

                       Percy Cudlipp

Ave Maria

Mothers of America
            let your kids go to the movies!
get them out of the house so they won't know what you're up to
it's true that fresh air is good for the body
                      but what about the soul
that grows in darkness, embossed by silvery images
and when you grow old as grow old you must
                    they won't hate you
they won't criticize you they won't know
                  they'll be in some glamorous
                          country

they first saw on a Saturday afternoon or playing hookey
they may even be grateful to you
                                        for their first sexual experience
which only cost you a quarter
                                        and didn't upset the peaceful home
they will know where candy bars come from
                                        and gratuitous bags of
                                                                popcorn
as gratuitous as leaving the movie before it's over
with a pleasant stranger whose apartment is in the Heaven on Earth Bldg
near the Williamsburg Bridge
                                        oh mothers you will have made the little
                                                                tykes
so happy because if nobody does pick them up in the movies
they won't know the difference
                                        and if somebody does it'll be sheer gravy
and they'll have been truly entertained either way
instead of hanging around the yard
                                        or up in their room
                                                        hating you
prematurely since you won't have done anything horribly mean yet
except keeping them from the darker joys
                                        it's unforgivable the latter
so don't blame me if you won't take this advice
                                        and the family breaks up
and your children grow old and blind in front of a TV set
                                                        seeing

movies you wouldn't let them see when they were young

                                                        Frank O'Hara

A Grand Night

When the Film *Tell England* came
To Leamington, my father said,
'That's about Gallipoli – I was there.
I'll call and see the manager . . .'

[111]

Before the first showing, the manager
Announced that 'a local resident . . .' etc.
And there was my father on the stage
With a message to the troops from Sir Somebody
Exhorting, condoling or congratulating.
But he was shy, so the manager
Read it out, while he fidgeted.
Then the lights went off, and I thought
I'd lost my father.
The Expedition's casualty rate was 50%.

But it was a grand night,
With free tickets for the two of us.

D. J. Enright*

Continuous

James Cagney was the one up both our streets.
His was the only art we ever shared.
A gangster film and choc ice were the treats
that showed about as much love as he dared.

He'd be my own age now in '49!
The hand that glinted with the ring he wore,
his father's, tipped the cold bar into mine
just as the organist dropped through the floor.

He's on the platform lowered out of sight
to organ music, this time on looped tape,
into a furnace with a blinding light
where only his father's ring will keep its shape.

I wear it now to Cagneys on my own
and sense my father's hands cupped round my treat –

they feel as though they've been chilled to the bone
from holding my ice cream all through *White Heat*.

Tony Harrison*

What You Have Come to Expect

The worn plush of the seat chafes your bare legs
as you shiver in the air-conditioned dark
watching a man embrace his wife at the edge
of their shadowy lawn. It is just past dusk
and behind them their house rises white and
symmetrical. Candles burn in each window,
while from the open door a blade of light jabs
down the gravel path to a fountain. In the doorway
wait two children dressed for sleep in white gowns.
The man touches his wife's cheek. Although
he must leave, he is frightened for her safety and
the safety of their children. At last he hurries
to where two horses stamp and whinny in harness.
Then, from your seat in the third row, you follow him
through battles and bloodshed and friends lost
until finally he returns home, rides up the lane
as dusk falls to discover all that remains of his house
is a single chimney rising from ashes and mounds of debris.
Where is his young wife? He stares out across
empty fields, the wreckage of stables and barns.
Where are the children who were the comfort of his life?

In a few minutes, you plunge into the brilliant light
of the afternoon sun. Across the street, you see your bike
propped against a wall with your dog waiting beside it.
The dog is so excited to see you she keeps leaping up,
licking your face, while you, still full of the movie,
full of its colors and music and lives sacrificed to some
heroic purpose, try to tell her about this unutterable
sadness you feel on a Saturday afternoon in July, 1950.
Bicycling home, you keep questioning what happened
to the children, what happened to their father standing
by the burned wreckage of his house, and you wish
there were someone to explain this problem to, someone
to help you understand this sense of bereavement and loss:
you, who are too young even to regret the passage of time.
Next year your favorite aunt will die, then your

grandparents, one by one, then even your cousins.
You sit on the seat of your green bike with balloon tires
and watch your dog waiting up the street, a Bayeux
tapestry dog, brindle with thin legs and a greyhound chest –
a dog now no more than a speck of ash in the Michigan dirt.
From a distance of thirty years, you see yourself paused
at the intersection, a thin blond boy in khaki shorts;
see yourself push off into the afternoon sunlight,
clumsily entering your future the way a child urged on
by its frightened nurse might stumble into a plowed field
in the dead of night, half running, half pulled along.
Behind them: gunshots, flame, and the crack of burning wood.
Far ahead: a black line of winter trees.

Now, after thirty years, the trees have come closer.
Glancing around you, you discover you are alone;
raising your hands to your face and beard, you find
you are no longer young, while the only fires
are in the fleck of stars above you, the only face
is the crude outline of the moon's – distant, as any family
you might have had; cold, in a way you have come to expect.

Stephen Dobyns

The Pictures

Threepence on Saturday afternoons,
A bench along the side of the hall –
We looked like Egyptian paintings,
But less composed.

Sometimes a film that frightened us
And returned at nights.
Once *Noah's Ark*, an early talkie
We took for non-fiction.

Cheapest was the home kino.
Lying in bed, you pressed on your eyes,
Strange happenings ensued.

But the story was hard to follow
And your eyeballs might fall in.
Fatigued, you fell asleep.

                D. J. Enright*

Autobiographical Note

Beeston, the place, near Nottingham:
We lived there for three years or so.
Each Saturday at two o'clock
We queued up for the matinée,
All the kids for streets around
With snotty noses, giant caps,
Cut down coats and heavy boots,
The natural enemies of cops
And schoolteachers. Profane and hoarse
We scrambled, yelled and fought until
The Picture Palace opened up
And we, like Hamelin children, forced
Our bony way into the hall.
That much is easy to recall;
Also the reek of chewing-gum,
Gob-stoppers and liquorice,
But of the flickering myths themselves
Not much remains. The hero was
A milky wide-brimmed hat, a shape
Astride the arched white stallion;
The villain's horse and hat were black.
Disbelief did not exist
And laundered virtue always won
With quicker gun and harder fist,
And all of us applauded it.
Yet I remember moments when
In solitude I'd find myself
Brooding on the sooty man,
The bristling villain, who could move
Imagination in a way

The well-shaved hero never could,
And even warm the nervous heart
With something oddly close to love.

Vernon Scannell

Rosedale Theatre, 1938

Feet on the parapet of the balcony,
We cup free sacks of penny candy, gum,
And unshelled peanuts, all included in
Our dime admission to the Saturday
Kids' matinée, and see the *Bounty* heave
And creak in every block and halyard. Waves
Of raw sensation break upon each white
Face that reflects the action, and our ears
Eavesdrop upon the commerce of a more
Real world than ours. The first big feature ends;
We trade reactions and gumballs with friends
Above the marching feet of Movietone,
Which now give way to a twin-engine plane
That lands as we half watch, and Chamberlain
Steps out, in his teeth, Homburg, and mustache,
A figure of some fun. We laugh and miss
His little speech. After the Michigan–
Ohio game, Buck Rogers will come on.

L. E. Sissman

Dream Song 7

The Prisoner of Shark Island with Paul Muni

Henry is old, old; for Henry remembers
Mr Deeds' tuba, & the Cameo,
& the race in *Ben Hur*, – *The Lost World*, with sound,

[116]

& *The Man from Blankley's*, which he did not dig,
nor did he understand one caption of,
bewildered Henry, while the Big Ones laughed.

Now Henry is unmistakably a Big One.
Fúnnee; he don't féel so.
He just stuck around.
The German & the Russian films into
Italian & Japanese films turned, while many
were prevented from making it.

He wishing he could squirm again where Hoot
is just ahead of rustlers, where William S
forgoes some deep advantage, & moves on,
where Hashknife Hartley having the matter taped
the rats are flying. For the rats
have moved in, mostly, and this is for real.

John Berryman*

Midweek Matinée

The lunch hour ends and men go back to work,
Plumbers with long bags, whistling office boys
With soup on their ties and pee on their shoes,
Typists with a sandwich and a warm coke.

The indolent or lucky are going to the cinema.
There too go the itinerant heavy drinkers,
Who take the piss out of bus conductors
Or fall asleep in public reading rooms

Over unlikely learned periodicals.
They come in late, just after closing time,
And sprawl in the cheap front seats
Dressed in the raincoats of a thousand wet nights,

Muttering with the lips of the unknown kisses.
Legendary, undeserving drunks, beggarly

And good for pity or laughter, you show
What happens to men who are not good at life,

Where happiness is demanded and lives are lived
For entertainment. I watch you sleep,
Grey humps in an empty cinema. You're dangerous.
All wish you were not there, cramping the style.

You are very bad, you are worse than civilized,
Untouched by seriousness or possessions,
Treading the taxpayers' roads, being found
Incapable in public places, always hungry,

Totally unlike what people should be – washed,
Happy, occupied, idle only in snatches
Of paid-for amusement or cynical truancies.
You have cut yourself off from barbers and supermarkets.

I don't want you here on my page, pink faces
Under spit and stubble, as fools or martyrs.
You are not new, you have nothing to sell.
You are walking evictions. You have no rentbooks.

You never answer telephones or give parties.
If you have a sense of humour, I want to know.
You claim the right to be miserable
And I can't stand what you bring out into the open.

Douglas Dunn

A Matinée

The shops, the banks, the bars are shut.
The square smells like a cinema,
All breath and chocolate and sweat.

The islands' washed-out distance
Means the fifties' rotten movies
Where I learned how to be bored

With love and money on location,
Postcard Europes, plots I couldn't grasp.
The starlets in their wide white skirts

Were always speeding on the cliffs
Or flinging into rooms to weep
At letters or the lack of them,

While stationed in the cypresses
Their leading men would smoke and stare
At nightfall, as the orchestra

Cranked up its fatuous claims
That the issue was passion,
Which seemed even worse than the adverts.

The stylists of never and nowhere
With nothing to do but rehearse
To the vacant plush darkness

And me with my headache and choc-ice.
Tedious wealth, I sympathised.
So when today I'm dull enough

To be Rossano Brazzi, let me sing,
Desert you, loom in archways, ask
About the past or unctuously show you

How the fishermen eat fish, then pose
Beside the ocean, signifying grief.
White girls in white skirts

With invisible legs and no sex,
Sealed in your villas being old,
Since all that I can manage is

To run those afternoons again,
I've left my number at the desk:
What better offers are there now?

Sean O'Brien*

The Weepies

Most Saturday afternoons
At the local Hippodrome
Saw the Pathe-News rooster,
Then the recurring dream

Of a lonesome drifter
Through uninterrupted range.
Will Hunter, so gifted
He could peel an orange

In a single, fluent gesture,
Was the leader of our gang.
The curtain rose this afternoon
On a lion, not a gong.

When the crippled girl
Who wanted to be a dancer
Met the married man
Who was dying of cancer,

Our hankies unfurled
Like flags of surrender.
I believe something fell asunder
In even Will Hunter's hands.

Paul Muldoon

Double Feature

My mum was holding up a Pyrex pie-dish
(lined with plump apple lumps) in her left hand,
flopping the pastry lid on with her right,
trimming the droopy overlaps and jabbing
steam-vents. She wiped a floured hand on her apron
and tuned the wireless — what Roy Fuller calls
'Some inexplicable, imperial,

Elgarian sadness' filled the scullery:
His Majesty, King George VI, is dead.

The following year we single-filed from school
down to the flicks to see a double feature
(stark Everest with Tenzing on its top
and the Queen crowned). The Regal, I recall,
was gaudy, faded, had seen better days.

                                        Peter Reading*

At the Regal

Is there nothing better to do
On a Monday afternoon
Than watch a film about caribou
Waiting for the western to come on?
I munch sweets in the stalls and think
This is the worst film I have ever seen
As the caribou migrate across
Acres of tundra on the screen,
Cold tired and cadaverous
And as near as makes no odds extinct.

In preference to junk like that
Give me the cowboy any day –
Living where he hangs his goddam hat
and playing poker for his pay –
Yup, he could make me a brand new man
If he just complied with three small ifs:
1) if he had acne on his chin,
2) he were a part-time pacifist
And 3) he once had to ask the heroine
'Say honey, sorry, where's the can?'

That's the sort of thing I want,
Loads of authenticity:
Viz. the couple courting hard in front
Whose stifled brute activity

Excites me more than every horde
Of Hollywood Apache braves
Repelled by the US Cavalry.
Those lovers can at least paraphrase
Both my lust and jealousy,
And they aren't either hired or bored.

Duncan Forbes

Come Home from the Movies

Come home from the movies,
Black girls and boys,
the picture be over and the screen
be cold as our neighborhood.
Come home from the show,
don't be the show.
Take off some flowers and plant them,
pick us some papers and read them,
stop making some babies and raise them.
Come home from the movies
Black girls and boys,
show our fathers how to walk like men,
they already know how to dance.

Lucille Clifton

A Film Review in the Form of a Poem

'Drive your cart and your plow over the bones of the dead.'
A wise ruthless proverb, but no match for nostalgia.
On Hollywood Boulevard bones never stop our progress;
we congregate over star-shaped names of shadows
summoned at the revival house, NuArt or Encore.
And at the Chinese Theatre hands inset into cement

[122]

still abide the reverent claspings of pilgrims.
Even a reviewer on routine assignment can be moved
with a seizure of piety for immoderate glamor,
the *elixir vitae* of every filmgoer's days.
Who in this place would call me mad if I sought out
Merle Oberon and easing my palms into hers felt a grasp
like Cathy Earnshaw's cold grip of a more passionate world?

As a child I loved the hand-hammered gold leaf
and hand-woven carpet of the Chinese Theatre,
prayed like the thief of Baghdad that by miracle
I could vault toward Asia to beard Fu Manchu.
And yet *be* Fu Manchu also, Jewish yellow peril,
mastermind, ultimate power of the universe, *Superman!*
How that red-caped muscular titan usurped my God!
My lips intoned the manna-like prose of comic books,
syntax of a city boy for whom *The Daily Planet*
glowed with unsullied virtue like the American past.
And here I am, Clark Kent with no redeeming underwear,
Narcissus in horn-rims, revisitant of oriental camp.
O reader, I was born to review this preposterous film!

What is *Superman* about? One subject only,
the desire to rise into the air by human strength.
Star Wars confused this with hot rods in space,
an impure mixture never my own archaic dream.
Like one of those boys commanded by a Renaissance prince
to flap weighted arms hour after hour, year after year
until his pectoral muscles hardened and he could fly,
I waited for the irresistible impulse to break free,
by downstrokes soar to a rarefied place, and hover.
So I understood Lois Lane's ecstasy in this movie's best scene
when the comic-strip struts of plot were pulled away
and she became airborne on the support of a superhuman arm,
to *be* in flight the secret she had wanted as mere news.
What is cinema for if not to suspend us in such hope?

And plummet downward in horrifying fall!
The wit of Lois's rescue prompted applause,
not so that other violation of common sense,
the lewd farce of Superman's near-fatal drowning.

Kryptonite is no laughing matter, is the gravity
of human nature, green danger of origins, inescapable.
Think how much better *The Man Who Fell to Earth*
expressed the star-orphan's bondage to his doomed nest.
Krypton is a prophetic planet, its annihilation
in spite of Jor-El's eloquence and craft
a figure – who can doubt it? – of our decease.
Uranium-like gem, kryptonite is no simple
Achilles heel of the otherwise perfect Paul Bunyan
but implacable history, in motion every frame of film.

(Cleveland boys with big dreams, nineteen years old,
what blowup did Jerry Siegel and Joe Shuster foresee?
Every moment I sense your presence in this metropolis,
blind Joe unable to watch your boy outrace a train,
Jerry with a heart crippled by the syndicate's greed.
I who write this ephemeral review, hunting and pecking,
know the fatality of art, the descent into Grub Street.
How much more bitterly the makers of Superman's first words
who bartered bird-selves for $130, then plunged to the depths.)

But I digress. 'Back to the movie,' I hear you say.
Reader, so many themes distract me from my task.
The obliteration of Krypton is a pretty flash of light
and you will enjoy the incandescent moment when
our hero prevents catastrophe along the San Andreas fault
which threatens Hollywood itself with untimely ruin.
And you get the happy ending you desire.
Yes, it's only a movie. You'll forgive me
if I have been unnerved by the dissolution of limits
even in movies, the change of matter into terrifying force.
Earthquakes, fire, flood, ravages of apocalypse;
humans dismembered in slow, *slow* motion;
psychos plunge their knives, fountains of gore
pool in small minds like madness from stroke.
Why do people see such films? I have no choice.

Homo filmex, endangered by species who act their desire,
take heart from this messianic man of celluloid.
Such movies are Kryptonite which we embrace,
dandies of the post-industrial era,

that we may never grow old in one mirror at least,
never lose power so long as remake and sequel beckon.
A wonderful movie. When I emerged from the Chinese
sunlight spangled the inlaid names of the Boulevard.
I testify here I felt at home with the laws of nature,
reconciled to my addiction, my occupation, and my fate.

Laurence Goldstein*

Double Feature

With Buck still tied to the log, on comes the light.
Lovers disengage, move sheepishly toward the aisle
With mothers, sleep-heavy children, stale perfume, past
   the manager's smile
Out through the velvety chains to the cool air of night.

I dawdle with groups near the rickety pop-corn stand;
Dally at shop windows, still reluctant to go;
I teeter, heels hooked on the curb, scrape a toe;
Or send off a car with vague lifts of a hand.

A wave of Time hangs motionless on this particular shore.
I notice a tree, arsenical grey in the light, or the slow
Wheel of the stars, the Great Bear glittering colder than snow,
And remember there was something else I was hoping for.

Theodore Roethke

Nostalgia

In the dumbest movie they can play it on us with a sunrise and a passage of
   adagio Vivaldi –
all the reason more to love it and to loathe it, this always barely choked-
   back luscious flood,
this turbulence in breast and breath that indicates a purity residing
   somewhere in us,

[125]

redeeming with its easy access the thousand lapses of memory shed in the
    most innocuous day
and canceling our rue for all the greater consciousness we didn't have for
    past, lost presents.
Its illusion is that we'll retain this new, however hammy past more
    thoroughly than all before,
its reality, that though we know by heart its shabby ruses, know we'll mis-
    place it yet again,
it's what we have, a stage light flickering to flood, chintz and gaud, and we
    don't care.

C. K. Williams

Movie

While you arrange yourself and set your eyes
Like spectacles upon your nose,
Out of the cool contented dark the long
Aeolian gales of music rise
And finger at your nerves; the data flows
Evenly upward with the names of hands,
The dress designer, master of decor,
Historian and lyric writer, bands,
The cast, the great Director. Then no more.

The silence mediates the pause, then flings
The window of your interest
Wide open on the street. Lean out and look,
He's coming! he's the guy who brings
That book to life exactly as you guessed;
Goodlooking too, all over kisses, clean,
And knows how to behave; he'll never die;
They'll save him for the close-up closing scene;
We want it that way; all of us know why.

A woman sits beside you, so intent
You'd think she was a breathless child;
Your knee is touching hers, light as a nod;
She'll wonder later what it meant

Because she didn't mind; it was a mild
Impersonal pressure, curiously polite,
Dim as the Exit sign upon the wall.
Outside she wouldn't even glance goodnight –
Perhaps you haven't touched her after all.

But up there she has cast her simple spell:
Sweet mouth, sweet eyes, sweet angry hair,
Chiaroscuro flawless as the moon,
Round as the face of Raphael.
O blend of mortal instinct, if we stare,
Let us; we tell you secrets that we dream
Of you, Astarte! (for we know your past).
But now in the dark be only what you seem,
Sugar us with your kisses while you last.

The world swallows your pill, quack that it is,
And loves it. Yes, it works a cure,
It makes us turn our heads, like smelling salts;
We think, *We'll go slow after this.*
It was terrific: or perhaps more sure
Of what's unreal, Inside or Out, we sight
A skirt, and with an intimating cough
Follow it down the street; or else we light
A cigarette, and start to walk it off.

Karl Shapiro

Mrs Fanchier at the Movies

If I could reply, but once, to these many new and kindly companions I
  have found
(Now that so many of the old are gone, so far and for so long)
Overhearing them on the radio or the phonograph, or here in the motion
  pictures, as now –

These electrical voices, so sure in the sympathy they extend,
Offering it richly through the long hours of the day and the longer hours
  of the night

[127]

(Closer at hand, and although automatic, somehow more understanding
  than a live friend)
Speaking sometimes to each other, but often straight at me —

Wishing I could reply, if only once,
Add somehow to the final burst of triumphant music, or even in
  tragedy mingle with the promise of the fading clouds —

But wondering, too, what it really was I at one time felt so deeply for,
The actual voice, or this muted thunder? These giant shadows, or
  the naked face?
Or something within the voice and behind the face? —

And wondering whether, now, I would have the courage to reply, in fact,
Or any longer know the words, or even find the voice.

Kenneth Fearing

Cinema

Men with gaping mouths
& dazzled women shuffle
in the queue outside
the pocket atlas store

A black car
circles the block
the driver counts the laps
with horn-blasts
97 . . . 98 . . . 99 . . .

Beside each other
in the cinema
they cast their hooks
at the screen
their lines do not tangle

That inch between their elbows
is the grand canyon

Aidan Murphy

Far West

Among the cigarettes and the peppermint creams
Came the flowers of fingers, luxurious and bland,
Incredibly blossoming in the little breast.
And in the Far West.
The tremendous cowboys in goatskin pants
Shot up the town of her ignorant wish.

In the gun flash she saw the long light shake
Across the lake, repeating that poem
At Finsbury Park.
But the echo was drowned in the roll of the trams –
Anyway, who would have heard? Not a soul!
Not one noble and toxic like Buffalo Bill.

In the holy name *bang! bang!* the flower came
With the marvellous touch of fingers
Gentler than the fuzzy goats
Moving up and down up and down as if in ecstasy
As the cowboys rode their girl-sleek horses
Over the barbarous hills of California.

A. J. M. Smith

The Movies

She knows a cheap release
    From worry and from pain –
The cowboys spur their horses
    Over the unending plain.

The tenement rooms are small;
    Their walls press on the brain.
Oh, the dip of the galloping horses
    On the limitless wind-swept plain!

Florence Kiper Frank

Film Epic

Into the flamboyant cavern of the lonely screen
You, heavy and middle-aged, may always wander;
So exile the garish afternoon, and in you blunder.
Beyond the dim electric torches Life is ready to be seen,
Life where no one ever asks, What does this mean.
Where two foredestined hearts will never stay asunder.
Here you will be ravished by romance; amid recorded thunder
Its enormous kiss will smear you with saccharine.

This is the marriage; clutch your ticket stub. Now yield
To him, the husband once-removed . . . And now the torches flare,
And now, to seek in many a less than technicoloured field
For Prince Aeneas, Queen, you slowly forth must fare.
You may seem satiate enough and given to clerks, not books,
But glimpse yourself at the exit and know how Dido looks.

Carl Bode

Full Supporting Programme

Just at the most exciting part
of the film, as the secret agent
hiding in the coffin pushed up the lid –
suddenly, behind us, a woman screaming!
We followed the direction, turned heads miming
disgust: she had ruptured our paid-for dream.
Meanwhile, back on the screen, sinister
extras lurked in the vaults that took
half a day to light. We saw what a crude
bit of cutting did for a poor script.
But she was at it again: 'Help me.
I think my husband's dead!'
Sure enough, there was a dark
heap in the seat beside her. What
a way to go, before you even know

what's on next week. But there was little
we could do; it was the manager's problem.
Bad for business, that. Behind,
a nice bit part for a Nightingale usherette.
Luckily the heroine in a bikini
appeared in time to save her lover, because
there were only five minutes left to blow
up the castle and sell us ice-cream.
Next time I thought about it,
a boy who looked too young to watch
the main feature sat where the shrieker
had been. We left while a priest
was easing into the corpse's seat,
his folded coat carefully trailing across
the lap of the mesmerised boy, as more
death and seduction began.

                                    Bill Turner

Bijou

Huge, perfect creatures move across the screen
to the rhythms of hidden bands.
Small, imperfect creatures slouch in plush seats
and pull crystal tears from their eyes
when the intellectual dog is lost
or when the nearly nice supporting player
is culled from the action by a villain arrow
while saving the blond-souled hero.
They drop their tears and look around hopefully
when they hear the bugle of a rescue party.
But the aisles are empty. Odorless horses
spring onto the screen below waving flags.

                                    Vern Rutsala

The James Bond Movie

The popcorn is greasy, and I forgot to bring a Kleenex.
A pill that's a bomb inside the stomach of a man inside

The Embassy blows up. Eructations of flame, luxurious
cauliflowers giganticize into motion. The entire 29-ft

screen is orange, is crackling flesh and brick bursting,
blackening, smithereened. I unwrap a Dentyne and, while

jouncing my teeth in rubber tongue-smarting clove, try
with the 2-inch-wide paper to blot butter off my fingers.

A bubble-bath, room-sized, in which 14 girls, delectable
and sexless, twist-topped Creamy Freezes (their blonde,

red, brown, pinkish, lavender or silver wiglets all
screwed that high, and varnished), scrub-tickle a lone

male, whose chest has just the right amount and distribution of curly hair. He's nervously pretending to defend

his modesty. His crotch, below the waterline, is also
below the frame — but unsubmerged all 28 slick foamy boobs.

Their makeup fails to let the girls look naked. Caterpil-
lar lashes, black and thick, lush lips glossed pink like

the gum I pop and chew, contact lenses on the eyes that are
mostly blue, they're nose-perfect replicas of each other.

I've got most of the grease off and onto this little square
of paper. I'm folding it now, making creases with my nails.

May Swenson

A few lines about film buffs, critics and those of us who consume the stuff

Film melon-eaters are palpable people,
not sweet in some holy wood or other

or deliberately acid in print
and festival small talk
but as real as reel-wound footage,
threaded tight, facing up to action,
while sitting well back from it
and enjoying the sliced fruit
of the editor's cutting eyes
and mending fingers, in the dark.

Of course, the first and last thing
to say fast is that, understandably,
their inordinate thirst for images
of projected property is quenched
more than only now and then,
often, in fact, especially when
their own loose dreams keep running out
on them, spooling themselves down
beside the iron legs of the daily machine.

Andrew Salkey

Eddie's at the Movies Again

I'm at the old movies again,
safe in the warm dark
where the smoke serpents
into that shaft of light
the projector of dreams
where clichés fall
like rain in Ireland
and they even dress for breakfast.
Where girls keep their Marcel waves
unruffled in the jungle
and dresses tear
in just the right places.
Where the light's always on
in a home-town porch
like an entrance to a Greek temple,

and there's always appropriate music:
Somewhere Over the Rainbow for thinking
and *There's a Small Hotel* for love itself.
Where if you've got two girls
the brassy one dies,
but not before giving you
something to remember her by,
and where the murderer sends flowers
to your funeral and gets caught.
It's certainly such stuff
as dreams are made on.
A new opium of the people?
Not to worry –
with my girl beside me
and my hand in her blouse
I'll not lose touch.

John Cotton

Moving Pictures

You came in in the mid-
dle in those days and of course
it was foreign, but the images
wrapped in music were doing as
we'd just been doing unaccompanied.

It was an afternoon of rain
on London, and drips fell
on us, the stalagmites of that dark hall,
surrounded by frustrated scholars
waiting for loins to stop and tongues begin.

We moved some rows away. The screen
being wordless still, we watched who sat
next in our leak of water and light.
Who swaggered in, alone? The right
person exactly for our story line.

We left before his eyes got used
to the comfortable dark. The shadows
with all the time there is
continued to rub against the brightnesses.
Elsewhere again I nuzzled at your breast.

I missed the end of Bertolucci's endless film
and I missed you. My consolation
must be: though you are gone,
you left somewhere a still more perfect one
to know the end, to come and tell me.

Alistair Elliot

Snow White Meets the Wolfman

In memory of François Truffaut

From your mother's best china,
Lapsang Souchong,
We're off now, hand in glove,
Down lovers' lane:
The back row of the local cinema.

Not Lon Chaney Jnr, no,
The Song of Bernadette
For you. Truffaut,
Baisers Volés for me:
For both the petty larcenies of love.

Hollywood mythologies.
Tonight's B feature
Must be a creepy.
Son of Chimera
Begins to darkening applause.

We turn to higher things.
A paper dove
Drifts down its silver beam,
Provokes
Wolf-whistles from the Gods.

Up front a creature,
Lion's head, snake's tail,
Hairy, heavy-breathing,
Body of a goat,
Is moving through the stalls.

Gooseflesh rises to the occasion,
A tight-lipped scream:
In the dark around us
Perspiration gleams
And fun-fur collars close

Around flushed throats.

                    Leon McAuley*

Vincent and I Inaugurate a Movie Theatre

Now that the Charles Theatre has opened
it looks like we're going to have some wonderful times
Allen and Peter, why are you going away
our country's black and white past spread out
before us is no time to spread over India
like last night in the busy balcony I see
your smoky images before the smoky screen
everyone smoking, Bogart, Bacall and her advanced sister
and Hepburn too tense to smoke but MacMurray rich enough
relaxed and ugly, poor Alice Adams so in-pushed and out
in the clear exposition of AP American or Associated
Paranoia and Allen and I getting depressed and angry
becoming again the male version of wallflower or wallpaper
or something while Vincent points out that when anything
good happens the movie has just flicked over to fantasy
only fantasy in all America can be good
because all Alice Adams wanted was a nose
just as long as any other girl's and a dress
just as rustly and a mind just as empty so America
could fill it with checks and flags and invitations
and the old black cooks falling down the cellar stairs

for generations to show how phony it all is
but the whites didn't pay attention that's slaving away
at something, maybe the dance would have been fun
if anyone'd given one but it would have been over
before Alice enjoyed it and what's the difference
no wonder you want to find out about India take
a print of *Alice Adams* with you it will cheer them up

Frank O'Hara*

Further Decline of Western Civilization

I'm at the Odium in Hollywood, watching
a double bill: *Gorky Park* and *Angel*.
Two old ladies – one red-haired, the other, blue –
take seats behind me, loaded down with popcorn and Pepsi.

Lee Marvin, *Gorky*'s villain, stalks on screen, lethal and haughty.
'He's such a crumb,' Blue says, admiring.
'He's a crumb in real life is what I hear,' says Red.

Now we see the contraband sables,
all teeth and fur and snarl, leaping around
their cages hissing like dynamite about to blow.
'Aren't they cute,' says Blue.
'I gotta get my tooth fixed,' Red declares. 'It's painin' me.'

Now the Anatomy Professor reconstructs the faceless heads of the corpses
   from Gorky Park.
'Ugh, that's disgusting,' snaps Blue.
'That doctor was a dwarf in the book,' Red declares.
'Why didn't they get a dwarf?' Blue wants to know.
'That guy's pretty short,' Red allows.
'He's not a dwarf,' Blue says. 'My sister's son-in-law's a dwarf.
He's out of work, too. They could of got him.'

On to *Angel*, a 14-year-old orphan who goes to private
school by day, and pays by turning tricks on Sunset Strip.
'Why'd they want to make a movie about this?' Blue demands.

'It's awful,' Red agrees.
Their chewing accelerates.

Now Angel's meeting friends: hookers, a crazy cowboy, a lesbian, a drag
    queen.
'Is a morphadite the same as a transvestual,' asks Blue.
'A pervert's a pervert,' pronounces Red.

The camera lingers on pogoing Hari Krishnas.
'I wonder about that guy,' says Red.
'What guy?' asks Blue.
'That Harry Krishner.'

The crazed slasher knifes a hooker,
decks her out like a bride, and spreadeagles her on a motel bed.
He bends to kiss her.
'Ugh, that's sick,' says Blue.
'Nothing shocks me any more,' says Red.

Charles Webb*

Why I Like Movies

For Charlotte

I

I like movies because
people get to mug their faces in movies
or walk around with bad posture
and no one yells
'Stop that mugging' or 'Stand up straight!'

2

I like movies because
faces become monuments to promise.

3

I like movies because
they spark nationalistic conversations
such as

'I never go to French movies, they're
so pretentious and intellectual.'
or
'Italians must be terribly affected by sex.
Just think of those voluptuous women, always
waiting. Anna Magnani, what a face!'
'There's nothing like an American movie musical.
All that razzle dazzle disguising the petit anguish
beneath the smiles. Blah, blah, blah.'

4

I like movies because
they say a lot about the Other.
Like Black Folks in America. Those natives in Tarzan
movies with processes and straightened hair. That buffoon
rolling his eyes towards the coming thunder or talking
casually to spooks, saints and children. The women who
tended the house of the seemingly rich with gestures meant
for either tenderness or reproach. Secrets studded in
their enormous flesh.

5

I like movies because
I never saw myself in them.
I saw the dreams of a people
who looked like spooks, saints
and acted like children.

6

I like movies because
as the last reel winds back upon itself:
image on image
time turns away
a revolution terrified of the dark.

Patricia Jones

Reel One

It was all technicolor
from bullets to nurses.
The guns gleamed like cars
and blood was as red
as the paint on dancers.
The screen shook with fire
and my bones whistled.
It was like life, but better.

I held my girl's hand,
in the deepest parts,
and we walked home, after,
with the snow falling,
but there wasn't much blue
in the drifts or corners:
just white and more white
and the sound track so dead
you could almost imagine
the trees were talking.

Adrien Stoutenburg

Brief Encounter

She'd quite a cupid mouth between World Wars
and thighs comely enough for five live kids,
and two dead, to heave from darkness to light.
An unromantic life, her one shy affair
was with Fred Astaire: 'Never, never change . . .
I love you, just the way you look tonight'.
End of flashback. All I know of her stands
trembling in my way – lost, half-deaf, senile,
a gummer made out of chicken gristle,
a terrible turning-up of the real.

Just popped on her coat and shuffled out,
leaving the fat-arsed staff frantic.

'I'm going to the pictures, I am'.
Time torn up like a ticket on entrance,
but only old features are being shown,
recurring dramas of the long dead.
Trevor Howard and Celia Johnson;
real people, plausibly symbolic.
So young, so lovely; a sad plot. You can
touch them, surely, just reach out. You cannot.
A veil of light separates art from life,
living from the dead, with nothing behind
that white screen, nothing to comfort longing
for imperishable images: *Beloved Husband*,
A Dearly Loved Son, gone into that world
alongside Film Stars of the Forties.

There, there, it's only a film. A weepy.
In the fresh air of indifferent daylight,
a film-struck girl trapped inside the hag-husk;
one of The Living Dead, to be returned,
given lukewarm tea from a feeding cup
as she waits in the dark for The End.
Can it be helped, what the decades have done,
this terrible turning of the reel?
What can her audience do about it?
We want to get back to our own storylines,
unfolding before us at spiral speed.
Farewell, on Rachmaninov's swelling chords.

Jules Smith*

Arizona Movies

I

Rosetta, her new boy friend
and all four kids

[141]

are going to the drive-in
down in San Manuel.

'One more beer,' they tell the kids
'and then we'll go.' The kids
want a quarter a nickel
another dime – the kids

are a pain in the ass
the movie is about a dog
and the boy friend wears glasses
baggy double-knit slacks

and a white belt. Rosetta,
on the other hand, is beautiful,
elegant, altogether sweet
in her new blue sweater

and when she reaches in her purse
to buy another round,
I spot her little silver gun.
'That's just in case,' she says,

'just in case.'

2

Sometimes
even in the middle
of the year's best movie
you can hear coyotes
at the San Manuel Drive-In.

Tonight, they are far away
and merely barking at the moon . . .

but Rosetta tells me
that when they chorus close
and suddenly together

hysterical, high pitched, furious

it means something is dying
in the dark foothills
behind the shaky screen.

3

After the bad movie
Rosetta wants to finish off
what's left of the tequila
drop off the kids

and then go dancing . . . !

But I don't know about Fred.
I think Fred sells mobile homes —
convenient, air conditioned,
catastrophically fragile,

I pass them everyday
and try to imagine myself
living there: the tv on
all the kids at school

and Rosetta, just lying
on the couch, just watching,
through the picture window,
some Apache ghost dance
cavalry of thunderheads
advancing slowly out
from between Mount Lemmon

And a pigeon blue wing
of the Catalinas.

4

No one is dancing
up at Pop-A-Tops. No one
is speaking. The tv's on
and in the Merry Christmas

snow flaked mirror, Fred
is shooting pool. Rosetta,
on the other hand, shreds
her matches into tiny bits

then looking up, her look
slides sidelong into mine —
the tense, unsteady look
I think, of children

getting lost . . . but what
was it that I thought to say?
Something dumb, mindless
a remark about the movie

or at my best, to notice
on that long, small arm
her careful, bar-room bracelet
of pink and yellow straws.

Whatever it was, she answers
to the whole place – loud,
and before I say a word:
'Nope, I'm not dead yet'

and the fuzzed up mirror
keeps still, stays quiet
as the slow blue echo
of a pistol shot.

5

Rosetta says she's 32
but Fred looks younger.
Fred's even younger partner
works the graveyard shift

at Magma Copper
and behind us all
the Falstaff clock
turns counter clockwise

towards eleven. 'One more game,'
they tell Rosetta, 'and then
we'll go.' *The Lariat?*
The Hangman's Tree?

'Why not Rosetta's place?'
Fred's partner whispers.
A joke perhaps. But still
it's curious, frightening

that I should also hear
in the shy nylon whisper

of Rosetta's thighs
in the click of small ice

something dangerous, random,
confused as kitchens,
cupboards where the knives
are kept, bedrooms

in the Apache Trailer Court
with real bullet holes
above the door.

6

Like Rosetta
I too hear voices.

Tonight, they are speaking
the frazzled language

of neon, the cindered
impossible language

of parking lots, static
and revolving lights . . .

but sometimes, it's Rosetta –
her voice still angry

clear, above the voices
of the graveyard shift

who slam their doors
like Fred or anyone

going off half drunk
to work tonight

in knee deep water
and the hot acidic dark

one full mile
underground.

Michael Van Walleghen

Drive In Movie

Lifesize in a car,
I watch tall faces
outdoors on a screen.

Across the way,
two people
– floundering
above a dashboard –
go down under their own weight.

I've come here
to be out of place.
One when everyone's two,
I'm the reason why locks click;
I'm anybody's guess.

The sun in the movie
goes down after dark
and a moon comes up over
the screen.
It's time now: the end.
Doris and Cary kiss;
couples rise; backs arch –
rearview mirrors fill with lips.

As gravel is scurried,
and cars – throwing light
at one another – pass by,
I wait to fall behind.

A hundred warm speakers hang
speechless from their poles.

Gary Sange*

At the Drive-In:
'John Wayne vs. God'

The sound of faint thunder
was silenced by the volume
of his voice.

But black clouds rolled in;
lightning hit the power lines,
and John Wayne vanished.

God won,
and the red-necks
dumped the beer cans
and tore out in their
American-flagged pickups,
looking for some ass.

A. A. Dewey

Dear John Wayne

August and the drive-in picture is packed.
We lounge on the hood of the Pontiac
surrounded by the slow-burning spirals they sell
at the window, to vanquish the hordes of mosquitoes.
Nothing works. They break through the smoke screen for blood.

Always the lookout spots the Indians first,
spread north to south, barring progress.
The Sioux or some other Plains bunch
in spectacular columns, ICBM missiles,
feathers bristling in the meaningful sunset.

The drum breaks. There will be no parlance.
Only the arrows whining, a death-cloud of nerves
swarming down on the settlers
who die beautifully, tumbling like dust weeds

into the history that brought us all here
together: this wide screen beneath the sign of the bear.

The sky fills, acres of blue squint and eye
that the crowd cheers. His face moves over us,
a thick cloud of vengeance, pitted
like the land that was once flesh. Each rut,
each scar makes a promise: *It is
not over, this fight, not as long as you resist.*

Everything we see belongs to us.

A few laughing Indians fall over the hood
slipping in the hot spilled butter.
The eye sees a lot, John, but the heart is so blind.
Death makes us owners of nothing.
He smiles, a horizon of teeth
the credits reel over, and then the white fields

again blowing in the true-to-life dark.
The dark films over everything.
We get into the car
scratching our mosquito bites, speechless and small
as people are when the movie is done.
We are back in our skins.

How can we help but keep hearing his voice,
the flip side of the sound track, still playing:
*Come on, boys, we got them
where we want them, drunk, running.*
They'll give us what we want, what we need.
Even his disease was the idea of taking everything.
Those cells, burning, doubling, splitting out of their skins.

Louise Erdrich

Motion Pictures

Of all locations to park, my car prefers
country drive-in theatres:

those fields fenced off in the dusk
echoing with the noise of speakers attached to poles
where every vehicle faces the same way
except a few pickups
containing hardy individuals settled down in the back
under coats and blankets.
                    My car especially enjoys
films about characters on the road
that include travelogue sequences as filler:
shots of strange North American cities
or European landscapes my car will never visit.
My car likes to observe these distant places
without having had to roll that far,
pistons rising and plunging,
all systems functioning, alert
for any failure.
What my car isn't happy about
are chase scenes: vehicles smashing
together, or swerving onto sidewalks
or down embankments to end in flames.
My car has passed too many overturned trucks
and police flares at other accidents
to successfully remind itself this is just a movie.
And my car seems indifferent
if the plot involves only people
indoors. But when this occurs
it loves to look higher than the screen
and the hills around,
up at the massed stars,
and recollect certain nights
it spent away out on the earth
in gear and travelling.
                My car is always a little regretful
when the films conclude
and it has to get in line
down the usual hard highway.

Tom Wayman

On Seeing a Movie Based on an Episode
from President Kennedy's Life

Tonight we took
the boys to see
PT Boat 1
09 at the
Dryden Drive-In
3 boys in the
Volkswagen and
our daughter of
course. Before that
we had to watch
Bob Mitchum chase
a tiger with
a torch and then
like Wilson in
Hemingstein's best
story steal the
girl indifferent
ly. Jack Hawkins
tried to shoot him
too. The boys sd
this was scary.
In the next car
a man shoved
his girl down in the
seat and had at
her; I turned the
mirror and watched
his shirt going
up and down, it
took about eight
or ten minutes.
Maybe it was
their first time, they
lit cigarettes
then Jack, dead Jack
came on and we

saw him choose his
PT boat, paint
er up and head
for battle. Av
rom had to pee
just then and wd
nt go outside
on the gravel
so we had to
leave. I loved Jack
Kennedy, he
wanted better
for us than these
Drive-In thumpings.
Under the great
stars of Amer
ica there shd
be better. We
were choked on car
fumes; to go down
town wd be worse.
On the way home
we passed trailer
parks, the sad young
marrieds inside
watching TV.
Why shdn't they
give up and hug
in those shoebox
havens, pullman
bunks and porta
ble blue heavens
if they can't walk
out into the
night without get
ting gassed? They know
their dreams are put
to sleep like pups.

David Ray*

Stumptown Attends the Picture Show

on the first attempt at desegregation in Canton, Georgia

Word has come and Martha the ticket girl
stands behind the candy counter
eating popcorns and smoking Salems.
Beside her the projectionist,
having canned Vivien Leigh
and come downstairs to watch the real show,
leans folding chairs against the theater doors,
guards his glass counter
like saloon keepers in his Westerns
guard the mirrors hung above their bars.

Outside, good old boys line the sidewalk,
string chain between parking meters
in front of the Canton Theater,
dig in like Rebs in a Kennesaw trench.
From the street policemen and sheriff's deputies
address their threats to proper names,
try to maintain any stability.
Someone has already radioed the State Boys.

Through a glass door Martha watches
the moon slide over Jones Mercantile.
In front of Landers' Drugstore
a streetlight flickers like a magic lantern,
but Martha cannot follow the plot,
neither can the projectionist.
Only one thing is certain:
elements from different worlds are converging,
spinning toward confrontation,
and the State Boys are winding down some county road,
moving in a cloud of dust toward the theater marquee.

David Bottoms

Triple Feature

Innocent decision: to enjoy.
And the pathos
of hopefulness, of his solicitude:

— he in mended serape,
she having plaited carefully
magenta ribbons into her hair,
the baby a round half-hidden shape
slung in her rebozo, and the young son steadfastly
gripping a fold of her skirt,
pale and severe under a
handed-down sombrero —

      all regarding
the stills with full attention, preparing
to pay and go in —
to worlds of shadow-violence, half-
familiar, warm with popcorn, icy
with strange motives, barbarous splendors!

                  Denise Levertov

Movie House

View it, by day, from the back,
from the parking lot in the rear,
for from this angle only
the beautiful brick blankness can be grasped.
Monumentality
wears one face in all ages.

No windows intrude real light
into this temple of shades,
and the size of it,
the size of the great rear wall measures
the breadth of the dreams we have had here.

It dwarfs the village bank,
outlooms the town hall,
and even in its decline
makes the bright-ceilinged supermarket seem mean.

Stark closet of stealthy rapture,
vast introspective camera
wherein our most daring self-projections
were given familiar names:
stand, stand by your macadam lake
and tell the aeons of our extinction
that we too could house our gods,
could secrete a pyramid
to sight the stars by.

John Updike

The Shooting of John Dillinger Outside the Biograph Theater, July 22, 1934

Chicago ran a fever of a hundred and one that groggy Sunday.
A reporter fried an egg on a sidewalk; the air looked shaky.
And a hundred thousand people were in the lake like shirts in a laundry.
Why was Johnny lonely?
Not because two dozen solid citizens, heat-struck, had keeled over backward.
Not because those lawful souls had fallen out of their sockets and melted.
But because the sun went down like a lump in a furnace or a bull in the Stockyards.
Where was Johnny headed?
Under the Biograph Theater sign that said, 'Our Air is Refrigerated.'
Past seventeen FBI men and four policemen who stood in doorways and sweated.
Johnny sat down in a cold seat to watch Clark Gable get electrocuted.
Had Johnny been mistreated?
Yes, but Gable told the D.A. he'd rather fry than be shut up forever.
Two women sat by Johnny. One looked sweet, one looked like J. Edgar Hoover.

Polly Hamilton made him feel hot, but Anna Sage made him shiver.
Was Johnny a good lover?
Yes, but he passed out his share of squeezes and pokes like a jittery masher
While Agent Purvis sneaked up and down the aisle like an extra usher,
Trying to make sure they wouldn't slip out till the show was over.
Was Johnny a fourflusher?
No, not if he knew the game. He got it up or got it back.
But he liked to take snapshots of policemen with his own Kodak,
And once in a while he liked to take them with an automatic.
Why was Johnny frantic?
Because he couldn't take a walk or sit down in a movie
Without being afraid he'd run smack into somebody
Who'd point at his rearranged face and holler, 'Johnny!'
Was Johnny ugly?
Yes, because Dr Wilhelm Loeser had given him a new profile
With a baggy jawline and squint eyes and an erased dimple,
With kangaroo-tendon cheekbones and a gigolo's mustache that
   should've been illegal.
Did Johnny love a girl?
Yes, a good-looking, hard-headed Indian named Billie Frechette.
He wanted to marry her and lie down and try to get over it,
But she was locked in jail for giving him first-aid and comfort.
Did Johnny feel hurt?
He felt like breaking a bank or jumping over a railing
Into some panicky teller's cage, to shout, 'Reach for the ceiling!'
Or like kicking some vice president in the bum checks and smiling.
What was he really doing?
Going up the aisle with the crowd and into the lobby
With Polly saying, 'Would *you* do what Clark done?' And Johnny saying,
   'Maybe.'
And Anna saying, 'If he'd been smart, he'd of acted like Bing Crosby.'
Did Johnny look flashy?
Yes, his white-on-white shirt and tie were luminous.
His trousers were creased like knives to the tops of his shoes,
And his yellow straw hat came down to his dark glasses.
Was Johnny suspicious?
Yes, and when Agent Purvis signalled with a trembling cigar,
Johnny ducked left and ran out of the theater,
And innocent Polly and squealing Anna were left nowhere.
Was Johnny a fast runner?

No, but he crouched and scurried past a friendly liquor store
Under the coupled arms of double-daters, under awnings, under stars,
To the curb at the mouth of an alley. He hunched there.
Was Johnny a thinker?
No, but he was thinking more or less of Billie Frechette
Who was lost in prison for longer than he could possibly wait,
And then it was suddenly too hard to think around a bullet.
Did anyone shoot straight?
Yes, but Mrs Etta Natalsky fell out from under her picture hat.
Theresa Paulus sprawled on the sidewalk, clutching her left foot.
And both of them groaned loud and long under the streetlight.
Did Johnny like that?
No, but he lay down with those strange women, his face in the alley,
One shoe off, cinders in his mouth, his eyelids heavy.
When they shouted questions at him, he talked back to nobody.
Did Johnny lie easy?
Yes, holding his gun and holding his breath as a last trick,
He waited, but when the Agents came close, his breath wouldn't work.
Clark Gable walked his last mile; Johnny ran half a block.
Did he run out of luck?
Yes, before he was cool, they had him spread out on dished-in marble
In the Cook County Morgue, surrounded by babbling people
With a crime reporter presiding over the head of the table.
Did Johnny have a soul?
Yes, and it was climbing his slippery wind-pipe like a trapped burglar.
It was beating the inside of his ribcage, hollering, 'Let me out of here!'
Maybe it got out, and maybe it just stayed there.
Was Johnny a money-maker?
Yes, and thousands paid 25¢ to see him, mostly women,
And one said, 'I wouldn't have come, except he's a moral lesson,'
And another, 'I'm disappointed. He feels like a dead man.'
Did Johnny have a brain?
Yes, and it always worked best through the worst of dangers,
Through flat-footed hammerlocks, through guarded doors, around
    corners,
But it got taken out in the morgue and sold to some doctors.
Could Johnny take orders?
No, but he stayed in the wicker basket carried by six men
Through the bulging crowd to the hearse and let himself be locked in,
And he stayed put as it went driving south in a driving rain.

And he didn't get stolen?
No, not even after his old hard-nosed dad refused to sell
The quick-drawing corpse for $10,000 to somebody in a carnival.
He figured he'd let *Johnny* decide how to get to Hell.
Did anyone wish him well?
Yes, half of Indiana camped in the family pasture,
And the minister said, 'With luck, he could have been a minister.'
And up the sleeve of his oversized gray suit, Johnny twitched a finger.
Does anyone remember?
Everyone still alive. And some dead ones. It was a new kind of holiday
With hot and cold drinks and hot and cold tears. They planted him in a
    cemetery
With three unknown vice presidents, Benjamin Harrison, and James
    Whitcomb Riley,
Who never held up anybody.

                                                    David Wagoner*

Grace at the Atlanta Fox

Whenever, in that ceiling sky,
Familiar clouds once more go by,

And in the restrooms, far below,
One half the lamps of Islam glow;

When, overweight but overawed,
Undying Grace, eternal Maude,

Once more are *en rapport* – are one –
With Myrna Loy and Irene Dunne

(Irene as essence, Maude; *Ur*-Myrna:
Now the new star Annapurna,

Nepalese and thick of tongue);
Or when, pure movie, pure, brave, young,

The Foreign Legion dare and do,
Each year is 1932;

Pre-Eleanor, pre-war, pre-Fala;
Time as place: the Garden of Allah,

Near whose entrance, chill with Freon,
That time's great sign resists still neon,

To be through Moorish, Hoover nights
This fugue of incandescent lights;

As if to make some statement yet;
As if the tan brick minaret

Were point and counterpoint; not theme,
But theme to be, that when the dream

Maude dreams is ours, and we too nod,
States then 'There is no God but God . . .'

Turner Cassity*

Movie-Going

Drive-ins are out, to start with. One must always be
Able to see the over-painted Moorish ceiling
Whose pinchbeck jazz gleams even in the darkness, calling
The straying eye to feast on it, and glut, then fall
Back to the sterling screen again. One needs to feel
That the two empty, huddled, dark stage-boxes keep
Empty for kings. And having frequently to cope
With the abominable goodies, overflow
Bulk and (finally) exploring hands of flushed
Close neighbors gazing beadily out across glum
Distances is, after all, to keep the gleam
Alive of something rather serious, to keep
Faith, perhaps, with the City. When as children our cup
Of joys ran over the special section, and we clutched
Our ticket stubs and followed the bouncing ball, no clash
Of cymbals at the start of the stage-show could abash
Our third untiring time around. When we came back,
Older, to cop an endless series of feels, we sat

Unashamed beneath the bare art-nouveau bodies, set
High on the golden, after-glowing proscenium when
The break had come. And still, now as always, once
The show is over and we creep into the dull
Blaze of mid-afternoon sunshine, the hollow dole
Of the real descends on everything and we can know
That we have been in some place wholly elsewhere, a night
At noonday, not without dreams, whose portals shine
(Not ivory, not horn in ever-changing shapes)
But made of some weird, clear substance not often used for gates.

Stay for the second feature on a double bill
Always: it will teach you how to love, how not to live,
And how to leave the theater for that unlit, aloof
And empty world again. 'B'-pictures showed us: shooting
More real than singing or making love; the shifting
Ashtray upon the mantel, moved by some idiot
Between takes, helping us learn beyond a trace of doubt
How fragile are imagined scenes; the dimming-out
Of all the brightness of the clear and highly lit
Interior of the hero's cockpit, when the stock shot
Of ancient dive-bombers peeling off cuts in, reshapes
Our sense of what is, finally, plausible; the grays
Of living rooms, the blacks of cars whose window glass
At night allows the strips of fake Times Square to pass
Jerkily by on the last ride; even the patch
Of sudden white, and inverted letters dashing
Up during the projectionist's daydream, dying
Quickly – these are the colors of our inner life.

Never ignore the stars, of course. But above all,
Follow the asteroids as well: though dark, they're more
Intense for never glittering; anyone can admire
Sparklings against a night sky, but against a bright
Background of prominence, to feel the Presences burnt
Into no fiery fame should be a more common virtue.
For, just as Vesta has no atmosphere, no verdure
Burgeons on barren Ceres, bit-players never surge
Into the rhythms of expansion and collapse, such
As all the flaming bodies live and move among.
But there, more steadfast than stars are, loved for their being,

Not for their burning, move the great Characters: see
Thin Donald Meek, that shuffling essence ever so
Affronting to Eros and to Pride; the pair of bloated
Capitalists, Walter Connolly and Eugene Pallette, seated
High in their offices above New York; the evil,
Blackening eyes of Sheldon Leonard, and the awful
Stare of Eduardo Cianelli. Remember those who have gone –
(Where's bat-squeaking Butterfly McQueen? Will we see again
That ever-anonymous drunk, waxed-moustached, rubber-legged
Caught in revolving doors?) and think of the light-years logged
Up in those humbly noble orbits, where no hot
Spotlight of solar grace consumes some blazing hearts,
Bestowing the flimsy immortality of stars
For some great distant instant. Out of the darkness stares
Venus, who seems to be what once we were, the fair
Form of emerging love, her nitrous atmosphere
Hiding her prizes. Into the black expanse peers
Mars, whom we in time will come to resemble: parched,
Xanthine desolations, dead Cimmerian seas, the far
Distant past preserved in the blood-colored crusts; fire
And water both remembered only. Having shined
Means having died. But having been merely real, and shunned
Stardom, the planetoids are what we now are, humming
With us, above us, ever into the future, seeming
Ever to take the shapes of the world we wake to from dreams.

Always go in the morning if you can; it will
Be something more than habit if you do. Keep well
Away from most French farces. Try to see a set
Of old blue movies every so often, that the sight
Of animal doings out of the clothes of 'thirty-five
May remind you that even the natural act is phrased
In the terms and shapes of particular times and places.
Finally, remember always to honor the martyred dead.
The forces of darkness spread everywhere now, and the best
And brightest screens fade out, while many-antennaed beasts
Perch on the housetops, and along the grandest streets
Palaces crumble, one by one. The dimming starts
Slowly at first; the signs are few, as 'Movies are
Better than Ever,' 'Get More out of Life. See a Movie' Or

Else there's no warning at all and, Whoosh! the theater falls,
Alas, transmogrified: no double-feature fills
A gleaming marquee with promises, now only lit
With 'Pike and Whitefish Fresh Today' 'Drano' and 'Light
Or Dark Brown Sugar, Special.' Try never to patronize
Such places (or pass them by one day a year). The noise
Of movie mansions changing form, caught in the toils
Of our lives' withering, rumbles, resounds and tolls
The knell of neighborhoods. Do not forget the old
Places, for everyone's home has been a battlefield.

I remember: the RKO COLONIAL; the cheap
ARDEN and ALDEN both; LOEW'S LINCOLN SQUARE's bright shape;
The NEWSREEL; the mandarin BEACON, resplendently arrayed;
The tiny SEVENTY-SEVENTH STREET, whose demise I rued
So long ago; the eighty-first street, sunrise-hued,
RKO; and then LOEW'S at eighty-third, which had
The colder pinks of sunset on it; and then, back
Across Broadway again, and up, you disembarked
At the YORKTOWN and then the STODDARD, with their dark
Marquees; the SYMPHONY had a decorative disk
With elongated 'twenties nudes whirling in it;
(Around the corner the THALIA, daughter of memory! owed
Her life to Foreign Hits, in days when you piled your coat
High on your lap and sat, sweating and cramped, to catch
'La Kermesse Heroïque' every third week, and watched
Fritz Lang from among an audience of refugees, bewitched
By the sense of Crisis on and off that tiny bit
Of screen) Then north again: the RIVERSIDE, the bright
RIVIERA rubbing elbows with it; and right
Smack on a hundredth street, the MIDTOWN; and the rest
Of them: the CARLTON, EDISON, LOEW'S OLYMPIA, and best
Because, of course, the last of all, its final burst
Anonymous, the NEMO! These were once the pearls
Of two-and-a-half miles of Broadway! How many have paled
Into a supermarket's failure of the imagination?

Honor them all. Remember how once their splendor blazed
In sparkling necklaces across America's blasted
Distances and deserts: think how, at night, the fastest
Train might stop for water somewhere, waiting, faced

Westward, in deepening dusk, till ruby illuminations
Of something different from Everything Here, Now, shine
Out from the local Bijou, truest gem, the most bright
Because the most believed in, staving off the night
Perhaps, for a while longer with its flickering light.

These fade. All fade, Let us honor them with our own fading sight.

John Hollander

Skin Flick

The selfsame surface that billowed once with
The shapes of Trigger and Gene. New faces now
Are in the saddle. Tits and buttocks
Slide rattling down the beam as down
A coal chute; in the splotched light
The burning bush strikes dumb.
Different sort of cattle drive:
No water for miles and miles.

In the aisles, new bugs and rats
Though it's same Old Paint.

Audience of lepers, hopeless and homeless,
Or like the buffalo, at home
In the wind only. No
Mushy love stuff for them.

They eye the violent innocence they always knew.
Is that the rancher's palomino daughter?
Is this her eastern finishing school?

Same old predicament:
No water for miles and miles,
The horizon breeds no cavalry.

Men, draw your wagons in a circle. Be ready.

Fred Chappell

Adam, Eve and the Big Apple

Don't you love farce? All those bedroom doors –
Feydeau, Astaire, those sketches at the Palace,
All have revolved around them: erotic wars,
A Dionysiac tribute to the phallus!
More lighthearted romps these than skin flicks
With leather and chains to titillate the senses –
Lubitsch himself provides more cheerful kicks
Than X-rated peep shows for the jocks and wenches.

Send in the clowns, as Sondheim aptly puts it –
A delightful round, those smiles of a summer night:
Even a Bergman lover lightly foots it
When the Stockholm sun's still up and the music's right.
    For sex, the commodity of the Times Square man,
    Once was champagne and laughter, Lunt and Fontanne!

Edward Watkins

First NY Showing

Think of those homosexuals at the Park-Bryant, think of them
At the All-Male Film Festival, Continuous 9:45 a.m.
To Midnite. Think of them in a transport of being received
By their kith, their kind, in being invited to
A show of their own, a show of their flag; of being deceived
By the tempter, the pander, the spectacled speculant who
Bids on, at lost-property auctions, the shape of their self –
Their only shape, really, preoccupation with self –
In brown-paper wrappings and ticketed, there on that shelf.

L. E. Sissman

Leicester Square: May 1974

Will Shakespeare leans at ease,
his right arm on a pillar topped with books,
his stone cloak unruffled in the breeze,
as constantly across the square he looks,
where letters five feet high,
announce Fitzgerald's *Gatsby*
and what we take to be
the eyes of Dr Eckleburg.
But these are brown not blue?
We look again
to find they are the two
enormous boobs of Jenny,
'a ride like you never had before',
the *Swinging Stewardess*
of the film that's shown next door;
and, as if to stress
the confusion of fantasies and themes,
and, still, a good wine needs no bush,
while *Gatsby* seems
to have no more than lettering,
Jenny's full-frontal dreams
are cut short at the hips.
Though Shakespeare always had it sorted in his head:
for the one a tragedy, for the other
the second-best bed.

John Cotton*

Night London

The pubs were out, the evening's takings done,
box-office hatches tightly closed. The girls
and boys of Theatre-land waited for their
release, hustling their patrons to the Strand.
'All out?' the firemen asked, huge padlocks

in their hands. The day's last workers left
by stage doors set in alleyways.
The night began . . .

A steel-blue lightness in the half-dark
of the Charing Cross Road marked the Classic's foyer –
all-night horror and coffee – three fifty.
The Chinese usher handed little packs
of sickly shortbread buttons to the queue,
then disappeared behind a hatch to dole
out plastic cups of coffee – frothy pale –
sugar and milk compulsory. Two films
and a reel on in the musty dimness
a ticketless straggler wove the side aisle;
bottles dropped from his sodden carrier-bag.
The balding plush soaked Cyprus sherry up.
A policeman, manoeuvring, got him
by the intact elbow of his pee-stained mac.
The emergency exit's long bolt scraped
on concrete. Lamplight flooded in.

The river wind chilled the brightness of squares
and bridges, lifting the sick garbage smells
from stores and restaurants, drying the grimed dew
of parks and monuments. Next day's papers
lay in the great old stations, fresh with print.
Outside, the streets were bare, light, free,
the Tubes all latticed shut.

Fiona Pitt-Kethley

Old Movies

How I loved those old movies
they would show in the Roxys
and Regals amongst all that
gilt plaster, or in the Bijou
flea-pits smelling of Jeyes.
The men sleek haired and suited,

with white cuffs and big trilbies,
their girls all pushovers,
wide-eyed with lashes
like venus fly traps and their
clouds of blonde candy floss
for hair. Oh those bosoms, hips
and those long long legs
I never saw in daylight!
And their apartments,
vast as temples,
full of unused furniture,
the sideboards bending with booze,
and all those acres of bed!
She, in attendance, wearing
diaphanous, but never quite
diaphanous enough, nightwear.
And their lives!
Where the baddies only,
if not always, stopped one,
and they loved and loved
and never ended up married.
Every time I get a whiff
of that disinfectant
I feel nostalgic.

John Cotton

On the Demolition in 1980 of the Roxy, Old Dover Road SE3

For John Betjeman on his seventy-fifth birthday

One day from the alley I often walk down,
I look over the car-park and see the roof
Of the cinema has gone, as with the wind:
A scree-littered slope – the Circle *al fresco*.

Seldom we three sat there, liked to be nearer.
Besides, in early days couldn't afford it –
Time now of almost dynastic measurement.

[166]

I had forgotten the walls were dirty green;
Perhaps thought them hueless in the encircling gloom
(Eyes on the screen, or even the lit curtain):
No more than I grasped that the pillars rising
On the walls were mock and mauve, and grubby, too;
The fenestration false, and almost
Pathetic today, artily *art nouveau*.

Scrap-men's torches already make livid scars.
What an amount of iron from the ruin!
No need at all to sit beyond the Circle's
Projection, as my nervous nature prompted.
It jibes with the moral background of those days –
Fade-outs discreet; goodies triumphant; naive
Celebration of bourgeois democracy
Exasperating my Marxist bias then.
But did I excuse *Mr Deeds Goes To Town*,
Though arrant sentimentality, I'm sure?
Expect so, being the first film attended
By that future buff, my son; though nothing he
Saw of it, being borne sleeping in our arms.

In the nearby greengrocer's, moved, I touch on
The oft-told family tale. 'Built Thirty-five,'
They say, 'wa'n't it?' 'This was Thirty-eight,' I say,
'I didn't come to Blackheath till Thirty-eight.'
– Days of our youth, atrocious days, joyous days.
'Di'n't half make a row when they knocked that roof in,'
They say. Bad action Hitler failed to bring off.
'Pity,' they say, across the cress and beetroot,
'We could do with some'ink like that round here.'
Yes, but, dear neighbours, just what would it display?
Where is, and how vanished, art's morality?
Instead of my own ancient Lancastrian,
I almost fall into your demotic speech,
Imitable after two and forty years.

Suburban old John of Gaunt, I wheel away
Edwards and carrots. *This land is now leas'd out.*

[167]

And all share the blame sound bricks, and sad, come down
– Except, of course, that other time-honoured John.

Roy Fuller

On the Demolition of the Odeon Cinema, Westbourne Grove

Never one for the flicks, I did not frequent the place:
Though I recall the *Voyage of the Argonauts*,
And a second feature – some twaddle about
A daughter of King Arthur, otherwise unrecorded
By history or tradition. Now, each day,
I pass it, and I hear the brutal noise
Of demolition: clatter of falling masonry,
Machines that seem to grit and grind their teeth,
And munch in gluttony of destruction.

Its soft innards, I guess, are gone already:
The screen, the lighting, the plush seats; the ghosts likewise –
Shadows of shadows, phantoms of phantoms,
The love goddesses, the butcher boy heroes,
The squawking cartoon-animals.

This odeon – I should regret it? –
In which no ode has ever been recited.
Yet there's a pang – for I've lived long enough
To know that every house of dreams
Must be torn down at last.

John Heath-Stubbs*

Gutting the ABC

After years of corporate mismanagement
it's over, box-office slumping to a few
Maltesers melting from hand to mouth.

[168]

The whole facade is down. I stand
where the screen used to be, adding
a soundtrack to events as I see them –
the earth-movers ripping out seats.

My backside would numb just waiting
for the feature: globs of swirling colour
were accompanied by Easy Listening Hits.
Then *Pearl and Dean.*
                    Is memory doomed
to be disembowelled when I'm old, hard
of hearing and with failing sight,
or will a colossal bottle of *Gordon's*
still pour its juniper cascade
and a voice-over sell me a carpet
whose gash pattern you wouldn't believe?

Paul Munden*

Sunday Observance

Sunday afternoon, and the votary rejoices;
   Whispers in the dark from the ranks of the devout;
'Shush!' says somebody – down go the voices,
   Up goes the tension as the lights flicker out.
Eager are the sighs that escape from the faithful,
   Eager are the eyes for a symbol, a sign;
Eager are the ears, and the minds are attentive;
   Brisk are the brains. The exception is mine.

It's the sixth time I've seen *Caligari*;
   I've boarded *Potemkin* before;
Birth of a Nation's a long operation,
   But must I be midwife once more?
Intolerance makes me intolerant,
   Turksib is a tedious train –
I grant you that *Greed* is impressive, but need
   I sit through the whole thing again?

I've seen quite enough of the savage
   (*Tabu* and *Moana* and such),
And though Maxim Gorki's a theme for a talkie,
   A trilogy's frankly too much.
To Pabst I addressed panegyrics
   And Eisenstein's praises I sang –
But now I have *no* time for Erich von Stroheim,
   And little for Lubitsch or Lang.

Sunday afternoon, and the Film Club is meeting;
   'Cinema's an Art' is the credo they profess:
'But,' says somebody – then starts repeating
   Cracks from the critics in the Sunday press.
Members are aware of the cutting and the lighting,
   Members are aware what a film should be;
Even the tenth time they find it exciting –
   Nobody's bored. The exception is me.

Anthony Brode*

The Phantom Agents

We need more data re our example, Earth – how it would behave in a
crisis, under pressure,
or simply on a day no one had staked out for unrest
to erupt. What season would fit its life style
most naturally? Who would the observers, the control group be?

For this we must seek the answer in decrepit cinemas
whose balconies were walled off decades ago: on the screen
(where, in posh suburbia, a woman waits),
under the seats, in the fuzz and ancient vomit and gum wrappers;
or in the lobby, where yellowing lobby cards announce
the advent of next week's Republic serial – names
of a certain importance once, names that float
in the past, like a drift of gnats on a summer evening.

Who in the world despises our work
as much as we do? I was against campaigning again,

then my phone started ringing off the hook. I tell you . . .
But to come back to us, sanded down to the finer grain
and beyond – this is what books teach you, but also
what we must do. Make a name, somehow,
in the wall of clouds behind the credits, like a
twenty-one-vehicle pileup on a fog-enclosed highway.
This is what it means to be off and running, off
one's nut as well. But in a few more years,
with time off for good behavior . . .

                                        John Ashbery

NOTES

'A Grand Night' (Enright). Adapted by writer-director Anthony Asquith from a novel by Ernest Raymond, *Tell England* (1931) is a patriotic movie celebrating the gallant British soldiers who fought and died at Gallipoli in the Dardanelles campaign of 1915. Asquith's father was liberal Prime Minister from 1908 to 1916, and this costly, ineffectual action against the Turks contributed to unseating him. (111)

'Continuous' (Harrison). In Raoul Walsh's *White Heat* (1949), James Cagney has one of his last, and greatest, gangster roles as the psychotic, mother-fixated Cody Jarrett, who dies atop an exploding gas tank after shouting triumphantly, 'Made it ma, top of the world.' (112)

'The Pictures' (Enright). Directed by Michael Curtiz, the epic early talkie *Noah's Ark* (1929) was the Warner Brothers' longest, most expensive movie to date. It cut back and forth between the biblical flood of Genesis and a Great War love story and in the spectacular flood scenes several of the vast crowd of extras were drowned. (114)

'Dream Song 7' *The Prisoner of Shark Island* (Berryman). Henry is John Berryman's *alter ego* in the 'Dream Songs'. The film that gives the poem its title, *The Prisoner of Shark Island* (1936), is a minor John Ford film about Dr Mudd, the physican who inadvertently tended the wounds of President Lincoln's assassin and was jailed as an accessory after the fact. He was played by Warner Baxter, not Paul Muni. In the first stanza Henry recalls films of the 1920s and 30s, including *The Lost World*, which lies behind his friend Randall Jarrell's nostalgic Hollywood poem, and *The Man From Blankley's* (1930), a satirical, rather talkative social comedy starring John Barrymore. The second stanza concerns fashionable foreign movies shown in art houses during Henry's manhood. The third stanza evokes the Hoot Gibson and William S. Hart Westerns of his youth. (116)

'A Matinée' (O'Brien). Rossano Brazzi (born Bologna, 1916) was the principal Italian dream lover employed by Hollywood in the 1950s, playing opposite Ava Gardner (*The Barefoot Contessa*), Jean Peters (*Three Coins in the Fountain*), Katharine Hepburn (*Summer Madness*), Sophia Loren (*Legend of the Lost*), Mitzi Gaynor (*South Pacific*). (118)

'Double Feature' (Reading). The final assault on Mount Everest by the British Commonwealth team led by Colonel John Hunt in June 1953 was gauged to coincide with the Coronation of Queen Elizabeth II, who had succeeded her father, George VI, in February 1952. The live television coverage of the

Coronation was a milestone in broadcasting history. But that was in black and white. Preconceived, rapidly edited colour documentaries, one of them with a poetic commentary written by Christopher Fry and spoken by Laurence Olivier, were sped around the world. They were accompanied by triumphant film of Edmund Hillary and Sherpa Tenzing's conquest of Everest. (120)

'A Film Review in the Form of a Poem' (Goldstein). Grauman's (much later Mann's) Chinese Theater on Hollywood Boulevard is as famous as Rick's Café Américain in Casablanca. Merle Oberon played Cathy in the 1939 Goldwyn production of *Wuthering Heights*. Nicolas Roeg directed the SF allegory *The Man Who Fell to Earth* (1976). Jerry Siegel and Joe Shuster created the comic-strip hero Superman in the 1930s, sold out their rights and died penniless. (122)

'Snow White Meets the Wolfman' (McAuley). In several Universal horror films, Lon Chaney Jr played Lawrence Talbot, the Wolf Man. *The Song of Bernadette* (1943), directed by the great Hollywood veteran Henry King, is a serious, reverential, accomplished, and far from despicable film about the French saint Bernadette (Jennifer Jones) whose visions created the shrine at Lourdes. *Baisers volés* (1968) is the third movie featuring Jean-Pierre Léaud as François Truffaut's cinematic *alter ego* Antoine Doinel. (135)

'Vincent and I Inaugurate a Movie Theatre' (O'Hara). Allen and Peter are O'Hara's peripatetic beat friends, Allen Ginsberg and Peter Orlovsky. *Alice Adams* (1935), directed by George Stevens, stars Katharine Hepburn as a social-climbing middle-western woman. Updated from a 1922 novel by Booth Tarkington (author of *The Magnificent Ambersons*), it is one of the most acute studies of class in American cinema. (136)

'Further Decline of Western Civilization' (Webb). In the 1983 Cold War thriller *Gorky Park* (directed by Michael Apted, based on a novel by Martin Cruz Smith, set in Moscow, filmed in Finland), William Hurt plays an honest Soviet homicide detective investigating a series of brutal murders that bring him into contact with honest American cop Brian Dennehy and corrupt fur trader Lee Marvin. Not to be confused with at least two other movies with the same title, writer-director Robert Vincent O'Neil's *Angel* (1983), a slick, low-life melodrama, centres on a female highschool student leading a double life as a Hollywood Boulevard prostitute. Cliff Gorman plays a compassionate cop. (137)

'Brief Encounter' (Smith). In the David Lean–Noël Coward film *Brief Encounter* (1945), English housewife Celia Johnson and married English doctor Trevor Howard meet on a provincial railway station, embark on a romantic, unconsummated affair, and finally part at the same station. (140)

'Drive In Movie' (Sange). Doris Day and Cary Grant appeared together in one film, playing a primly virginal secretary and her lecherous boss in the Delbert Mann comedy *That Touch of Mink* (1962). (146)

'On Seeing a Movie Based on an Episode from President Kennedy's Life' (Ray). *PT 109* (1963, director Leslie Martinson) is a Warner Brothers reconstruction of the World War Two incident in the South Pacific when Lieutenant John F. Kennedy's torpedo boat was sunk after an encounter with a Japanese destroyer. Cliff Robertson played Kennedy with the family's approval. The supporting film in this drive-in double bill is *Rampage* (1962, director Phil Karlson), another Warner film, in which Robert Mitchum and Jack Hawkins play rival white hunters transporting a rare cross between a leopard and a tiger from Malaysia to a German zoo. The plot has a certain resemblance to Hemingway's story 'The Short Happy Life of Francis Macomber' (filmed in 1947 as *The Macomber Affair* with Gregory Peck as Wilson the white hunter). (150)

'The Shooting of John Dillinger outside the Biograph Theater' (Wagoner). The Indiana bank robber and FBI Public Enemy Number One John Dillinger (1902–1934) was killed by G-men as he emerged from watching the MGM gangster movie *Manhattan Melodrama* (1934, director W. S. Van Dyke) starring Clark Gable and William Powell as childhood friends who grow up to become a hoodlum and a district attorney. The death of Dillinger has been recreated in numerous films including *Dillinger* (1945, director Max Nosseck), *The FBI Story* (1959, director Mervyn LeRoy), *Dillinger* (1973, director John Milius), and *The Lady in Red* (1979, director Lewis Teague). (154)

'Grace at the Atlanta Fox' (Cassity). The Atlanta Fox in Atlanta, Georgia, was among the grandest cinemas in the American South, a Spanish-Moresque palace that enhanced, and not infrequently overwhelmed, the movies shown there. It was embarked upon when the pioneer Hollywood mogul William J. Fox was creating his empire in the 1920s and became part of the 20th Century-Fox organization that Darryl Zanuck put together in the wake of Fox's downfall. 'Pre-Eleanor and pre-Fala' refers to Eleanor Roosevelt and FDR's dog Fala; the 'Hoover nights' alludes to the time before the coming of the New Deal. (157)

'Leicester Square: May 1974' (Cotton). Jack Clayton's version of *The Great Gatsby* had its premiére at the Odeon, Leicester Square. Nearby, at a now-defunct cinema opening on to Charing Cross Road, was to be seen the lesser known *Die Stewardessen* (aka *The Swinging Stewardesses*), a 1972 German movie about the amorous adventures of the air hostesses Jenny, Frances and Evelyn, directed by one Michael Thomas. The British censor cut the film from 85 minutes to 65 to protect local audiences from its continental erotic excesses. (164)

'On the Demolition of the Odeon Cinema, Westbourne Grove' (Heath-Stubbs). The Odeon, Westbourne Grove in West London, was one of the cinemas in Britain's largest, most architecturally significant national movie chain, created in the 1930s by the Birmingham-born Oscar Deutsch (1893–1941). Its name, happily coinciding with ancient Greek and more recent American precedents, was derived from his initials. Designed and embarked upon before the advent of World

War Two forced its temporary abandonment, this 1,750-seat cinema was finally opened in August 1955. In 1983 the Rank Organization, which had acquired the Odeon chain after Deutsch's death, sold the cinema to the small Coronet company, and it was demolished in 1985.

The double-bill of British 'U' Certificate adventure movies the poet recalls was shown there in August 1963. In *Jason and the Argonauts* (directed by Don Chaffey), a retelling of the search for the Golden Fleece, the American performers Todd Armstrong (Jason) and Nancy Kovack (Medea) head an otherwise British cast. The script was by the playwright and opera librettist Beverly Cross (later to be the husband of Dame Maggie Smith), the special effects were created by Ray Harryhausen, and the score was provided by Bernard Herrmann, who wrote the music for *Citizen Kane*, numerous Hitchcock films, and Scorsese's *Taxi Driver*. Directed by the American Nathan Juran, *Siege of the Saxons* has a wholly British cast led by Janette Scott as King Arthur's daughter Katharine, who is assisted by a Robin Hood-style outlaw to repel the Saxon enemy. The invaders are helped by the treacherous regicide Edmund, played by Ronald Howard, son of the more famous Leslie, whose death is memorialized in a poem by Maurice Lindsay in this anthology. (168)

'Gutting the ABC' (Munden). The Associated British Picture Corporation was one of the biggest producers of films in Britain and through its ABC cinemas (where MGM and Warner Brothers films were screened) the principal competitor in Britain to the Rank Organization's Odeon and Gaumont chains. The company ceased production and its dwindling number of cinemas passed into the hands of EMI and the Cannon company; those that now survive bear the name MGM. Pearl and Dean was the chief national company responsible for producing and distributing advertisements in British cinemas, their glittering logo preceding packages of commercials, making them as famous, if not as respected, as the great Hollywood studios. (168)

'Sunday Observance' (Brode). The legendary Film Society was launched in London in 1925, with H. G. Wells, George Bernard Shaw, J. B. S. Haldane and Julian Huxley among its charter members, and held its first screening (Paul Leni's *Waxworks*) at the New Gallery Kinema, Oxford Street, on the afternoon of Sunday 25 October. Its Sunday performances continued until April 1939, becoming a sabbath institution and being widely copied around the country. (169)

IV

The Stars and the Supporting Cast

Provide, Provide

The witch that came (the withered hag)
To wash the steps with pail and rag,
Was once the beauty Abishag,

The picture pride of Hollywood.
Too many fall from great and good
For you to doubt the likelihood.

Die early and avoid the fate.
Or if predestined to die late,
Make up your mind to die in state.

Make the whole stock exchange your own!
If need be occupy a throne,
Where nobody can call *you* crone.

Some have relied on what they knew;
Others on being simply true.
What worked for them might work for you.

No memory of having starred
Atones for later disregard,
Or keeps the end from being hard.

Better to go down dignified
With boughten friendship at your side
Than none at all. Provide, provide!

Robert Frost

The Film Star

Donnez à manger aux affamées
It is a film star who passes this way
He is looking so nice the women would like

To have him on a tray
Donnez à manger aux affamées.

Stevie Smith

Girl in Films

The girl had the nothing talked out of her,
was given the black hat, and made a star:
new films were made in hours, and she cried

in the executive producer's car
while being driven smiling to the door.
There was an engine and a well inside,

it cost a hundred dollars just to peer
over the edge, far more to wind the tar
up to the surface: when an actor died

the girl talked quietly. Behind the bar
the ample barman taped what he saw
and sold it to the network for a ride

inside some woman's cadillacky fur.
The girl froze up and moved in with the czar,
who'd lace one cup in six with cyanide.

Glyn Maxwell

Movie Actress

I sit a queen, and am no widow, and shall see no sorrow

She is young and lies curved on the velvety floor of her fame
Like a prize-winning cat on a mirror of fire and oak,
And her dreams are as black as the Jew who uncovered her name;

She is folded in magic and hushed in the pride of her cloak
Which is woven of worship like silk for the hollows of eyes
That are raised in the dark to her image that shimmered and spoke;

And she speaks in her darkness alone and her emptiness cries
Till her voice is as shuddering tin in the wings of a stage,
And her beauty seems wrong as the wig of a perfect disguise;

She is sick with the shadow of shadow, diseased with the rage
Of the whiteness of light and the heat of interior sun,
And she faints like a pauper to carry the weight of her wage;

She is coarse with the honors of power, the duties of fun
And amazed at the regions of pleasure where skill is begun.

Karl Shapiro

The Movie Beauties

Forever twenty,
The promise of kohled eyes stares from the past.
What thickets of memory and experience
Have we hacked through
To reach this arousing of emotion,
Denied even the salutary kiss?
No Prince Charming,
The projectionist threads film
And they awaken as they were,
Pearl, Dolores, Lillian and Jean,
Those delectable sex-pots of the screen
We could never touch
Except by proxy.
And now to the distance of their flesh
Is added time.
Desire so latent,
What is this that wakes in us?
My sleeping beauties
You sleep deeper now,
In memories of how
It never was.

John Cotton

Movie Actors Scribbling Letters Very Fast in Crucial Scenes

The velocity with which they write –
Don't you know it? It's from the heart!
They are acting the whole part out.
Love! has taken them up –
Like writing to god in the night.
Meet me! I'm dying! Come at once!
The crisis is on them, the shock
Drives from the nerve to the pen,
Pours from the blood into ink.

Jean Garrigue

Inside Sally

First off, there were the fans,
Flashes of pure blond, blue
Lights and Clair de Lune

The crouching quarterback

The fans, that taut balloon,
And movement, movement
On the stage, the lights,
The frozen room, the fans

A roaring in the circling stands,
The crouching quarterback,
A Princeton boy, arms striped

'I never quite understood it,
This sex symbol,' said Marilyn
Monroe before she died. They named
A life preserver for Mae West.
Jean Harlow, her platinum hair, died
Of her kidney, and Brigitte Bardot,
At thirty years, is still troubled
By acne.

[182]

There was, of course, music,
Au Clair de Lune, and fans,
A thousand fans, blond rhythm
In those curling wings

The crouching quarterback,
A Princeton boy, striped arms,
Calls Inside Sally, his wingback
Takes the ball, a play as naked
As the moon,
                    and understands.

                              R. H. W. Dillard*

The Blue Angel

Marlene Dietrich is singing a lament
for mechanical love.
She leans against a mortarboard tree
on a plateau by the seashore.

She's a life-sized toy,
the doll of eternity;
her hair is shaped like an abstract hat
made out of white steel.

Her face is powdered, whitewashed and
immobile like a robot.
Jutting out of her temple, by an eye,
is a little white key.

She gazes through dull blue pupils
set in the whites of her eyes.
She closes them, and the key
turns by itself.

She opens her eyes, and they're blank
like a statue's in a museum.
Her machine begins to move, the key turns
again, her eyes change, she sings

– you'd think I would have thought a plan
to end the inner grind,
but not till I have found a man
to occupy my mind.

Allen Ginsberg

15th Raga For Bela Lugosi

Sir, when you say
Transylvania or wolfbane
or
I am Count Dracula,
your eyes become wide
&, for the moment, pure
white marble.

It is no wonder that
you were so long a junkie.

It's in the smile. The way
you drifted into Victorian bedrooms
holding up your cape like skirts,

then covering her face
as you bent over her to kiss
into her neck & sup.

It is no wonder & it was
in good taste too.

David Meltzer*

Bela Lugosi: Three Lines

1   1930

To be dead, to be really dead,
That must be glorious.
But you cried like a man undone
When the stake broke in:
The truth of Dracula
In that last sound, off camera,
Somewhere to the right of focus.

2   1933

A simpler truth: *Death*
Is always very close.
In the liver, the heart,
The room across the hall,
The food in the jar,
The unexpected call
Late at night.

3   1934

Master of old fly eaters,
King of the rats, batwing
And red eye, you knew
The lesson of the veins,
The secrets of circulation.
Any way you cut it,
It was always the same:
Supernatural, perhaps.
Baloney, perhaps not.

R. H. W. Dillard

Ode to Groucho

1 INVOCATION

Pindarick, a great gorblimey Ode
Soaring on buzzard wings, ornate,
Or tottering titanic on feet of clay,
It would have to be, to be adequate –
With the neo-gromboolian overtones
And the neo-classic gimmicks:
Pat gags cadenced from 'Mauberly'
In platinum-plated timing,
And tendrils convolvulating
To clutch the dirty cracks and hold the house up!

O flaking Palladian Palladium!
On a back-cloth rattled by oom-pah –
All our nostalgias, Hey there! the old vaudeville circuit.
Proscenium buttressed with brutal truths
Where sleek myths lean in manneristic attitudes,
Chalk-white in the chastest diction,
Sequined with glittering metaphysicality.
And massive ambiguities
Endlessly rocking a whole way of life.

2 PRESENCE

What you had was a voice
To talk double-talk faster,
Twanging hypnotic
In an age of nagging voices –
And bold eyes to dart around
As you shambled supremely,
Muscular moth-eaten panther!

Black eyebrows, black cigar,
Black painted moustache –
A dark code of elegance
In an age of nagging moustaches –
To discomfit the coarse mayor,

Un-poise the suave headmaster,
Reduce all the old boys to muttering fury.

A hero for the young,
Blame if you wish the human situation –
Subversivest of con-men
In an age of ersatz heroes:
Be talkative and shabby and
Witty; bully the bourgeois;
Act the obvious phoney.

3 APOTHEOSIS

Slickness imposed on a rough beast,
A slouching beast and hypochondriac.

Great Anarch! Totem of the lot,
All the shining rebels

(Prometheus, of course, and that old pauper
Refusing cake from Marie Antoinette,
And Baudelaire's fanatical toilette,
And Rimbaud, striding off to Africa,
And Auden, scrowling at a cigarette . . .)

Bliss was it etc. Smartish but fair enough.
We stammered out our rudenesses

O splendid and disreputable father!

Martin Bell*

To the Lady Portrayed by Margaret Dumont

Now that high, oft-affronted bosom heaves
A final sigh, crushed by the wrecker's ball;
Like a definitive mansard, it leaves
Our view an empty lot. Before the fall,
The camp was to make sex grotesque, but when
Was anything more grave? For us, our grace

[187]

Was being the yoohooed-at, naughty men
Whose eyes would lower, finally, from that Face.

Death, be not bowed by that solidity
But bear her ever upward, cloud by cloud,
To where she sits, with vast solemnity,
Enthroned; and may we, some day, be allowed
  If not a life of constant flight there, then a
    Glimpse of that fierce green land of mink and henna.

John Hollander*

Villanelle for Harpo Marx

True oracles say more than they suppose.
Your very dumbness makes your message clear.
The clown may speak what silent Hamlet knows.

A harmless droll is what the camera shows,
The children's friend whom parents need not fear.
True oracles say more than they suppose.

In your fake world of frantic gag and pose
We see our real despair come striding near.
The clown may speak what silent Hamlet knows.

Your wasteful slapstick is a dig at those
Whose cash can buy the strength that most revere.
True oracles say more than they suppose.

You say that terror pays what pleasure owes.
What makes it real is that they cannot hear.
The clown may speak what silent Hamlet knows.

You tell them no man loves the dice he throws.
It is a zany world that calls you queer.
True oracles say more than they suppose.
The clown may speak what silent Hamlet knows.

John Wain

To Harpo Marx

O Harpo! When did you seem like an angel
   the last time?
   and played the gray harp of gold?

When did you steal the silverware
   and bug-spray the guests?

When did your brother find rain
   in your sunny courtyard?

When did you chase your last blonde
   across the Millionairesses' lawn
   with a bait hook on a line
   protruding from your bicycle?

Or when last you powderpuffed
   your white flour face
   with fishbarrel cover?

Harpo! Who was that Lion
   I saw you with?

How did you treat the midget
   and Konk the Giant?

Harpo, in your recent nightclub appearance
   in New Orleans were you old?
   Were you still chiding with your horn
   in the cane at your golden belt?

Did you still emerge from your pockets
   another Harpo, or screw on
   new wrists?

Was your vow of silence an Indian Harp?

                        Jack Kerouac

Harpo Marx

Harpo Marx, your hands white-feathered the harp —
the only words you ever spoke were sound.
The movie's not always the sick man of the arts,
yours touched the stars; Harpo, your motion picture
is still life unchanging, not nature dead.
You dumbly memorized an unwritten script . . .
I saw you first two years before you died,
a black-and-white fall, near Fifth in Central Park:
old blond hair too blonder, old eyes too young.
Movie trucks and five police trucks wheel to wheel
like covered wagons. The crowd as much or little.
I wish I had knelt . . . I age to your wincing smile,
like Dante's movie, the great glistening wheel of life —
the genius *happy* . . . a generic actor.

Robert Lowell

La Plus Blanche

JEAN HARLOW, YOU ARE IN BEAUTY ON DARK EARTH
WITH WHITE FEET! MICHAEL
slaying the dragon is not more wonderful than you. To air
you give magical sleekness. We shall carry you into Space
on our shoulders. You triumph over all with warm legs and a
smile of wistful anxiety that's cover for the honesty
spoken by your grace! Inner energy presses out to you in warmness —

you return love. Love returned for admiration! Strangeness
is returned by you for desire. How. Where
but in the depth of Jean Harlow is such strangeness
made into grace? How many women are more beautiful
in shape and apparition! How few can /have/

draw such love to them? For you are the whole creature of love!

Your muscles are love muscles!

Your nerves — Love nerves!

And your upturned
comic eyes!
Sleep dreams of you.

Michael McClure*

To Celebrate Eddie Cantor

The flesh is brittle, alas,
And ever-modish time, that fiend, is slee:
The Goldwyn Girls of Nineteen Thirty-Three
Also must go, must fade beyond nostalgia,
Vanish when celluloid crackles.

That year, not less constrained,
We strained the other way to find the future –
Eager and awkward, tried to look sixteen,
Be full initiates into the life of the time
And shuffle into the LYRIC, the local flea-pit.
We howled and whistled, fidgets on iron seats.

Our coming-in was brisk to music
Strident through raucous light along the slanting floor,
Underfoot rubbish and everywhere sweet disinfectant
Stinking like LADIES and GENTLEMEN –
The whole place blatant and blaring,
Usherettes sullen and louts obstreperous.

And, slumping back in seats, to see a flick,
Shadows to look at shadows, not expecting luck,
Amazed then, caught in your outrageous joy,
Dear Eddie!
          Blank looming screen
And then you whirled from its imagined wings –
A small impassioned man who could hardly wait for his music,
A master, from Vaudeville, an accomplished master.

Voice soaring in gleeful lubricity,
Scandalous coloratura at full tilt!
Excited wide eyes rolling

[191]

And hands that have to clap that joy's too much.
Energy, wanton small bright ball
Leaping on top of the fountain –
Living water, extravagant
Flooding and cleansing the movie-house.

No endless exits down the sad perspectives,
The avenues of infinite regrets,
For you, Sir, No Siree!
Palmy Days, ample a blue sky
And the gross bull lulled to an euphoric calm,
Contented cows, O Don Sebastian –
The lineaments of gratified desire
Making whoopee with the whooping red-skins.

Thinly we rustled, ears of unripe corn –
You could have gathered us up in the palms of your hands.
Singing and dancing, you came out more than real,
Potent Revivalist, strong drink for shadows –
For you at the end of the picture
Bunches and baskets of flowers, all of them girls.

Martin Bell*

Mae West

Westward the course of vampire moves its way;
The concave bosom sinks into eclipse;
Everywhere happy endings flatter Mae,
And ape the pace that launched a thousand hips.

Ogden Nash*

Mae West

She comes on drenched in a perfume called Self-Satisfaction
from feather boa to silver pumps.

She does not need to be loved by you,
though she'll give you credit for good taste.
Just because you say you love her
she's not throwing herself at your feet in gratitude.

Every other star shows how worthless she feels
by crying when the hero says he loves her,
or how unhoped for the approval is
when the audience applauds her big number,
but Mae West takes it as her due –
she knows she's good.

She expects the best for herself
and knows she's worth what she costs
and she costs plenty –
she's not giving anything away.

She enjoys her admirers, fat daddy or muscleman,
and doesn't confuse vanity and sex,
though she never turns down pleasure,
lapping it up.

Above all, she enjoys herself,
swinging her body that says, Me, Me, Me, Me,
why not have a good time?
As long as you amuse me, go on,
I like you slobbering over my hand, big boy,
I have a right to.

Most convincing, we know all this
not by her preaching it
but by her presence – it's no act.
Every word and look and movement
spells independence.
She likes being herself.

And we who don't
can only look on, astonished.

Edward Field

Reflections on a Bowl of Kumquats, 1936

The exemplar of the calculating squint
and the surreptitious kick to the shin,
of the fight to the finish, no holds barred;
the juggler with billiard balls and oranges,
interchangeable in a blur –
like Life&Death at the heart of the farce:
bite into the wrong thing in the dark and watch
the teeth fly like sparks, everybody laughing . . .
Sly, slyer than cats and lady druggists,
more familiar than house dicks with the bright evil
gritted into the fabric of things, of 'everyday life',
so many places to avoid, and dreams,
the man in the four-way mirror outflanking his insomnia,
pockets stuffed with bankbooks,
closely shaven even at two a.m.
Let double-talk patch the fearsome wind,
a crazyquilt of insults and anxious asides,
only the children, who threatened him, equipped
to read the barometer of that face,
the short degrees between spite and rage,
degrees of applause and betrayal,
of the dinginess of rooms, of the lost years
notched with a penknife on his traveling trunk.
Now see the sun setting behind the palms,
see the weedless lawn and the Florentine fountain,
see the clay court steaming through the vines,
see Hollywood to the north dirty and pink;
tailored in white with rakish Panama, chewed corona,
the nimble fat man sips gin from a halved tennis ball,
shows the vicious backhand patented for laughs, for winning.
Only the stray dogs at the gate can appreciate that.
Never give a sucker an even break.

Nicholas Christopher*

In Person: Bette Davis

At the Music Hall
last week, the most varied audience
   ever assembled in Detroit –
   its gay populace émergé,
auto profiteers, idolators from Kalamazoo, shut-ins
blinking from urban and suburban
   TV caves

all came, Bette
(and I could go on listing their fates,
   each $8.50 seat yearning . . .
   for what? two-bit matinees,
the remembered ecstasy of your caustic tongue, the swivelling
cigarette-shaking spitfire
   that is you),

all were on time.
When you entered and said, 'What a dump!'
   they shrieked for a wrecking ball
   but you restrained them with love.
They were mike-shy but your fluent witchery again enchanted
again excited to speech all
   wanting grace.

'I can't believe
('Yes, it's true, darling'), I can't believe
   I'm talking to Bette Davis!'
   'Bette, which was your *favorite*,
was it Margo Channing or Judith Traherne or Mildred or Jane?'
'They were all such *won*derful roles,
   all of them.'

'O Bette, why?
After so many fabulous parts
   why did you degrade yourself
   and play Baby Jane?' 'No, No!
It was a *beau*tiful role, I had a *ball* doing Jane. Remember
I was never a glamour-puss.'
   O Bette

You won't autograph
but when a fanatic hurls to the stage
   you proffer your hand; he kisses
   and swoons to the quotidian . . .
Here is erudition scholars would envy: the meek hypothesis,
the forty-year old rumor; here
   those questions

you have answered
all your life – your co-stars, directors,
   feuds, Oscars, jealousies, kids,
   the *Fortune* poll in '40,
the offer of *Gone With The Wind* passed by (but *Jezebel* remains),
the longing for *Virginia Woolf*
   unfulfilled.

There is nothing
they do not know or will not ask, no film
   they cannot correct you on,
   no secret they have not guessed.
'Bette, why aren't there more tributes for you?' 'I don't want tributes,
   when
they see you stumbling to your grave
   they give you

tributes. No thanks!'
Questions persist, no one dares to leave.
   They would gladly use you up
   but when you dismiss, they obey,
each with his or her internal film of you (in black dress and shoes),
the *person* of you at last, and
   forever.

Laurence Goldstein*

Dick Powell

      I saw him in Hollywood yesterday and I asked
      him why he even considered acting in those little

TV dramas where he was cast as a farmer and
some tow-headed little bastard who wanted to grow
up to be a potato called him Pa and he was too
old to ever get the creamy ingenue.

And whatever happened to the Dick Powell everybody
loved in *Gold Diggers of 1933* where Ruby Keeler
and Joan Blondell never wore bras but he was too
cool to fall for that because all he wanted to
do was tickle those ivories.

He didn't answer, of course, just stared
until I turned to leave. Then he came for me.

The police separated us eventually and I apologized
for being rude and he mumbled something about
unusual pressures.

But that was days ago and I should have forgotten
all about it but at night and sometimes in the
afternoons and even as I write this I can still
feel those cold, yellow teeth in my bones.

Ron Koertge*

Shirley Temple Surrounded by Lions

In a world where kapok on a sidewalk looks like an 'accident'
– innards – would that freckles could enlarge, well, meaningfully
   into kind of friendly brown kingdoms, all isolate,
with a hero's route, feral glens,
   and a fountain where heroines cool their mouths.

Scenario: an albino industrialiste, invited to the beach at noon
(and to such old exiles, oceans hardly teem with ambiguities)
   by a lifeguard after her formulae, though in love –
'Prop-men, the gardenias, the mimosa need anti-droopage stuffing.'
Interestingly slow, the bush and rush filming.

[197]

Hiatus, everyone. After the idea of California sort of took root,
we found ourselves in this cookie forest; she closed the newspaper,
groped past cabañas, blanched and ungainly.

The grips watched Marv and Herm movies of birds tweeting,
fluttering around and in and out an old boat fridge, on a reef,
when eek, the door – or was it 'eef' – 'Shirl' said the starling, end of –

The janitors are watching movies of men and women ruminating.
Then a cartoon of two clocks, licking. Chime. Licking, chime. *Then* a?
   After that, photos of incinerators in use moved families more than
the candy grass toy that retches. Dogs. For the dressers, 'Mutations',
about various feelers. For the extras, movies of revenge that last.

This spree *has* to last. 'Accept my pink eyes, continual swathing,'
Shirley rehearsed. 'Encase me in sand, then let's get kissy.'
   Do children have integrity, i.e. eyes? Newsreels, ponder this.
How slow the filming is for a grayish day with its bonnet
   bumping along the pioneer footpath, pulled by – here, yowly hound.

Kenward Elmslie*

Nobody Dies Like Humphrey Bogart

Casual at the wheel, blinding rainstorm,
The usual blonde doll alongside – only
This time our man knows she's talked,
The double-c, and by his cold eyes
We can tell it's the end of the line for her.

It's all in the corner of his mouth:
Baby if we're gonna go we'll both go
My way, and his foot deep on the gas
With the needle (close-up) leaping to eighty.
She's shaky but ready to call his bluff.

Rain and the wipers clearing the glass
And dead ahead the good old roadblock.
Quick shot moll – the scream forming.

Quick shot Bogey – that endearing look
Which was his alone, face and soul.

Any way we go, baby, one or the other,
You'll look a lot prettier than me
When we're laid out in the last scene,
You in pink or blue with the angels,
Me with the same scar I was born in.

Norman Rosten*

Bogey

san quentin, sing sing, alcatraz.
if he busted out the slammer once
he did it a dozen times.
the smoke he pushed at you
no hazard to your health, mild even,
against narrowing eyes, flared nose,
lip curled so nasty.
robinson, cagney, raft were no match.
he'd whistle down bacall,
and hepburn was easy.

think of him – leeched tugging the QUEEN.
trenching the MADRE, crazy for gold.
grounds in his coffee, nails or glass.
but what about CASABLANCA?
the song sam played wasn't just any song,
ilsa just another dame
when rick grazed her eyes,
clinked her wine, said
'here's looking at you kid.'

Lee L. Berkson

Bogart

I grew up on Humphrey Bogart movies; it was like church.
I liked the way he would look tired muscles at wickedness
And smoke cigarettes existentially, better than Europeans.
'To Have and Have Not' was what his eyes always said;
No matter what the picture was (Queeg as well as The Downer
Of the Drink to Forget Ingrid) the Great Rub was there:
That to have was not to have and not to have was to have.
He granulated that Rub till I could sprinkle it on toast;
In a big feast scene he would see to it that I, a cult of one
In the middle row, got the right feeling for the leftovers;
His empathy was like a nun's, it fed on eternals and grit.
Good wouldn't always win so much as grandeur would,
Grandeur as seen from the squinting empathetic eye he was.

Nicholas Flocos

John Garfield

The heat's on, dead wind shoots up
9th Avenue, flutters the T-shirt
On the convertible's antenna, lulls
The stragglers into Billy's Pool Parlour.
The city's last tough guy
Sidles down 44th Street,
Bumming a smoke, feinting a punch –
Used to show a good left, they say . . .
Later, hat doffed, fingers drumming,
He watches East River tugs
Link the bridges with foam;
Whatever left Brooklyn Harbor
In the last war died, or
Maybe is still out at sea.
After Hollywood, the big money,
The girls with the roulette eyes,
He's blacklisted out of pictures

When he won't give names —
'A matinee socialist', McCarthy calls him.
His voice a hoarseness,
Health gone to hell,
The good looks rumpled into anonymity,
He holes up in West Side hotels
With ex-society girls and B-actresses,
In the end drinks
For nine months straight,
Blacks out regularly at dawn,
Dead at 39, journalists delighted
To report an English girl,
Under-aged and on junk,
In bed with him at the time.
Uptown in a Bronx trainyard
Three kids play blackjack
Under a bridge, blow dope
And belt cough medicine,
Tend a low fire — the fastest one,
In black, keeps losing,
Can't pay up, leans back
And watches rain come down
On a southbound express.

Nicholas Christopher*

The Sidney Greenstreet Blues

I think something beautiful
and amusing is gained
by remembering Sidney Greenstreet,
but it is a fragile thing.

The hand picks up a glass.
The eye looks at the glass
and then hand, glass and eye fall away.

Richard Brautigan*

Carmen Miranda

Backstage, eating bananas
with Carmen Miranda, she offers me
her hat. I thank her and take
a bunch of purple grapes, 3 hardboiled
eggs, a muskmelon and four
ears of corn. She says, Frank,

it wasn't always this way.
There were lean years in Madrid, Marseilles,
Cuernavaca, when dancing didn't pay
and my dear hats went unrefrigerated.
Fruit can be expensive to a poor girl . . .
Anyway, I danced as best I could
with pears, beans, and tangerines shaped
from wax or wood, but it wasn't
the same. You know what they say about
the heart that wears a false face
and vice versa, but why go into it?
It's enough to say I suffered
to dance with no hat at all. Better that
than a cheap imitation! Darling,
try a quince. Persimmons? Have a cumquat!
But, the disgrace of those days
forced me to sing as an escape. And now
my hats and I sing and dance, and do well.
Oh, there are times I feel the fruit
salad is, well, ridiculous; but it's the thing
I do best, if you know what I mean . . .

Before I left, I kissed her
on the cheek, and said, I'm no spokesman
but I think we'll always love you for it . . .
And back on the streets that night
I split the sky with cherry pits.

Frank Polite*

On *Imagerie*: Esther Williams, 1944

only in the
milkiest
emulsions, the deepest
silvers, would
that

mirror open, the
tips

of the elbows
flare.   combs, lotions . . .
her sleeves
would

float over the
foam-
white bowls with their
na-

creous blossoms.   hair
shaken, hands
posed, each
glint's

a splinter, a ray I'd
pull from
those

gray, grain-
in-

flected spaces . . .
warped
oceans, our
ob-
fuscated worlds.   would
feed on

those fires, that light
that

> pours in a
> limp
> clatter of black,
> unfastened corals . . .
>
> Gustaf Sobin*

Why That's Bob Hope

The comedian, holding a chunk of flaming shale.
If only *Der Bingle* could see him now! He looked
so puffed and sleepy in that Texaco hardhat,
I could've popped a fuse. Well, like the oil,

here today and gone today. In *my* good old days
Hope was on Sullivan's 'shew' so often us kids
dropped TV for longhair sex and smoking weeds.
What a mistake! But now we're past our wild phase

and Bob's back with this burning rock, funny
for a change. No, no old quips now about Dean's double
vision, Phyllis Diller's breasts or Sinatra's aging treble.
He says if we all squeeze the rock together real money

will drip out. We'll live real good and still afford a war
where he'll bust our boys' guts on tour in El Salvador.

William Hathaway*

Poem

Lana Turner has collapsed!
I was trotting along and suddenly
it started raining and snowing
and you said it was hailing
but hailing hits you on the head
hard so it was really snowing and

[204]

raining and I was in such a hurry
to meet you but the traffic
was acting exactly like the sky
and suddenly I see a headline
LANA TURNER HAS COLLAPSED!
there is no snow in Hollywood
there is no rain in California
I have been to lots of parties
and acted perfectly disgraceful
but I never actually collapsed
oh Lana Turner we love you get up

Frank O'Hara*

Cross My Heart

I always feel that Sonny Tufts
Is something rather large from Cruft's:
Which gives his work, in moderation,
A certain dogged fascination.

C. A. Lejeune*

The B Movie

At a preview of *That Hagen Girl* in 1947, when actor Ronald Reagan became the
first person on screen to say 'I love you, will you marry me?' to the nineteen-year-
old Shirley Temple, there was such a cry of 'Oh, no!' from the invited audience that
the scene was cut out when the film was released.

Lap dissolve. You make a man speak crap dialogue,
one day he'll make you eat your words. OK?
Let's go for a take. Where's the rest of me? '*Oh, no!*'

Things are different now. He's got star billing,
star wars, applause. Takes her in his arms.
I'm talking about a *real* weepie. Freeze frame. '*Oh, no!*'

[205]

On his say-so, the train wipes out the heroine
and there ain't no final reel. How do you like that?
My fellow Americans, we got five minutes. *'Oh, no!'*

Classic. He holds the onion to water such sorrow.
We need a Kleenex the size of Russia here, no kidding.
Have that kid's tail any time he wants to. *Yup.*

Carol Ann Duffy*

Valerio

A poem-film, starring Anthony Quinn

Valerio gets down from his mule.
He holds a leather lung to his mouth.
It is the wine of his country.
As he drinks it, he looks down on
A valley that was seldom green
In the days when he, too, dug and hoe'd.
It was the Irrigation Project
Delivered this green outlook.
For years they demanded such a thing.
Five years ago, the government
Turned up and turned on water.
Men went to jail in 1928,
Demanding water and a few pipes.
Men went to jail in '32,
After two men died in the scuffle.
What were their names? Brave men, anyway . . .
Priests don't like Valerio.
Who *does* like him? Nobody does.
He bawls insults at the lawyer.
'Your feet', he yells, 'disturb the dust
And spiderwebs of fascism!'
Everybody laughs at him.
He insults the wife of the mayor.
'Your father sent men to their deaths!'
'Why don't you forget, Valerio?

Why don't you forgive and forget?'
Valerio walks away, tugging
His mule on its halter, grunting.
'And why did he never marry, eh?'
He tows his mule into the village
Surrounded now by new houses.
By a wall he can hear young bathers
In the swimming-pool of the hotel.
There's nothing for him at the Post Office.
Valerio, who led the partisans,
There's no letter for Valerio.
He walks out of a page of
Silone's early stories, sunlight
Redesigning the dust from the building-site.
'Who'd write to *him*?' everybody asks.
'Can he even *read*?' 'They say he fought
Two years in the hills, up there.'
A young man watches him go by
Then takes a seat with an open view.
He sees Valerio climb the old track.
'They say he still lives up there,'
Says his uncle. 'It's a sad story.
Personally, I preferred to survive.'
Valerio sits on a boulder
And looks at yellow earth-movers
Nudge and butt at the landscape
In which, for years, he lay concealed.
He goes higher, and farther away.
The young man watching him turns
To look at a girl on a bicycle.
When he turns back, Valerio's gone.
He doesn't know why, but a tear
Drips down the young man's cheek, and falls
Into the dust, where, soon, it dries.
It was over there, by the sluice
Of the Irrigation Project
Valerio ran with a girl
That night when everything went wrong.
Demented Germans were burning farms,
Burning everything they couldn't eat

Or take with them, and the sky heaved
In illuminated rumbles.
And he had six bullets left
Out of the twelve he had to start with.
Six times he'd missed, and ten friends dead.
If only one had lived! Just one.
Even the Englishman who'd come
Out of the sky by parachute
With his bad Italian, his promises,
And who was shot jumping the dry stream-bed.
Who ever heard of such a thing –
A dead, long-jumping Englishman?
If he had lived, Valerio thinks,
Then he, at least, would write to me.
Valerio lost a boot and breath.
There was a noise where there should have been none.
She sighed. Her grip was tight.
A minute went by and then she fell.
He didn't even know her name, not then,
Not now, a courier from somewhere.
Fear and courage without a name!
The dead, anonymous as furniture . . .
He hid and waited for two Germans,
Who tapped her body with their boots,
Then turned her over, tearing off
Her covert crucifix.
He's seen so much of his country
Through rifle-sights. Now, as he looks,
He sees the German metal shine,
Not quite reflections, but more like
Reflections in disguise, dull light.
Two shots towards the metal.
A door bangs in the village and
He twists the halter which he drags his mule by.
He carried the girl into the hills
And buried her at dawn beside
The spring, where goats drink. Their bells,
He was told, as a child, inspired
A poet from Rome to write a sonnet.
Since then, he dreams of lovers

With bells around their throats,
And, cradled in his palm, his warm
And miniature Christ still suffers.
Only Valerio knows, his lips on the water,
His knees among picnic litter.
Whenever he remembers her
He looks at his four bullets with
The agony of Christ – one for
The lawyer, and one for the lawyer's wife;
One for the lawyer's father who
Was worse than his fat son; one for
The priest. The man in the Post Office
Who claims he has had no letter
Will be taken care of with a knife.
Valerio puts the lung of wine
To his mouth that has not kissed
His mouth shut tight on a secret
A mouth which refuses to speak
A mouth which gave up cursing years ago
A mouth which mumbles when drunk
A mouth wise in wine and water
A mouth which chokes on its insults.
Foreign tourists have rented the summer.
Valerio does not know why
They are responsible – he scans
The car-park through German binoculars –
All he knows is that they are.
And he, Valerio, is honoured in that country,
and in other countries where
They clench their fists for Valerio
Without knowing the name of Valerio.
He counts his bullets. He guards his spring.

                                    Douglas Dunn*

Twice As Many Gorillas

For Ava Gardner

Now listen here, Guinevere, one more shot
like that and you're inside the lizard noose,
I'll string you up with the iguana, or ship
you to a convent – see if you can get
the cleric's collar off your neck when you're
frazzled, spooked, and all played out.
No more midnight swims with your two handy men
and beach boy lancelots, Misters Urge and Purge.
Admit it baby, you begin your nightly
scenes with traces of a noble Spanish accent,
but soon you've dropped it altogether, sometimes
snarling a remark in Spanish slang, trotting
around the animal compound in high heels.
And by the end you're a dancing barefoot contessa,
your fingernails just exuding peals
of take-me/forsake-me polish, as your curls and earrings
and black satin skirt make shakey orbits
around the one salacious plea your eyes
can offer. You have a plan for every
sleeping purpose: to rouse it until another
victim comes slinking back, expecting
some damage in the dark and then some rest.
Yes, I know the businessman master planner
made us all monkeys' uncles with our urges,
but you have twice as many gorillas
bounding through your supposedly civilized brain,
and you can't soothe them 'til they break the bars,
make a big mess, and cower back inside again.

Jack Skelley*

The Newlyweds

After a one-day honeymoon, the Fishers rushed off to a soft drink bottlers' convention, then on to a ball game, a TV rehearsal and a movie preview.

Life

'We're married,' said Eddie.
Said Debbie, 'Incredi-

ble! When is our honey-
moon?' 'Over and done,' he

replied. 'Feeling logy?
Drink Coke.' 'Look at Yogi

go!' Debbie cried. 'Groovy!'
'Rehearsal?' 'The movie.'

'Some weddie,' said Debbie.
Said Eddie, 'Yeah, mebbe.'

John Updike*

To G. K.

Princess, whose magic pen was dipped
   In radiant colours of romance
To write the wonder of your script,
   Your fairy-tale of chance?

Bring us Beauty, Art and Grace
   Be welcome to this land of ours
And with our homage take your place
   'Mid song and flowers.

Long may you play your golden part,
   Not only to en-sky your name,
But to be throned in every heart
   With heart-fire fame.

A people we, proud of our Past,
   From modern urgency afar,
Long have we hoped with faith steadfast
   To hail with ecstasy a Star.

Sweet Princess, may our dream come true –
Our Star be You.

                              Robert Service*

Ballade for a Wedding

Moments exist for you and me
   Of solitude that's not for those
Within the fringe of monarchy:
   They have the thorns and we the rose.
   We could abide perhaps the prose
Of pressmen and the trumpets' blare,
   The flashlights and the public pose,
But Father Tucker will be there.

Deep diving in the Middle Sea,
   Where friendly langoustes wave and doze
And cuttle-fish suck tenderly
   Points of a prince's rubber toes,
   In that green world where no tide flows,
Far from the *plein* and the *impaire*,
   Dreams he of love? for nothing shows
That Father Tucker will be there.

Now at the Hôtel de Paris
   The open friends and secret foes,
By that stone cavalier where we
   Used to discuss our winning throws,
   Gather for gossip: Hopper knows
Why Garbo's missing and the fair
   Jane and Marlene, but all suppose
That Father Tucker will be there.

Envoi

   Prince, you may draw your curtains close
And set your sentries on the stair,
   Then lie down by the bride you chose,
But Father Tucker will be there.

Graham Greene*

Marilyn

that last take – not MISFITS, them.
she and clark under a fine moon, posse of stars.
the colt bolts to the mountain, finds innocence.
monty broods by the corral.
she loves them all, even monty.
she says goodbye, as if tomorrow . . .

suppose she slept easy without the pills.
suppose the call got through to bobby or jack.
imagine joe in the on-deck circle
menacing in yankee pinstripes, batting cleanup,
always cleanup. arthur in the wings.

suppose she packs, grabs her poodle
slips out the side door, incognito
as she can be in silver lamé,
top cut low enough to jar the dullest memory.
suppose she flies into morning
lands in Majorca, hops a single engine
some island off the map.

say she practices her spanish
words like 'buenas noches' and 'adios'
fading into orange roofs, papaya
a shell's throw from the water
the sand and sun. a bird sings to her
wants no autograph.

Lee L. Berkson*

[213]

Marilyn and You

From one of her sky-high heels, Marilyn
would lop off
a quarter of an inch,
a horse-shoe in miniature,
so that she could toe the line
the more unsteadily
between insanity and lunch,
or walk a high-tension wire
she could never see the end of
(they always gave her too much, or too little rope);
she went skeetering, all ass-wiggles,
hip-swayings, thigh-jiggles,
down a shocking slope
to the bed where they found her jack-knifed.

Photographs would have her looking well-dressed
in black high-heels
and not much else.

You wear yours to parties – that little lift –
and only look unsteady when you're drunk, or bored
off-balance.
You've never used them to pin any part of a man
to the floor, or stamp a military tattoo
on his chest.
I've seen them flung anyhow in the cupboard
among the bras and pants
and given them a second glance.
I've watched you, after half a mile, totter
and almost fall. Go barefoot rather than.

Alan Jenkins

The Earth: To Marilyn

hey brassy baby whose switched-on hair
made them glow in the dark
call for a brand-new smile to wear
in the long nights when the geiger counters
praise you, when dream goal
of a thousand quick-buck loud tuft hunters
you go down measured/call
for a trickier hip swivel
to flick the slow worm fingers off, drop out
the ball from the socket, the joint
from its fleshbound background, tune
the strings away

from their fixed tonality/call
a halt to that plumed tale
of wealth they caught fluttering out of your walk
(made needles rise, that crazy click
go-go: we've struck the mother-lode)/call for
a girdle of stainless steel
fitted with three padlocks, seven sharp spikes to stick
whatever plunders you/for a quick
mind feel.

　　　　lady of spending in dreams when I see
under your put-on costumes of intellect
how rich
delicious you were made
madonna of money, my promised score
when the sound tracks
out when the blind hair screen
screams black and nothing's
paying i detest the waste
of life, loin's hurry, mind's fast
that came to this long feast
for you and me
now we two are filled

your mouth with me
mine with you

Judith E. Johnson

Marilyn

Bleached, plucked, and flaccid, heavily insured,
You burn upon the filament of night.
The palm-lined canyon where your heart is mured
Echoes your kinship to hermaphrodite.
The jewelled toad is cousin to your house
And squats within the eucalyptus wood;
Enjoin the moth, the lizard, and the mouse
From dwelling in your white-walled neighborhood.
Compel the traffic of the commonplace
To pass demurely by your redwood door.
Evangelists, discerning in your face
Their tickling fever, pause to call you whore.
Your friends, arriving drunk but well advised,
Invade your emptiness and dub it quaint.
Eager as children for the advertised
Seductions of a perfume or a paint,
They stare upon the cherubs of your bed,
Steal swizzle-sticks and larger souvenirs,
Take notes for memoirs of a maidenhead
And name the fog a distillate of tears.
But you, the Messalina of the arts,
Sitting alone with milk and sleeping pills,
Retch in the bowl when death and morning start
To close your eyes upon the eunuch hills.

Lawrence P. Spingarn

Patriotism

Mr Robert Newton, British-born actor, became a resident alien in America. While filming in Australia he told Press interviewers he could not understand the figure of £46,300 which the British income tax authorities were claiming he owed. He was not, he said, a business man, and the whole thing was in the hands of his lawyer. Mr Newton added that he still loved Britain.

Breathes there the man, with soul so dead,
Who never to himself hath said,
  'This is my own, my native land'?
Not Newton! – though officials itch
To question him on matters which
  He simply doesn't understand.

The Revenue declares: 'You owe
Forty-six thousand pounds or so' –
  Yet, hunted, harried, sorely smitten
By bureaucrats obsessed with tax,
Bob cries to all the world, 'Relax!
  In spite of them, I still love Britain!'

Granted, while chaps like Bob for years
Pile up their income-tax arrears,
  Somebody's got to hold the baby.
Need that his peace of mind destroy?
Artistic temperament, old boy!
  And some time he will settle, maybe.

Bob, you are not a business man.
Why fret yourself, when others can
  Cope with necessities so sordid
As trying to make both ends meet,
And keeping Britain on her feet?
  Let them be plucked, and you, applauded!

Act on, in glorious Technicolor,
While the more dutiful, but duller,
  Stolidly foot the fiscal bill!
Your words have brought a hard-pressed nation
More than sufficient compensation:
  Great Newton loves small Britain still!

Breathes there the man, with soul so sick,
Who'd sneer, 'This patriot lives on tick –
  'Twere better he should hold his tongue'?
Let all who such prim notions cherish
Primly pay up, and primly perish,
  Unwept, unhonoured, and unsung!

Percy Cudlipp*

Mentioning James Dean

I

'Who?'

2

Lilacs drifted into my nostrils
like small dirigibles. I brushed
my twelve-year-old haircut carefully.
The impossibility of talking to anyone,
so you mumble, sometimes you whine, but
some things you will outgrow. All of us
have tripped into dark rooms, banging
into still objects, sweating, &
there she was – Mother,
rabbit sounds squirt, come
from inside of your eyes, squinting,
the pain of new light
shredded in thin air.

3

They saw your body in dreams. They saw
it intact, your face blown off or
a clown's, & holding services
they knew you were among them, scrambling
for some sweet love, flesh, or
just a friend's arm, & the swollen
park on Sundays.

4

You took a wrong turn, but
we followed, our eyes nailed
to the bone screen. Take us
back, or let us
feel the seance table
fall apart in our dead fingers.

Terry Stokes*

Charlton Heston

Granite –
a granite slab.
He has survived earthquakes,
doomed 747's, sunken submarines,
japanese carriers and the wrath of god.
He can stand and watch cities
filled with his children,
his wife, his mistress, his dog
crumble into greasy flame.

He is beyond irony.
His mouth doesn't twitch.

He will go on.
His numb cobalt eyes
stare at the horizon.

Better than anyone, he knows
what must be done
to save us.

Elliot Fried*

Rescue with Yul Brynner

Appointed special consultant to the United Nations High Commissioner for
Refugees, 1959–60.

'Recital? "Concert" is the word',
and stunning, by the Budapest Symphony –
    displaced but not deterred –
listened to by me,
        though with detachment then,
            like a grasshopper that did not
            know it missed the mower, a pygmy citizen;
                a case, I'd say, of too slow a grower.
There were thirty million; there are thirteen still –
healthy to begin with, kept waiting till they're ill.
History judges. It will
salute Winnipeg's incredible
conditions: 'Ill; no sponsor; and no kind of skill.'
    Odd – a reporter with guitar – a puzzle.
    Mysterious Yul did not come to dazzle.

    Magic bird with multiple tongue –
five tongues – equipped for a crazy twelve-month tramp
    (a plod), he flew among
the damned, found each camp
        where hope had slowly died
            (some had never seen a plane).
            Instead of feathering himself, he exemplified
                the rule that, self-applied, omits the gold.
He said, 'You may feel strange; nothing matters less.
Nobody notices; you'll find some happiness.
No new "big fear"; no distress.'
Yul can sing – twin of an enchantress –
elephant-borne dancer in silver-spangled dress,
    swirled aloft by trunk, with star-tipped wand, Tamara,
    as true to the beat as *Symphonia Hungarica*.

    Head bent down over the guitar,
he barely seemed to hum; ended 'all come home';
    did not smile; came by air;
did not have to come.

The guitar's an event.
    Guests of honor can't dance; don't smile.
'Have a home?' a boy asks. 'Shall we live in a tent?'
    'In a house,' Yul answers. His neat cloth hat
has nothing like the glitter reflected on the face
of milkweed-witch seed-brown dominating a palace
that was nothing like the place
where he is now. His deliberate pace
is a king's, however. 'You'll have plenty of space.'
    Yule – Yul log for the Christmas-fire tale-spinner –
of fairy tales that can come true: Yul Brynner.

Marianne Moore*

George C. Scott

There is a conspiracy in this country
That men are unromantic
Rather dull
Aggressive
Money wanters
Moneymakers
Money spenders.
Now, let us discuss George C. Scott.
I was not a fan of General Patton
– Or of any military man
But, George C. Scott in *Petulia*
With his broken nose, spindly legs, neck like a truck driver,
And, in his shorts
Well
He is a man!
He made me forget poems, prose, and my intellect.
I mean he was, and is, gorgeous
He is midwestern, an actor, much married
But *gevalt* – I'd change it all
All my middle-class ideologies about men
With that beast – Scott –
I notice Colleen Dewhurst married him twice!

[221]

Now marriage is not my favorite
But you can't lose too much with him — I mean really —
I notice Julie Christie has never been the same
        I'd even start saluting the flag
       For
        George C.
         And that's a lot
          For even Scott!

                Paula Morgan*

Brigitte Bardot: Soured Recluse

Allergy: exaggerated or pathological reaction to substances, situations, or physical states that are without comparable effect on the average individual.

The sexpot of the sixties
is allergic to humanity.

'I see no one.
I don't go out.
I am disgusted with everything.
Men are beasts.'

See how all great philosophies
sway on the point of a pin,
how all great reactions
begin with an irritant as small
as a grain of pollen
or a nodule of dust.

Does she sneeze, itch,
break out in a rash,
experience respiratory embarrassment?
As one thing leads to another,
the chain reaction lashes
and links the delicate balance
of metabolism until it goes crazy.

She could have been another Mao
given the right irritant,

[222]

'without comparable effect on
the average individual.'

38 years old and
her whole arm begins to swell,
the chart lights up
like a war planning board.
Mold, dust, feathers, egg yolk,
you name it.
She has named it:
                    'Men are beasts.'

So reserve your pity, I tell myself,
for those who deserve it.
This is a case history
as common as the cold.
It can be cured by higher altitudes
or a dryer climate:
                    'Her fascination with men is drying up.'

She has the answer for herself.
The rest of us can wait.
She has the answer.
She doesn't need any of mine.

                              Kathleen Wiegner*

La Route

A poem-film, starring Jean-Paul Belmondo

Whether or not the man driving
Is really my chauffeur – he is
A pal who happens to like caps –
Is unlikely, at this speed, to
Bother anyone we pass on
These country roads.
                    This is the speed
We go at: illegible notices,
A gate half-open to a lane

Where . . . Hand on a shutter that's . . .
Someone's jumping off a tower
On a château that's blinked by sun.
No. It's a child who's throwing
Newspapers out of a window.
Is it? Why is he doing that?
Swift dapples of lime-shade are
Left behind, cool places for *boule*,
Old men who shuffle in the dust.
A silent weir; a fisherman
Snapped in the frame of pouring out
His glugless wine . . .
           And in here it's
Smoke, which has no words, despite mouths
Blowing it out; and no one wonders
Out there in the houses, up there
In the villas which have survived
The holidays and good times of
Their smart owners, that inside here
Is a man sitting on the back-seat
Notorious for fifty crimes,
For whom old peasant women in
Their hats are a multitude of
His own mother and several aunts;
Or that the young men in cafés –
Blurred, talking – are as fragile straws
He wishes he could catch with his eyes.
For I need to be one of them
Again, and stripped entirely clean
Of infidelity, this silk,
This speed and all that I have done.
These obsolete advertisements,
Each populated hole in the shade . . .
And it is not anonymous
Even at this speed which can make
A cigarette seem longer, or
The radio a function of
Travelling, a voice of nowhere
And no one at a microphone.
The seat's leather is heating up;

An open book is fast asleep.
She has left her hairbrush. It is
Rocking gently in a corner of
The hot back-seat. To take it back
Would not be gallantry, but
A waste of petrol. So why did
She choose to remain there, with them?
Nadine . . . Ruthless and beautiful:
She looks like both ideals. It is
A better trip without her; she, she . . .
How many women have I known?
If only, Nadine, you were not a liar . . .
That boy in the nylon overalls
Who is . . . that little bridge; these trees;
These children on stilts. She would have
Turned the radio up, too loud,
And chattered like the tart she was,
A fishwife slimmed for luxury,
A swimming-pool girl, a girl made by
Advertisements, my kind of girl
Who tastes of other men's champagne.
I doze like an open book, open,
Where my real life is written, told,
Told and shown, lying in two halves
And hinged, so, like the door I did
Not go through; and I think I am
A man who had no mother, who,
Therefore, is bad, and going to
A city where Max is standing
In a doorway, thinking that life
Is a dandy with a flick-knife
And a certain self-confidence
In clever cuts with it – up-cut,
Into the belly, and throat-cut,
For the kill. He thinks I don't know.
I know who paid him kill you, Jean.
I know he told you it was me,
But it wasn't, and you knew it.
Why, friend, do I weaken before
This dutiful revenge, as if

I've had enough, and this the last?
We are passing the houses of
Doctors and Professors. Sight
Is not what it was on this journey.
Max I see more clearly as
An executioner, or, if
Not that, then, at least, destiny
Who stands well-dressed in a shadow;
And faces, certainly, are not
So beautiful, nor are gardens
Anything like what I have seen
Today, with all the little quirks
People share, twitches, quarrels, food,
Their affections, their crazed sweetness
Accusing me. So, it is true:
There is a deep hole in the world.
Friend, you were with me, under the trees,
That summer we decided to reap
The pious franc instead of hay.
We did it with laughter. We were *good*.
It's a long road back; there were thefts
Conducted in the name of Law
Everywhere along it, making me
Almost a good man, who, sunk
In the ghost of my personality
Cannot remember my last drink
Or when I lit this cigarette.
It could have been years ago
Before the multitudes of mothers.
'Try a schoolmistress. She'll mother you.'
You used to say that, Jean, teasing me.
I aged like a ballad, always young.
No matter what I did, or thought,
An innocence clung to me like
A skin, a lime-shade, or like hair:
A history of love and theft,
Those deals; a history of suits
And big tips left in restaurants,
The career of my machismo –
Never stuck for a dame, or lost

For introductions to the rich.
Why, Jean, do they like crooks so much
In France? What's wrong with honesty?
A long road, Jean, but I never met
Anyone like me; I never met
Myself among the handshakes.
Max, I am coming to get you,
But, you bastard, if you stick me
It will be just as well, for I
Have seen a big hole in the world
That's full of paymasters, and you,
And I know what you don't, which is
That I'll go back the way I came
As safely on this leather seat,
Unnoticed in a machine, driven
By a black-capped chauffeur who says
Nothing, who, whatever happens,
Either way, Max, will take me home,
Who will have the good sense to know
Where, in the country, that is.

                    Douglas Dunn*

The Day I Stopped Dreaming about Barbara Steele

The drizzle shifted,
A bird drowsy with rain
Yawned into song,
The foghorn ran down.

Below the castle walls
Her head grisly with masks
The long slices of her sides
And the heavy dog's howl
(I hear the clamor of horses
And the long rope to which I am attached
Buckles beneath me)
The knotted arm

And the long sinew
That lays itself along
The long curve of her side.

Blond, her legs curved
To the horse's flank,
Making the sun dance
To the blue of her eyes

(Is the last dream before waking
More flesh than real,
More real than the dark before?)

The horse dances
And she is as purely naked
As the pine-needled dawn
And the dogs run lazy and smooth
In the tall grass.

The bronze door,
Stone,
A muffled cry,
The iron maiden,
And the sun
Crazy with its own size
In the moving lake
Where her horse lowers its head to drink
And she sleeps on his arching spine.

R. H. W. Dillard*

Jim Brown on the Screen

is the past in a new package, in daylight sunlight
with the white woman of his savagery done up in brown
for advertising newness in the deadness and liveness
in the oldness, of punctured, rotting, maggot loving A
merica America America, my cunt
tree
what an odd arrangement

of nature, a
cunt
tree
where the 'one eyed bird' rules inside the heads of drylipped
slobberers
worshipping the blackwhiteness
of died Ann
Dyed Ann
who they killed anyway and shotup with their bulletejaculation
Dyed Annnnnnnnn who-muh they chang-ed into 'dem'
tho she has a sheen of black beneath and makes her anyway more
than they could ever hope to imagine even on the silver screek.
Jim Brown socked them. Socittoembabeeee
He knocked them down. Yea. Bad dude bad dude you dig him crack
that faggot in the mouth . . . yeh (hand slap) 'sa bad motofreaky
Jim Brown put his hand on a white woman . . . youmember he put his
hand on that gray bitch . . . the one with . . . yeh hell yeh, too much
oh man they doin that all overnow . . . Poitier kissed one in the
mirror . . . wat about that time Jimmy Brown kicked that sucker in
the nuts . . . (hand slap) yeh . . . yeh, knocked that motherfucker out

. . . in the space freakout station of our slavery
        mourn for us soldout and chained to devilpictures
        in this cold ass land of ruling doodoo birds and hairy ladies

I mean we walk in whiteness like the rest life sucked out on a
humble death eminent planned by whiteness to the white resolution
of all things. Jim Brown. Our man in space correcting the image
for now, with the old chain of whiteness forever, whiteness, for
ever, if he could escape, if he, could kill them all Jim, killem
Jim if he could, if he could race past any of them, again, like
he used to, in the real world, that image for us to build, among
the easy slickness of imitation, and accommodation. We know you livin
good Jim, we know you walk in stores and buy shit, (hand
slap, stomp, wheel) Yeh, we know you know all kinda hip folks
and talk easy in leather bars, and sashay through parties with
the eyes of our women and beastwomen glued to yo thang, Jim
you can be more than that anyway, more than a new amos in space
more than uncle thomas from inner plantation psychotic
cotton salvation you could be a man, Jim, our man on the land
our new creator and leader, if you would just do it and be it

in the real world
in the new world of yo own black people
I hope you do
it, Jim
I hope you unmaniquin yo
self, you can
do it, if you
want it, you can

you
sho
can, jim

Amiri Baraka*

Old Extras

Old extras never die or get the sack,
they simply go on file for horror films –
or so I was told in all seriousness
by a woman on *Tale of Two Cities*,
part of the Old Bailey mob, or, as one
assistant phrased it, (fearing the Union),
'Gallery personnel'.

As we sat in waist-crushing, hessian skirts,
hair under foul mob-caps, she told us how
she'd been put on that file – 'just by mistake',
and gone to Central Casting, hair fresh-dyed,
proffering new photos, begging 'Take me off.'
It worked. Now she was saving all the cash
for a good face-lift – one thousand pounds.
She looked all right to me, no real wrinkles
at forty odd, the only obvious flaw –
the ripple of a lousy nose-job.

Fiona Pitt-Kethley

Merging

In *Dogs of War* a Cockney extra gave me
some good tips for survival.

'Never put yourself forward –' he advised,
'we're in it just to be anonymous –
the more so, the better.' He'd merged enough,
he said, to fill the place of umpteen men
on the Titanic's decks. 'Crew, passengers,
waiters – the ruddy lot!' Eventually,
some young assistant sussed him out and pulled
him from behind the bar, saying: 'I never want
to see that ugly mug of yours again.'

'Just mingle, join any queue you see –
it's probably for grub . . .' – not quite such good
advice. Getting in line, I thought for tea,
I nearly got myself stuck with a beard
in *Reds*. His mingling, on the other hand,
brought him an extra day in some beer ad.
They left him gilded in an anteroom,
(one rower too many for the quinquereme),
to mind the others' clothes – he only had
a loincloth on – forgotten, sweating gold,
alone.

I've seen him since, I think, merging in films,
tucked away, round the corner from a set
in Pinewood, selling watches from a case.
I saw his brawny arm at Shepperton
amongst an octopus of hands stealing
the cream cakes from a tray while other men
confused the cook with change. And he was
one of six who leaned the table down,
left three accountants grovelling on the ground
for cash and chits, and took us into more
paid overtime.

Fiona Pitt-Kethley

Bond Girl

Back in my extra days, someone once swore
she'd seen me in the latest James Bond film.

I tried to tell her that they only hired
the really glamorous leggy types for that.
(My usual casting was 'a passer-by'.)

I've passed the lot in Pinewood Studios.
It's factory-like, grey aluminium, vast
and always closed. Presumably that's where
they smash up all the speedboats, cars and bikes
we jealous viewers never could afford.

I quite enjoyed the books. Ian Fleming wrote well.
I could identify *a touch* with Bond,
liking to have adventure in my life.
The girls were something else. All that they earned
for being perfect samples of their kind –
Black, Asian, White – blonde, redhead or brunette,
groomed, beauty-parlourised, pleasing in bed,
mixing Martinis that were shaken not stirred,
using pearl varnish on their nails not red –
was death. A night (or 2) with 007,
then they were gilded till they could not breathe,
chucked to the sharks, shot, tortured, carried off
or found, floating face downward in a pool.

Fiona Pitt-Kethley

Elegy for an Actor Drowned in Time of War

(Leslie Howard – 1 June 1943)

But this one man we mourn among so many
because he died upon a gentle cause,
who had not marched with horror for an ally,
nor levelled weapons to increase our loss.

The waves that joined across smashed fuselage
hid his green journey from our following eyes,
secured the seas' unfruitful patronage;
and closed the slender dossier of his days.

We who are harnessed in the limbs of killing
and cannot choose the act in which we move,
once honoured this man's intellectual spilling
of scorn upon the enemies of love.

So let us honour now his silent going,
whose gestures lent belief to muddied years;
who made his final exit little knowing
Death had let down the curtain unawares.

Maurice Lindsay*

The Flicker

Some silent movie star
was murdered late yesterday.
He was an old newspaper story,
yellow, torn and fading,
I found years ago
under the kitchen linoleum.
I wonder,
with the silence of his moving lips
(colorless in the ear and the eye),
if his celluloid body jerked to a stop
on the screen of the Douglas Art Theatre.

Lew Blockcolski

The Death of Marilyn Monroe

The ambulance men touched her cold
body, lifted it, heavy as iron,
onto the stretcher, tried to close
the mouth, closed the eyes, tied the
arms to the side, moved a caught
strand of hair, as if it mattered,
saw the shape of her breasts, flattened by
gravity, under the sheet,
carried her, as if it were she,
down the steps.

These men were never the same. They went out
afterwards, as they always did,
for a drink or two, but they could not meet
each other's eyes.

            Their lives took
a turn – one had nightmares, strange
pains, impotence, depression. One did not
like his work, his wife looked
different, his kids. Even death
seemed different to him – a place where she
would be waiting,

and one found himself standing at night
in the doorway to a room of sleep, listening to a
woman breathing, just an ordinary
woman
breathing.

Sharon Olds

Stan Laurel

Ollie gone, the heavyweight
Balletic chump, and now
His turn to bow out, courteous,

A perfect gentleman who
Tips his hat to the nurse

Or would, that is, if he were
Still in business. She
Adjusts his pillow, smooths
The sheets until their crisp-
And-even snow-white starchiness

Becomes his cue. It's time
For one last gag, the stand-up
Drip-feed: *Sister,*
Let me tell you this
I wish I was skiing,

And she, immaculately cornered
For the punch-line: *Really*
Mr Laurel, do you ski? A
chuckle –
No, but I'd rather I was doing
That than this,

Than facing death, the one
Fine mess he's gotten into
That he can't get out of
Though a nurse's helpless
laughter
Is the last he hears.

John Mole*

To Mourn Jayne Mansfield

(Decapitated in a car crash, June 1967)

I

SAIR SONNET

Cauld is thon corp that fleered sae muckle heat
Thae Babylon breists that gart the bishops ban

And aa the teeny titties grain and greet
That siccan sichts should gawp the ee o man.

Still are the hurdies steered sic houghmagandie,
The hips sae swack, their ilka step a swee,
That graybeards maun hae risen hauflin-randie
To merk them move and move the yirth agee.

Faan is thon powe that crouned her fairheid's flouer,
Hackit awa as gin by the heidsman's aix –
Our lust the blade has killed thon bonnie hure,
Puir Quine! that aince had reigned the Queen of Glaiks.

Owre aa the warld the standards canna stand,
Wauchied their strength as onie willow-wand.

II

HOLLYWOOD IN HADES

Jayne Mansfield, strippit mortal stark
  O' aa her orra duddies –
For thae that sail in Charon's barque
  Keep nocht aside their bodies –
Comes dandily daffan til Hades' dark,
  A sicht to connach studies.

Yet Pluto, coorse as King Farouk,
  Gies only ae bit glower –
She naukit, ilka sonsie neuk,
  But he's seen aa afore –
And turns to tell the t'ither spook,
  'Marilyn, move outowre!'

Alexander Scott*

judy garland is dead

judy garland is dead and everyone
is asking did she take an overdose?
murder made to look like suicide?
or was it just cirrhosis of the liver?

just? what's cirrhosis but suicide
on the installment plan? you know that you're
killing yourself, and you even know that you
could stop if you really put your mind to it,

but you don't stop, you don't stop
for the same reason that you started in
the first place, because without it you'd be
insane or the quicker kind of dead.

when i was a kid i dedicated a poem
to judy garland. in those days
i used to employ images and
syncopation, instead of just fucking around

and bullshitting as at present, anyway it began
somewhere somewhere over the rainbow a
wry old wizard and a wizened witch
conjure fumes of colors, orgies of

ice cream odors, etc. except that it
was spread all over the page – all over
fifteen pages – and i couldn't bring it to
a satisfactory conclusion. it

took her eventual suicide for granted,
let's say it took suicide as a way of life
for granted, but there was still
the delirium of the return to the Palace,

of the triumphal night at Carnegie Hall,
captured on a famous Capitol double l-p,
which i must have played fifteen times a day,
always with goosebumps . . .

look, i want it known that i am not
sitting down today drooling over
the opportunity to write an ELEGY,
i'm not rushing to scoop the two hundred fifty

thousand other poets who at this very moment
are calling upon NATURE to mourn at the bier
of the CHANTEUSE, untimely lopped, etc.
there are things i would rather be doing.

[237]

my girl is waiting at her apartment;
our little time together is wasting.
i have a stack of overdue recommendations to write.
by sundown i'll be too drunk to function.

not too drunk though to think upon the
judy garlands and the scott fitzgeralds,
john keats, john barrymore, alexander pope,
all those who live in suffering year after year

and then die. and now it's drugs too, and friends
of mine, fine funny guys, on whites in the morning,
reds at night, until the inevitable crash.
what kind of a fucking life do you call that?

that's all i had to say – if winter comes
can suicide be far behind? judy,
i'm glad it's over for you. go to sleep
now, little girl; sleep a rainbow sleep.

Gerald Locklin*

W. H. Auden & Mantan Moreland

In memory of the Anglo-American poet & the Afro-American comic actor (famed
for his role as Birmingham Brown, chauffeur in those ancient Charlie Chan
movies) who died on the same day in 1973

Consider them both in paradise,
discussing one another –
the one a poet, the other an actor;
interchangeable performers
who finally slipped backstage
of a play whose cast favored lovers.

'You executed some brilliant lines,
Mr Auden, & doubtless engaged our
innermost emotions & informed imagination,
for I pondered your *Age of Anxiety*
diligently over a juicy order of ribs.'

'No shit!' groans Auden, mopping his brow.
'I checked out all your Charlie Chan
flicks & flipped when you turned up again
in *Watermelon Man* & that gas commercial
over TV. Like, where was you all that
time in between? I thought you'd done
died & gone back to England or somethin.'

'Wystan, pray tell, why did you ever eliminate
that final line from "September 1, 1939"? –
We must love one another or die.'

'That was easy. We gon die anyway no matter
how much we love, but the best thing I like
that you done was the way you buck them eyes
& make out like you runnin sked all the time.
Now, that's the bottom line of the black
experience where you be in charge of the scene.
For the same reason you probly stopped shufflin.'

                                                    Al Young*

Duke Wayne Gazes back on the Ruins of Eden (A Movie Dream)

a few loyal polynesians left over from 'the hurricane'
propel the small craft away frm the sinking island

behind them, nothing but smoke & ash
ahead, grey drizzle of december

duke turns, he wears his old campaign hat
left over frm the indian wars
his face is deep-creased, ancient & sad

one tear hangs like a stalactite
from the corners of each eye

somewhere, if we listen carefully
we can hear 'red river valley'
accordion fading in & out on the wind

this is the final frame of the last movie
duke's face, a stone rushmore of regret,
turns away
staring into the mist

Michael Shepler*

Garbo Goodbye

The cheekbones, the jaw, the noble throat,
the sad mask of a mouth that still
knew how to laugh, to smile with pain –

until towards the end of your existence
you fled the light, the cyclop eye
of human avidity behind the camera lens –

and from time to time we glimpsed you
tracked for a moment like an almost
extinct species, a wild outcast

crossing the back lots of Central Park,
Venice, Klosters, Sweden, with mute desperation
of the Abominable Snowman across eternal snows

pursued by men, lovers like wolves –
to give yourself, at last, only to the unknown
in a final fade-out, without close-up.

James Kirkup*

Haiku

The blue angel flew
Up to heaven, where la vie
Est toujours rose.

James Kirkup*

NOTES

'Inside Sally' (Dillard). Born in Missouri as Helen Gould Beck, Sally Rand (1903–79) went to Hollywood via midwestern nightclubs and between 1925 and the coming of sound she appeared in numerous movies (e.g. Cecil B. DeMille's *The King of Kings* and Howard Hawks's *A Girl in Every Port*), mostly in supporting roles. Forced out of the cinema by her unsuitable voice, she became a chorus girl and in 1933 discovered her true métier at the Chicago World's Fair as a fan dancer. Her arrest for giving an allegedly 'obscene performance' brought her national fame and wealth, and she was still performing her act in nightclubs across America in her seventies. Rand returned only once to the screen to appear with George Raft and Carole Lombard in *Bolero* (1934), playing herself and doing a version of her newly notorious fan dance. She is memorialized in the song 'Zip' from the Rodgers and Hart musical *Pal Joey* (1940) – each refrain ends with the highbrow striptease artiste Gypsy Rose Lee disparaging one of her competitors, including:

> Zip! My intelligence is guiding my hand.
> Zip! Who the hell is Sally Rand? (182)

'15th Raga/For Bela Lugosi' (Meltzer). Bela Lugosi (1882–1956) left his native Hungary following the defeat of Bela Kun's shortlived leftwing Republic in which he organized an actors' union, and in 1921 emigrated to the United States. For three years he appeared as Count Dracula in a stage version of Bram Stoker's novel and re-created the role on screen in 1931. His Dracula and Boris Karloff's Frankenstein monster became iconic figures and together they dominated the Hollywood horror movie in the 1930s and 40s. After the war his career went into sad decline and he died penniless, his health undermined by years of drug abuse. He was buried in his Count Dracula cape. (184)

'Ode to Groucho' (Bell). Of the four (or five) Marx Brothers, Groucho (1890–1977) enjoyed the greatest success as a single act and an individual personality though his movies with Chico (1886–1961) and Harpo (1888–1964) are the high points of his career. Harpo (named Adolph at birth but known in the family as Arthur) was the first to appear in a movie (*Too Many Kisses*, 1925), and while he never spoke on screen, a character modelled on him called Banjo in the Kaufman and Hart comedy *The Man Who Came To Dinner* speaks a good deal. (186)

'To the Lady Portrayed by Margaret Dumont' (Hollander). Margaret Dumont (1889–1965) joined the Marx Brothers in their stage shows during the 1920s and her imperious society ladies, endlessly the objects of Groucho's obsequious wheedling and the butts of his jokes, were a mainstay of their films from *The*

Cocoanuts (1929) to *The Big Store* (1941). She also appeared in movies starring W. C. Fields, Laurel and Hardy, Jack Benny, Danny Kaye and Abbott and Costello. (187)

'La Plus Blanche' (McClure). Jean Harlow (1911–37) was the blonde star of Howard Hughes's *Hell's Angels* (1930) and then a leading lady at MGM until her untimely death. McClure's play *The Beard*, about a meeting in heaven between Harlow and Billy the Kid, concludes with an act of oral sex between the two legendary figures, and was one of the first plays presented publicly in London following the end of the Lord Chamberlain's theatrical censorship role in 1968. (190)

'To Celebrate Eddie Cantor' (Bell). The New York-born son of Russian Jewish immigrants, Cantor (1892–1964) became a professional vaudeville singer and comedian at the age of fourteen. He appeared in such lavish 1930s Goldwyn productions as *Whoopee!*, *The Kid From Brooklyn* and *Roman Scandals*, and was noted for his rolling poached-egg eyes and individual speech rhythms. (191)

'Mae West' (Nash). The Brooklyn-born West (1892–1980) attained considerable notoriety on Broadway before coming to Hollywood in 1932 to make a series of risqué comedies, most of them partly scripted by West herself, including *She Done Him Wrong*, *I'm No Angel* and *Belle of the Nineties*. They helped revive the ailing fortunes of Paramount and led to much stricter enforcement of the Hays Office Production Code from 1934 onwards. (192)

'Reflections on a Bowl of Kumquats, 1936' (Christopher). The anarchic W. C. Fields (1879–1946), born in Philadelphia, son of a British immigrant, started out as a juggler and was an international star by the beginning of the century. Although he made his movie debut in 1915, his great period as a movie star followed the coming of sound when he could give full vent to the sardonic wit that expressed the rebarbative, curmudgeonly on-screen and off-screen personality he had created. He wrote many of his own scripts under bizarre pseudonyms (e.g. Mahatma Kane Jeeves for the 1940 *The Bank Dick*) and co-scripted *My Little Chickadee* (1940) with Mae West. (194)

'In Person: Bette Davis' (Goldstein). Born into a middle-class New England family, Bette Davis (1908–89) came to Hollywood via Broadway success and appeared in over a hundred films and won two Oscars. A good many of her movies were made at Warner Brothers where she was a contract star, a situation against which she famously rebelled, resulting in her losing an action brought by the studio in the British high courts. Her caustic humour and outspokenness made her a favourite guest on TV chat shows and in her late sixties she began making public appearances in theatres, taking questions from fans. (195)

'Dick Powell' (Koertge). Dick Powell (1904–63) became a star as a crooner and dancer in Warner Brothers musicals playing opposite Ruby Keeler. In the mid-

1940s he switched to hard-boiled characters in *film noir* thrillers, his first role being Philip Marlowe in Edward Dmytryk's film of Chandler's *Farewell My Lovely* (shown in the US as *Murder My Sweet*). Although he continued to act he subsequently turned to producing and directing films, occasionally for the cinema but mostly for TV, and was president of his own highly successful Four Star company. (196)

'Shirley Temple Surrounded by Lions' (Elmslie). Born in Santa Monica, California in 1928, Temple made her first movie at the age of three and was a star at the age of six, winning a Special Oscar in 1934. She was an eerily accomplished performer (so much so that many doubted her age and the Vatican sent an emissary to check her out). But she never established herself as an adult star, retiring in her early twenties to become a housewife and then a diplomat. Of his poem, Kenward Elmslie had this to say in a letter to the editors: 'My first movie-star crush was Shirley Temple, 1936. I kept her photo by my pillow. I was absolutely dead certain we'd marry when I grew up – we were both born in April, the same age: a good omen. Her photo, and the fantasy intimacy it provoked, outshone memories of her movies, though I was captivated by certain scenes: her tap-dance duet, up and down stairs, with "Bojangles" Robinson, and by chats with an elderly British gentleman, Sir C. Aubrey Smith – a genuine Sir! She was succeeded in short order by Bette Davis . . . Vivien Leigh . . . Hedy Lamarr . . . Joan Bennett . . . Tyrone Power . . . Lon McAllister . . . John Derek . . . Delon . . . Brando . . . Clift. But only Shirley Temple achieved bedside photo status, plus a future role as my bride. While I never deliberately set out to work meanings into a poem, I suppose this poem circles around the marvellous and savage schism between dreamed mind's eye "films" that draw on the same hypnotic magic movies do *vs* the disillusioning thuds – and slowness – of wakeful reality. I was always being yanked out of thrilling movies and dreams into an abrasively tedious daylight that dragged out time mercilessly, particularly in childhood, but as an adult too.' (197)

'Nobody Dies Like Humphrey Bogart' (Rosten). Son of a leading New York surgeon, Bogart (1899–1957) began playing middle-class juvenile leads on Broadway, but made his name in Hollywood playing gangsters, private eyes and adventurers. With his fellow Warner Brothers stars Edward G. Robinson and James Cagney, he came to define a new kind of urban man. (198)

'John Garfield' (Christopher). Born Julius Garfinkle, son of Jewish immigrant New Yorkers, Garfield (1913–52) led a disorderly life before finding fame on Broadway and joining Bogart and Cagney at Warner Brothers in 1938, making his debut in *Four Daughters* as a new kind of brooding leading man, harbinger of Brando and Dean. After the war he formed his own production company, working (as he had done in the theatre) with leading members of the left. He was called before the House Un-American Activities Committee in the early 1950s, though he had never been a member of the Communist Party, and refused to discuss the political allegiances of his friends. HUAC began preparing a case against him for perjury and Garfield found himself virtually blacklisted. But before he could appear again before HUAC, Garfield died of a heart attack in the Manhattan apartment of a woman friend in May 1952 at the age of thirty-nine. (200)

'The Sidney Greenstreet Blues' (Brautigan). The stout, imposing British-born Sydney Greenstreet (1879–1954) made his movie debut in *The Maltese Falcon* at the age of sixty-two and subsequently appeared in *Casablanca* and other films, mostly at Warner Brothers and on several occasions teamed with the diminutive Peter Lorre. (201)

'Carmen Miranda' (Polite). The vivacious Portuguese-born singer and dancer Miranda (1909–55) was known as the Brazilian Bombshell. She enjoyed a considerable vogue in the 1940s through a series of 20th Century-Fox Technicolor musicals set in Latin America (e.g. *Down Argentine Way, That Night in Rio*) co-starring Don Ameche and designed as part of Hollywood's contribution to President Roosevelt's 'Good Neighbour Policy'. She was especially noted for her extravagant headgear featuring exotic tropical fruits. (202)

'On *Imagerie*: Esther Williams, 1944' (Sobin). Born in Los Angeles in 1923, Williams was a swimming champion and a performer in Billy Rose's Aquacade before being signed by MGM. *Bathing Beauty*, the first of her musicals featuring spectacular aquatic production numbers, appeared in 1944. Joe Pasternak, her producer at MGM, once remarked: 'I used to keep her in the water 99 per cent of the time. Wet she was a star.' In a letter to the editors, Gustaf Sobin writes: 'For the sake of anecdote, Esther Williams taught me how to swim in the summer of 1944 at the Beverly Hills Hotel where my family had a bungalow. I was only eight at the time and she – I imagine – in her early twenties. At seven in the morning, every morning, there were only the two of us in or about the pool. I can assure you, life has never been sweeter.' (203)

'Why That's Bob Hope' (Hathaway). The British-born comedian Bob Hope (b. 1903), after establishing himself in vaudeville, on Broadway and on radio, had a successful movie career in the 1940s and 50s, especially through the 'Road' movies he made with Bing Crosby ('Der Bingle'). From the late 1940s he worked also in TV. The super-patriotism that made him a much publicized entertainer of American troops overseas in three wars led him to take increasingly right-wing positions on political and social issues. (204)

'Poem' (O'Hara). Born in Wallace, Idaho, 1920, Lana Turner was taken to California at the age of nine by her mother after her father was murdered. She was a major star at MGM from the late 1940s until the 1950s, and her troubled private life (seven marriages, her daughter killed Lana's gangster lover and so on) was as familiar to moviegoers as her films. (204)

'Cross My Heart' (Lejeune). Miss Lejeune, movie critic of the *Observer* from 1928 to 1960, frequently reviewed movies in verse. This comment on Sonny Tufts

(1911–70), scion of a leading Boston banking family (who gave their name to Tufts University) and amiable Paramount star, was occasioned by the comedy *Cross My Heart* (1945, director John Berry). One of the handful of minor celebrities who turned out for the opening of the Flamingo, Bugsy Siegel's Las Vegas nightclub in 1946, Tufts became something of a joke, especially after Ethel Barrymore pronounced his name with incredulity when introducing him at a Tinseltown gathering and he became the butt of stand-up comics. (205)

'The B Movie' (Duffy). The 36-year-old Ronald Reagan was picking up the threads of his acting career after World War Two and the 19-year-old Shirley Temple was attempting to progress from child star to adult actress when they were cast in *That Hagen Girl* (1947, director Peter Godfrey), a dismal Warner Brothers comedy about a teenager's mistaken belief that she's the daughter of a teacher. In the 1960s both entered politics, running for office as Republicans in California. (205)

'Valerio' (Dunn). Born in Mexico in 1915 of a Mexican mother and an Irish father, Anthony Quinn has had a career in the movies lasting nearly sixty years. His early days were spent playing Indians and minor heavies in occasional major films (some directed by his father-in-law Cecil B. DeMille) and villains in B movies. He became a major star after winning an Oscar as Marlon Brando's brother in *Viva Zapata!* (1952, director Elia Kazan) and has specialized in larger-than-life characters from various ethnic backgrounds (Greek, Italian, Eskimo, Spanish, Russian, Mexican, Arab, Basque, Polish). He won a second Oscar as Gauguin in *Lust for Life* (1956, director Vincente Minnelli). (206)

'Twice As Many Gorillas' (Skelley). The North Carolina-born Ava Gardner (1922–90) was one of the key Hollywood stars – half-broad, half-aristocrat – of the late 1940s and 50s. She was a femme fatale of *film noir* (*The Killers*, *The Bribe*), a remote, alluring siren (*Pandora and the Flying Dutchman*, *The Barefoot Contessa*), the aloof, companionable Hemingway heroine (*The Snows of Kiliman-jaro*, *The Sun Also Rises*). In *The Knights of the Round Table* (1953) she played Guinevere; in *Night of the Iguana* (1964) she ensnared Richard Burton. (210)

'The Newlyweds' (Updike). In 1955 the 22-year-old movie star Debbie Reynolds married the 27-year-old crooner Eddie Fisher and they became the beaux ideals of a young married couple for the Eisenhower era. In 1959, however, Eddie left Debbie for her friend Elizabeth Taylor (starring with her the following year in *Butterfield 8*) and was himself dumped when Taylor met Richard Burton shooting *Cleopatra*. (211)

'To G. K.' (Service). Robert Service, the British-born balladeer of the Yukon where he arrived just after the Gold Rush and lived for six years, became famous for such poems as 'The Shooting of Dan McGrew'. After World War One ambulance service he settled in France and his last years were spent in Monaco. As an honorary Monégasque he wrote this poem to welcome Grace Kelly on the occasion of her wedding in 1956. (211)

'Ballade for a Wedding' (Greene). The Irish-American priest Father Francis Tucker, father confessor to Prince Rainier of Monaco, acted as go-between in arranging the Prince's marriage to Grace Kelly after the couple had met when she was appearing in Hitchcock's *To Catch a Thief* on the Côte d'Azur in 1955. Through his contacts in Philadelphia, where he had once served, Tucker was able to check out Kelly's family. Greene's Ballade is a pastiche of a poem by another British Catholic humorist, Hilaire Belloc, called 'Ballade of Hell and Mrs Roebeck' which has the refrain 'And Mrs Roebeck will be there'. Greene's squib appeared in the *Punch* of 16 April 1956, a number largely devoted by its editor Malcolm Muggeridge to cartoons and articles attacking the state visit to Britain by the Soviet leaders Bulganin and Khrushchev. (212)

'Marilyn' (Berkson). Born Norma Jean Mortenson in Los Angeles, Marilyn Monroe (1926–62) has probably been the subject of more poems, biographical studies and compilations of photographs than any other star or film-maker in the history of cinema. *The Misfits* (1961) was her last film. (213)

'Patriotism' (Cudlipp). Robert Newton (1905–56), one of the hellraisers of the British movie world, gave an understated performance as a suburban husband in the Noël Coward–David Lean *This Happy Breed* (1944), but is best known for his eye-rolling over-the-top character roles – as the Ancient Pistol in Olivier's *Henry V* (1944), the painter Lukey in Carol Reed's *Odd Man Out* (1947), Bill Sikes in Lean's *Oliver Twist* (1948) and Long John Silver in the Walt Disney version of *Treasure Island* (1950). His final role was the Scotland Yard inspector pursuing Phileas Fogg in Mike Todd's *Around the World in 80 Days*. (217)

'Mentioning James Dean' (Stokes). After bit parts in four minor films and starring roles in Elia Kazan's *East of Eden* (1955), Nicholas Ray's *Rebel Without a Cause* (1955) and George Stevens's *Giant* (1956), the Indiana-born James Dean (1931–55) entered the pantheon of legendary Hollywood stars on 30 September 1955 when he was killed in a car crash north of Los Angeles, driving his Porsche, on his way to take part in a motor race. (218)

'Charlton Heston' (Fried). Charlton Heston (born Chicago 1923) had his first major role as the circus manager in Cecil B. DeMille's *The Greatest Show on Earth* (1952) and has been especially associated with Westerns, historical epics, war movies and biblical films, playing Moses, John the Baptist, General Gordon, Michelangelo and Ben Hur. In the 1960s and 70s he was a major figure in Disaster and Group Jeopardy pictures such as *Planet of the Apes*, *Skyjacked*, *Earthquake*, *Airport 75* and *Two Minute Warning*. (219)

'Rescue with Yul Brynner' (Moore). Born on the remote Sakhalin Island off the Asian coast of Siberia, Yul Brynner (1915–85) had one of the most extraordinary lives of any actor, working as a musician, circus artist, wartime broadcaster for the American Office of War Information, radio and TV producer, before finding fame on stage and film as the shaven-headed star of *The King and I*. He served as a special consultant to the United Nations High Commissioner for Refugees and published a book arising from the experience, *Bring Forth the Children* (1961), in collaboration with the photographer Inge Morath. (220)

'George C. Scott' (Morgan). Born in Virginia in 1927, George C. (for Campbell) Scott embarked on an acting career after service in the US Marines and in 1959 made a striking double debut, first as a mad preacher in the Delmer Daves Western *The Hanging Tree*, then as an acerbic prosecutor in Otto Preminger's *Anatomy of a Murder*. He clinched his reputation as a character star playing the sadistic gambler Gordon in *The Hustler* (1961). He played opposite Julie Christie in Dick Lester's *Petulia* (1968) and two years later refused an Academy Award for his portrayal of General George S. Patton in Franklin Schaffner's *Patton*. He twice married and divorced the actress Colleen Dewhurst (1926–91), who made her last screen appearance with their son Campbell Scott in *Dying Young* (1991). (221)

'Brigitte Bardot: Soured Recluse' (Wiegner). After a dozen film appearances, Brigitte Bardot (born Paris 1934) achieved international fame as a 'sex kitten' for her role as the provocative teenager destroying older men around St Tropez in *Et Dieu créa la femme* (1956), directed by her then husband Roger Vadim. She subsequently worked with Henri-Georges Clouzot, Louis Malle and Jean-Luc Godard while leading a much publicized private life. She retired from the cinema in 1974 and has been a campaigner for animal rights. (222)

'La Route' (Dunn). Born outside Paris in 1933, the son of a well-off sculptor, Jean-Paul Belmondo achieved immediate fame as the dashing criminal anti-hero, modelling himself on Bogart, in Jean-Luc Godard's New Wave movie *A bout de souffle* (*Breathless*, 1960). Over the next decade he was an international art-house star, usually playing dangerous, insouciant, often anti-social charmers, working with Godard (notably in *Pierrot le fou*), Philippe de Broca, Vittorio De Sica (opposite Sophia Loren in *Two Women*), Jean-Pierre Melville, Truffaut, Louis Malle and Alain Resnais. From the early 1970s his films became less distinguished but he remained a big box-office draw in France. (223)

'The Day I Stopped Dreaming about Barbara Steele' (Dillard). After an inauspicious start in British movies, Barbara Steele (born in Trenton, Wirral, in 1938) became the cult heroine of continental horror pictures, starting in 1960 with a role as a witch in Mario Bava's minor classic *Black Sunday*. In addition to horror movies, she has also appeared in Fellini's *8½* (1963) and Malle's *Pretty Baby* (1978). (227)

'Jim Brown on the Screen' (Baraka). Born in 1935 in Georgia, raised in Manhasset, Long Island, Brown was a football scholar at Syracuse University and a star fullback for the Cleveland Browns (1957–67) before entering the movies. He has played mostly in tough action movies such as Gordon Douglas's Western *Rio Conchos* (his 1954 debut), Robert Aldrich's *The Dirty Dozen* (1967) and Tom Gries's *100 Rifles* (1969) in which he had a famous love scene with Raquel Welch. Film historian Ephraim Katz called him 'The first bona-fide black male "sex symbol" of the American screen'. (228)

'Elegy for an Actor Drowned in Time of War' (Lindsay). The archetypal Briton, though of Hungarian descent, Leslie Howard (1893–1943), star of *The Petrified Forest, The Scarlet Pimpernel* and *Gone With the Wind*, was shot down by the Luftwaffe in a civil plane flying from Lisbon to London. It was thought at the time that the Germans believed Winston Churchill was on board. It is, however, possible that Howard was targeted for his successful anti-Nazi propaganda as a broadcaster and film-maker. Josef Goebbels was especially incensed by Howard's *Pimpernel Smith* and in 1942 the German ambassador in Stockholm put pressure on the Swedish government to prevent further screening of the picture in the British embassy's cinema. Seeing *Pimpernel Smith* at one of these private screenings helped persuade Raoul Wallenberg to undertake his mission to save Hungarian Jews from Adolf Eichmann in Budapest. (232)

'Stan Laurel' (Mole). Born in Ulverston in the Lake District into a theatrical family as Arthur Stanley Jefferson, Laurel (1890–1965) made his stage debut at sixteen. In 1910 and 1912 he toured America with Fred Karno's company, understudying Charlie Chaplin, and remained there, making his first screen appearance in 1917. He teamed up with the American comedian Oliver Hardy (1892–1957) in 1927 and they became what many consider the greatest double act in film history, especially notable for their work in the early 1930s. In 1961 he was given a Special Academy Award 'for pioneering in the field of cinema comedy'. His final words as quoted in John Mole's poem are those recorded by Fred Lawrence Guiles in his biography *Stan*. (234)

'To Mourn Jayne Mansfield' (Scott). Alexander Scott was Professor of Scottish Literature at Glasgow University and wrote verse in the literary form of Lowland speech known as Scots or, more recently, as Lallans. Jayne Mansfield (1933–67), a buxom blonde beauty queen from Pennsylvania, briefly studied drama at the Universities of Texas and California before enjoying several Hollywood years of dubious success in the wake of Marilyn Monroe. The *reductio ad absurdum* of a decade obsessed with female breasts, Mansfield connived at the exploitation of her figure and blatant sexuality to comic effect by Frank Tashlin in *The Girl Can't Help It* (1956) and *Will Success Spoil Rock Hunter?* (1957). She did her best work in the downbeat Paul Wendkos *film noir* thriller *The Burglar* (1957) and came to Britain to appear with Kenneth More in the dreary comedy-Western *The Sheriff of Fractured Jaw* (1958). Her later years were mostly spent in dismal European films and in 1967 she was decapitated in a motor accident outside New Orleans. (235)

'judy garland is dead' (Locklin). Born Frances Gumm in Grand Rapids, Michigan in 1922, Garland died on 22 June 1969 after a remarkable, but very disturbed career as a child and adult star in movies and the concert hall. The coroner's verdict was accidental death due to an overdose of sleeping pills. (236)

'W. H. Auden and Mantan Moreland' (Young). Auden (1907–73) left Britain for the United States in 1938 and became an American citizen, though he returned to live in his old Oxford college, Christ Church, in 1972, and died of heart failure in a Viennese hotel on the night of 28/29 September 1973. Born in Louisiana, Moreland (1902–73) ran away from home at the age of twelve, became a stage and nightclub performer, and appeared in over 100 movies between the late 1930s and his death, his last role being in *The Young Nurses* (1973). (238)

'Duke Wayne Gazes back . . .' (Shepler). Born Marion Michael Morrison and nicknamed 'Duke' after a pet dog of childhood, John Wayne (1907–79) worked in movies from 1929 until 1976. John Ford gave him his first bit parts, retrieved him from B movie Westerns and made him a major star in *Stagecoach* (1939). In the last of his numerous films with Ford, *Donovan's Reef* (1963), Wayne played an American living on the Polynesian island where he had fought in World War Two. (239)

'Garbo Goodbye' (Kirkup). Born Greta Gustafsson in Stockholm in 1905, Greta Garbo worked at MGM in Hollywood from 1927 to 1941. She died in New York on 1 April 1990. (240)

'Haiku' (Kirkup). Marlene Dietrich (1901–92) was born in Berlin, starred there in Josef von Sternberg's *The Blue Angel* in 1930 and came to Hollywood the same year. Her movie and concert career spanned over sixty years and she died in Paris on 6 May 1992. (240)

V

Behind the Camera

Nepotism

Uncle Carl Laemmle
Has a very large faemmle.

Anon.*

Requiem for a Producer

Reuben Jewel, who got his start in silents, died on Wednesday.
I met him the year that he finished *Anna's Men*,
the blockbuster story of Russian passion
as suggested by the novel of Leo Tolstoy. 1937 –
R. J.'s first Oscar, that made him both 'struck and dumb'
as he said in his acceptance speech, with this recognition
that he brought to the screen 'great classics such as Anna Karen,'
an honor that made him goddamned proud, excuse me, ladies and
    gentlemen.
Let us gathered here in the Wee Kirk o' the Canyon
wish him one final happy ending.
Some people thought his movies were too syrupy –
since the heroes end up with their girls and all the money,
the deep kiss, the rescue, and the cup of cheer, and it's too much – maybe.
But who's here that's so happy he's tired of being happy?
Who'd hate a well-fed, white-toothed world? Not me.
Jewel's lowlifes lived in shining, painted slums, romantically,
his men and women stayed in love, their kids smiling, their heartbreaks
    temporary.
And more, R. J. found a sweetness in a public – unequaled in any history –
who paid good money to watch – sometimes twice – pictures of other
    people's joys.
Art is art, but I can't scoff at this man's fantasies.
The private man? Well, R. J. lived his life in the projection room,
the dark where there was no Warsaw or words, drunk wife, frightened
    son,

no bullied daughter running off to be a Carmelite nun.
I'm glad I could honor the last request, scrawled with a chewed-up
  ballpoint pen,
'a blanket of white narcissists for my coffin,
because I always loved their strong perfume,
this one last thing,' he asked, 'before I join the immorals, old man.'
Goodbye, R. J. What's here – suburban chateaux, leggy blondes,
the oceanic, endless present, the righteous gun in every hand –
is partly your creation.
You saw the covenant fulfilled; of your seed,
unnumbered as the stars, was made a nation.

Patricia Storace

The Filmmaker

(with subtitles)

He was a filmmaker with a capital F.
Iconoclastic. He said 'Non' to Hollywood,   1
'Pourquoi? Ici je suis Le Chef.'   2
A director's director. Difficult but good.

But when Mademoiselle La Grande C.   3
Crept into his bed in Montparnasse
And kissed him on the rectum, he
Had a rectumectomy. But in vain. Hélas.   4

And how they mourned, the aficionados.
(Even stars he'd not met were seen to grieve,
The Christies, Fondas, Streeps and Bardots.)
And for them all, he'd one last trick up his sleeve.

'Cimetière Vérité' he called it (a final pun).   5
In a fashionable graveyard in Paris 3ième.
He was buried, and at the going down of the sun
Premiered his masterpiece, *La Mort, C'est Moi-même*.   6

The coffin, an oblong, lead-lined studio with space
For the body, a camera and enough light

To film in close-up that once sanguine face
Which fills the monumental screen each night.

The show is 'Un grand succès'. People never tire   7
Of filing past. And in reverential tone
They discuss the symbolism, and admire
Its honesty. *La Vérité* pared down to the bone.   8

FIN   9

1 'No' 2 'Why? Here I am the chef.' 3 Miss the Big C. 4 Alas. 5 'True cemetery' 6 *The Death it is Myself.* 7 'A grand success'. 8 The Truth 9 End

Roger McGough

On British Films

Isn't it funny
How they never make any money,
While everyone *in* the racket
Cleans up such a packet?

J. B. Boothroyd

In Memoriam Busby Berkeley

Military straddle the pool.
A gasp of music. Everyone is here.
Thousands cross the street unseeing. Two hearts
Grow breasts. Swirling like a dream with top hat
And cane come eternal softnesses.

Wind them up and let them go. Spin
Little dancer. The rain is gold, and as
The eyes light up it's Keeler! Powell!
The audience, to a man, cry down their trousers.
The lights come on too bright, like chariots.

George Szirtes*

[255]

Elegy for Arthur Prance

'The Man Who Taught the Stars to Dance'

The toes that tapped through morning air
were once stand-ins for Fred Astaire.
The heels cool in the gutter where
the dancer lies up-ended.

The one time only Arthur Prance –
'The Man Who Taught The Stars To Dance' –
had reached his zenith with a jig
which once came over very big
on radio.

The feet that clicked from ten flights high
and danced flamenco down the sky
had once made Ginger Rogers cry
'His *entrechat* is splendid.'

The one time only Arthur Prance –
'The Man Who Taught The Stars To Dance' –
possessed an act of wide appeal
especially his eightsome reel
danced alone.

The one time only Arthur Prance –
'The Man Who Taught The Stars To Dance' –
performed his final pirouette
and heard applause he didn't get.

Pete Morgan

Into the Movies

The sidewalk creeper looks ahead to the Pacific,
To the peal of mission bells.
Stepping out of a drainage tunnel
Under Highway 41 he is happy.
Barges will not keep him up all night.

Someone else can claim his lean-to
And lie awake reading the papers he used for warmth.
Walking north against the suction-slap of semis,
He imagines a pal released from jail,
A worker out of luck,
Then cuts west on Covert. He slows down,
Squeezing the tire of a bike chained to a fence.
There is rain in the weather, the sweat of trees,
Some creature panting in an alley.

Now he's getting what he needs at this time each day
As he makes a withdrawal at Donut Bank.
At the counter, huddled over coffee,
He fidgets with the holes in his socks
And thinks of his favorite moviemaker, Preston Sturges.
He tells himself how Sturges knew the scruffy side
Of money, the steep slide from a stool.
Then he wonders whether Sturges ever stared
Through the window of a florist shop
While thinking of blue mountains above a patio
And alimony leveling the landscape out.

He thinks of the look his own wife
Found inside her the night she left –
That empty cash register look.
Dunking a glazed donut,
He plays a Sturges film in his head
And Great McGinty recalls his days as governor
While wiping down a South American bar.
'McGinty lost by playing for people
Instead of himself,' he says,
And he's thinking of that bicycle.

Back on the street he fingers a wire cutter,
Flinches as a black-and-white zooms by.
The chain snaps. A cat growls in a tree.
In a gust of wind the cables overhead
Sway back and forth, methodical as jump ropes.
He hears a child waking up.
Then he is peddling through a fine spray,
Through a chain-gang scene in *Sullivan's Travels*.

What does he try to forget?
Riding the rails to Hollywood in '46?
The nothing good that happened when he got there?
Fleeting jobs? Hammerhead police?
That last week peddling what he knew about stars –
Maps telling where they lived?
The smell of the trainyard counterpunches the past

And he brakes beside a blind man
Holding up the station house
Beside a dog that looks asleep, or worse.
'How does John Gilbert's house sound to you?' he says.
'I could take you there.'
'I'm anywhere,' the blind man says,
And makes his squeeze-box wail,
Which makes the dog's ear twitch,
Which agitates the fly on his brow.
'You can leave the bike,' he says.
'It's good to have conveyance.
Anywhere's OK, but there are places even after that.
I'd like a private way to get there should I go.
Maybe I could hook a basket up for dog.'
The creeper and the blind man laugh. The 6:05 blows by.

'Only in America,' the creeper says, 'could Sturges make it;
Laughter in an ambulance, everybody crooked but OK,
Easy marks, loose change, no change.
They say he liked to park his private car
In an alley and sing to himself all night.'
He leans the bike against the blind man's leg.
'I'm going to try,' he says.
'Now file those numbers off. I'll say
That southern chain-gang scene one more time,
The one with convicts laughing at cartoons.'
The creeper did that, crossed four tracks, and hopped the flyer west.

Robert McDowell*

Orson Welles, Are You Listening?

Even now, at this late date, when your future seems all
used up, I still sense
                    the top of your head
                                        about to explode.
25 years after *Citizen Kane*, two decades since
The Magnificent Ambersons was mutilated –
still you choose to suffer
frustrations of unfinished projects
                                (*Heart of Darkness*
                                    The Iliad)
forego what victories the system might allow.

Von Stroheim dies; you become
rogue elephant in the sausage factory,
man from Mars on CBS radio.
But I have questions to pose:

            Why have you dissipated your energy?
            What remains but an obese ego,
            limp carcass stuffed with roast lamb.
            What betrayal do you keep silent?
            Why did you, cineastic lion,
            cast that tab collar
            as Joseph K?
                        But let it go. You need
                        a touch of evil – confidential reports
                        written by strangers, distorted
                        in halls of mirrors. You
                        flee forever through Vienna sewers.

How much longer must you display your talents
for lesser men? How often must that iambic voice
ring out as Darrow, as Mapple, as Cagliostro,
as Ben Franklin in some Cinerama epic! Surely
you don't need *that* much money for your films.

(Remember Thalberg burning 14 reels of *Greed*
to extract 43 cents of silver per reel?)

Dress in sackcloth.

    Fire your flesh.

       Von Stroheim watches.

        William David Sherman*

It's All True

Always on the edge of carnival, RKO's Best Boy
flew down to Rio for Rockefeller and Whitney,
with camera crew, candybars and hootch, to gee-swell
the ever-expanding waistline of America.
He swallowed it all, sweating out the drink
in 'disreputable nigger neighbourhoods',
samba dancing at the Urca nightclub;
for 'Hemispheric Solidarity', a belly laugh.
He lost control . . . it was taken away from him.

The Mercury Theatre, *The Magnificent Ambersons*;
Kane, Falstaff, Hank Quinlan and a touch of Lime.

'You're a mess, honey', sherry-barrel-shape,
a freakshow of distortion, all about Orson
smashing up Rita, Lena, Rosebud's dressing rooms,
tilting at windmills when the money ran out.
Made up twenty to seventy, appearing in films
from time to time like a cuckoo-clock
amontillado-voiced; the professional disillusions
of an amateur illusionist cloaked in black humour.
Who else could announce an invasion from Mars?

        Jules Smith

Elegy for Jean Cocteau

You played your death with cigarette-smoke
And centaurs carried you away.
                                    A whiff of jazz,
The dry wind brought its own irreverence.
Now you're with Orpheus and the Chevaliers.

You're right, the mirror traps us all: death's oval mask
Steams the reflection over from the other side.
Now we can't see you any more. We call you dead
The way we called you hypnotized by death.

A poet has to die to rise as verse, you said.
All life you gave us nightbursts of your pain,
(Midnight made lucid) since you showed us
The flowers of your cinema had roots in blood.

Perhaps your Eurydice was death: perhaps
The grave's your new adventure and you've gone
To astonish silence with a forward look.

Harry Guest*

Losing Touch

In memoriam George Cukor, died 24 January 1983

The contact strip taken in 1975
during the filming of an
adaptation of Maeterlinck's play
The Blue Bird.

The Blue Bird was an American–
Russian co-production starring
Elizabeth Taylor, Jane Fonda,
Ava Gardner and Oleg Popov.

Tony Harrison wrote the lyrics
for the songs in the film.

George Cukor used to send
Tony Harrison contact strips
with scribbled notes. He wrote
on the back of this strip:
frame 1 'a character' and
frame 2 'the brooding poet'.

The top picture was used by
The Times in their obituary
of George Cukor on Wednesday,
26 January 1983.

I watch a siskin swinging back and forth
on the nut-net, enjoying lunchtime sun
unusual this time of year up north
and listening to the news at five past one.

As people not in constant contact do
we'd lost touch, but I thought of you, old friend
and sent a postcard now and then. I knew
the sentence starting with your name would end
'*the Hollywood director, died today*'.

You're leaning forward in your black beret
from *The Times* obituary, and I'd add
the background of Pavlovsk near Leningrad
bathed in summer and good shooting light
where it was taken that July as I'm
the one you're leaning forward to address.
I had a black pen poised about to write
and have one now and think back to that time
and feel you lean towards me out of Nothingness.

I rummage for the contacts you sent then:
the one of you that's leaning from *The Times*
and below it one of me with my black pen
listening to you criticize my rhymes,
and, between a millimetre of black band
that now could be ten billion times as much
and none that show the contact of your hand.
The distance needs adjusting, just a touch!

You were about to tap my knee for emphasis.

It's me who's leaning forward now with this!

Tony Harrison*

Point of View

Higgledy-piggledy
Christopher Isherwood
Looked on Berlin with a
Camera's eye,

But when his faith became
NeoDravidian
Hollywood lenses would
Moisten and cry.

Chris Wallace-Crabbe*

The Fall of the House of Hitchcock

Family Plot: born 1899, son of covered table legs,
Cocky of Shamley Green shaped like motherly Queen Victoria
by double-bass meals, ice-cream and Martinis,
his appetite for birds stuffed behind a wall of flesh,
recipes and restaurants spoken of as though
previous lovers, in ice-box tones. The house
of Hitchcock has skeletons in the food cupboard.
A fat boy dreams of opening it with the concealed key,
Mother, an absolute shocker who dies laughing.
Open windows disperse the heat of lunchtime liaisons;
gulp of voyeur and gourmet. Dali's figure
pushes libidinous shapes from the roof.

Female hip and automobile in Fifties curves,
cantilevers of bra and bridge. Vera Miles corseted

by contract, Doris Day waving her conscience bye-bye,
Kim Novak made over by Pygmalion's hair-dye.
Handsome male leads are looking down Janet Leigh's
mountainous cleavage from dizzy heights of desire,
falling in love, dangling from skyscrapers and rock,
spinning in erotic *Vertigo*, wanting the fallen woman
from the Golden Gate into San Francisco Bay,
climax approaching with a dreamer's compulsion –
vertiginous sensation, nocturnal emission.

Watch out, Hollywood Hitch is walking on,
surreal slasher at the eyeball's murderous gaze
(ACTION! *Rear Window*; *Spellbound*; *Frenzy*; *The Wrong Man*;
Shadow of a Doubt; *I Confess*. CUT!) seen last
as a shapely silhouette, Registrar of Deaths.

Jules Smith*

Five Poems on Film Directors

ANTONIONI

Trees are drowning in salt. The keyhole whines.
He's left his boat
in the reed-bed, her book
and idiotic gloves lie where she threw them.
Beyond the canal the tankers prowl
north to south, their call
lingers across the marshes.
'Why did you wait till the summer was over
before you came?' 'Why did you wait for me
if you'd rather have a boat than a woman?'
'It wasn't that. It isn't that.'
'I'm going.' 'Send back the car.'
'With Sandro? You're joking.' 'It's cold.'
The silver car between the poplars
like a fish in reeds.
He lives on peppermints and blues
or

He is tearing photographs for a living
or
He has been sent death, is opening it
or

GRIERSON

Then the nets rose and fell
in the swell. Then the dark water
went fiery suddenly, then black.
Then with a haul it was all
fire, all silver fire
fighting down the black. Then the fire
rose in the air slowly,
struggling over the side of the boat.
Then it was deck and hold.
Then it was the dance of death
in silver with grey gulls.
Then it was low clouds, bars of light,
high water slapping, choppy wake
and oilskin tea then.

WARHOL

We are turning orange. They are turning purple.
The spindle is turning out metamorphic rock.
Lighting a cigarette, he is turning she.
The Empire State is turning dark
all day. The beach has gods on it,
turning their backs on each other
as each one swivels on a visitor.
The pickup sparks and spits, two
stereo corners turn redhot.
In the glow she turns vague, bends,
and a split second turns her
in the next cycle of darkness.
They shriek like parrots, and as bright,
they are half turning into birds.
Two on a sofa turn a fanzine,
my dear. We turn on, off, on.
A wig drifts, she

[265]

turns he. He sh-
rieks in orange. We
drift to the door.
It turns. It turns out
the world after all,
steady as the Empire State
being blown by the wind.

KUROSAWA

Glade sword, glint running.
Tree shiver, choked cry.
River shadow, full quiver.
   Dust mounds, old wind.
   Grave mounds, cold wind.
Thatch fire, child running.
Plunder cart, thousand ashes.
Village rain, storm forest.
Storm gods, rain ghosts.
Restless fathers, prayer hearths.
Jogging banners, thrones dissolving.
Blood crop, dog pot.
   Dust mounds, old wind.
   Grave mounds, cold wind.
Cracked stave, slow crumple.
Moon blade, rolled skull.
Blood brother, spangled ambush.
Sun coins, bird calls.
Bent bow, man running.
Bent bow, body jumping.
Bent bow, neck streaming.
Bent bow, knees broken.
Bent bow, breast nailed.
Bent bow, bent bow.
Bent bow, bent bow.
   Dust mounds, old wind.
   Grave mounds, cold wind.

GODARD

– and the walls were very white, the girl
being interrogated was speaking slowly
but her words were lost in the gunbursts
coming up from the street–

> slumped in the café, featureless brown room
> with a radio blaring, one window
> opening on a filthy garden
> with a sort of chickenrun –
> whether he was only drunk, or dead –

>> 'the audience has no means of knowing
>> and that's it' / in the skyscraper lift
>>> at the nineteenth floor
>>> 'All right, 20 thousand
>>> cheap at the price'

– no, the interrogation was long before.
She went into the country –

>>> the junction not
>>> 'like' a spider's web
>>> keeps catching trains –
>>> the bridges he'd been over –
>>> really a blank sky

ALL REACTIONARIES ARE PAPER TIGERS

– she'd come to the bridge without knowing it
but it was already too late, they had their dogs,
easy even without searchlights –

BUT THEY ARE ALSO REAL TIGERS
WHO HAVE DEVOURED MILLIONS OF PEOPLE

> 'it isn't cinema at all
> without a flow of images,
> Godard's destroying the cinema'

BUT ON THE OTHER HAND THEY ARE PAPER TIGERS
BECAUSE NOW THE PEOPLE HAVE POWER

and the coupé slid over
in a cool cliché into the sea

Edwin Morgan*

Flowers for Luis Buñuel

What is the word for 'death'
in French?   What word triggers
laughter at slit eyes and guttered
cripples?
                    What is the word for
the language of eye, the montage of
blood?
                    Buñuel, Buñuel,
the musicians in the buildings play no tune
comparable to the whirring lens
of hideous glare of light and blood.
The knives and dwarfs and round firm tits
say death in French for a language too
strong to hold in the gut.
                    Buñuel, Buñuel,
is the world?   A place?
                              such dirty
cunts and open flies! an unwiped ass
editing the noise of the city,
the wind an instrument of long black hair,
all the mothers dying.

Let us go to the cinema.
Let us go
          to the sinema.
Every rock depends for life upon
the spilling of blood, and torn flesh.
Every death creates a small quiver,
a hatred of mirrors.
                    Who knew guilt
before this?   The eye, the eye,

burning too steadily through the ugly night
in the theatre dark with the smells
of all our hatred.   The cinema of
the slit, the wound, the crawling ants.
Buñuel, did you do it?   Did you?
Have you built the handless queer,
the only sighted murderer?   Have you
built them?
            Let the misshapen dance
around the rock.   Only a priest can eat
this shit and not vomit.   This is the
cross made of bones.   Prayers?   Never!
          Buñuel, Buñuel,
is the world?   Did you?

                    Stuart Z. Perkoff*

Ode to Fellini on Interviewing Actors for a Forthcoming Film

Wasps and flowers fill the 1910 confession box.
  Hot. Hot. But the lovely Witch of the North, wearing
    a Puritan black velvet hat
      and backless black bikini,
peddles slowly on her bicycle about the beach
  at St Tropez. Two Mercy nuns, whose fingers stink
    like stale blue milk or Labrador,
      herd us across the schoolyard
protected by the Swiss Guards of the snow;
      we kneel, itching

inside snowsuits, wet, around the marble altar rail.
  Monsignor floats in from the sacristy,
    pressing a glass relic box against
      his belly; we cry and kiss
the hairy knuckle of the virgin martyr. The hands
  of Christ are the muscles of the sun:
    they make flesh and bone from bread
      and blood from ordinary

table wine. There is another moon,
    its slow tides

the menstrual flow of the nuns. Around your office table
    crowd an old alcoholic circus clown,
        a Christmas doll and three umbrellas
        and Anita Ekberg's mother
in a photo. Rain falls on artificial flowers. What
    if everything comes from the sea? The angels
        are ecstatic fish. Or helicopters.
        And you, Fellini, are
a deep-sea diver, searching for the sex
        of God. Good luck.

                              Paul Carroll*

Bresson's Movies

A movie of Robert
Bresson's showed a yacht,
at evening on the Seine,
all its lights on, watched

by two young, seemingly
poor people, on a bridge adjacent,
the classic boy and girl
of the story, any one

one cares to tell. So
years pass, of course, but
I identified with the young,
embittered Frenchman,

knew his almost complacent
anguish and the distance
he felt from his girl.
Yet another film

of Bresson's has the
aging Lancelot with his

awkward armor standing
in a woods, of small trees,

dazed, bleeding, both he
and his horse are,
trying to get back to
the castle, itself of

no great size. It
moved me, that
life was after all
like that. You are

in love. You stand
in the woods, with
a horse, bleeding.
The story is true.

Robert Creeley*

Pasolini

Is there a limit to how many changes
A man can go through between his first love
And the one that bursts his heart?
And with those changes, a kaleidoscope of views –
From cellars and high balconies, sober and drunk –
Always the same city flanked by the same hills,
Washed by a sea as filthy as the shore.
But the rough boys grew suave; cheap fashions bought them,
Poor mutants of affluence and bigotry.

Each year, it seems to me, you altered colour –
Not as the chameleon to hide
But to be vivid like an ulcer or a bloom.
I follow after and – two decades late –
Look for your footprints in the shantytowns.
Here are the children of the child you loved
In endless transformations as he was,

[271]

And I see what dragged you in and out of guilt
Like a fish on a sharp hook but a weak line:
You boarded the midnight tram to what you wanted
Regardless of the price – which was your life.

I met you once at a reception in London
Held in a low-ceilinged room by the river
With writers you despised. You approached me
And said, 'How very English of you: an umbrella,
On such a night as this!' In your smile
I counted the teeth. I'd come down from Oxford
Not to hear you but Auden.
I'd not even seen your films, much less read
A word of yours in verse or prose.
You had a haggard look, also a hunger
To be out of there, back in your element.
I didn't understand your manner. 'Goodnight'.
I hurried off to Paddington for the train.

I wish I'd lingered at least a few minutes
In your solitude that evening in London,
Simply to learn your voice, to taste
The ashes of Casarsa from your lips. What errors,
What pain it might have helped me round, to hear
Just for a moment in that crowded room
The pure elixir of your egotism,
The Italy that coarsened your tongue with love.

Michael Schmidt*

Elegy for Pier Paolo Pasolini

(Murdered, Rome, 2 November 1975)

So Momma Roma got you in the end –
the bitch goddess and her instrument,
a bit of teenage rough trade, one of those
subproletarian ragazzi da vita you immortalized
in poetry and film – one of your own sorry passions.

[272]

Sex for you, as for so many of us,
was pure pleasure, uncontaminated by
the bourgeois shams of guilt, family and home;
but also a religious and political commitment –
each one-night stand a separate responsibility for life, and man.

I know too well the station where you picked him up (or he
picked you), that fascinating messenger from ancient furies.
The gay guides are filled with places just the same,
where lust and destiny, danger and boredom all
come together in a final massacre of loneliness.

Una vita violenta – your own title
for the sad brutality of fallen Rome
that is for ever ancient, ruined by the scandal of perverse
papal prohibitions, by the moon's castrating goddess
who allowed a first and final grope, then excommunicated you:

crushed you to death in the suburban cruelty and moonless dark
of Ostia, pathetic substitute and shabby back-projection for
what should have been mysterious and scented pagan groves,
with high priests chanting, dancing, performing a forgotten rite
on naked Adonises, chained and ravished on altars of marble flowers.

– Instead, courageous and confessed comrade of boys and men,
compassionate Marxist-Sodomist of all male Christian love,
you in a pious odour of sanctity were hypocritically laid to rest
in Rome, according to the last rites of a church that you so often
both loved and lashed, celebrated and despised.

– Yes, they fucked up the final cut, and the unkindest.
But in the memories of men, you, Pier Paolo,
the close-up victim of your own compulsions, hero
of your own divine poetic fantasies, forever cruise
infatuation's crowded boulevard of shadows

in your excessive chariot of love and death,
the moon-silvery Alfa Romeo, vehicle and property
of which your lonely genius and vision were the only stars,
and that you slowly faded out, in Ostia,
one Sunday night, in Scorpio, in winter, when the moon was dark.

James Kirkup

Godard's Women

For Philip Levine

You ask about Godard's Women
why do they titillate
is it their nonbodies
so brittle they could snap .
as a purse snaps shut
when she takes
a cigarette
& lights it

Their subject is
never the self
but illusion for a man
ladies whose body
is steel wire

Jeanne Lance*

NOTES

'Nepotism' (Anon.). This anonymous couplet, erroneously attributed to Ogden Nash, comments on the way the German-born Carl Laemmle (1867–1939), founder of Universal Studios, and his fellow pioneer Hollywood moguls employed their relatives. It was followed by the Tinseltown saying 'The son-in-law also rises', a joke allegedly inspired by the marriages of David O. Selznick and William Goetz to the daughters of Louis B. Mayer in 1930. (253)

'In Memoriam Busby Berkeley' (Szirtes). Born in Los Angeles, the child of theatrical parents, William Berkeley Enos (1895–1976) got his nickname from a turn-of-the-century actress and began his career as a choreographer working as an army drill instructor superintending mass parades during World War One. In the 1920s he staged musicals on Broadway and came to Hollywood in 1930 to work for Sam Goldwyn, before moving on to Warner Brothers where his extravagant, innovative, wholly cinematic choreography in *42nd Street* (1933), *Gold Diggers of 1933* and *Dames* (1934) transformed the movie musical, taking it far away from the proscenium arch of the theatre. From 1936 to 1949 he worked as a director, then returned to choreography, his last assignment being *Jumbo* (1962). (255)

'Into the Movies' (McDowell). Born into a wealthy Chicago family as Edmund Biden and educated privately in Europe, Preston Sturges (1898–1959) became a screenwriter in the early 1930s and was Hollywood's pre-eminent movie satirist as a writer-director in the 1940s. Among his films are his debut as director, *The Great McGinty* (1940), an account of a state politician's rise and fall starring Brian Donlevy, and *Sullivan's Travels* (1941), in which Joel McCrea plays an ace director of comedies who goes on the road as a late-Depression era hobo in order to find authentic material for earthy, real-life movies. (256)

'Orson Welles, Are You Listening?' (Sherman). Welles (1915–85) was born in Kenosha, Wisconsin, the son of a rich inventor and his beautiful pianist wife, who both died when he was young. The child prodigy grew up to be a boy genius and was a major figure in theatre and radio (internationally notorious for his broadcast version of *War of the Worlds* on Hallowe'en 1938). He brought his Mercury Company to Hollywood to make *Citizen Kane* (1941) and *The Magnificent Ambersons* (1942), though the latter was re-edited while he was in Latin America making the uncompleted documentary *It's All True*. He made a number of films in America and Europe (including a 1962 version of *The Trial* starring Anthony Perkins as Joseph K), several unfinished and unseen, starred in numerous pictures directed by others, worked sporadically in the theatre, and became a celebrity through his appearances on television and in commercials. Some think Welles a betrayer of his prodigious talents; others consider him a self-destructive victim of both the Hollywood system and of the early success that Scott Fitzgerald considered one of the great American traps; another view is that one way and another he fulfilled himself, but just happened to make his greatest work first.

During the silent era Erich von Stroheim had similar problems with the front office, most notably with the 'boy wonder' producer Irving Thalberg, subsequently the model for Monroe Stahr in Scott Fitzgerald's *The Last Tycoon*. As head of production at Universal, Thalberg cut Stroheim's *Foolish Wives* (1922) and replaced him on *Merry-Go-Round* (1923). Moving to MGM as vice-president, Thalberg inherited Stroheim's seven-hour *Greed*, took it out of the director's hands, reduced the duration to under two hours and subsequently had the discarded reels washed for their silver nitrate. (259)

'Elegy for Jean Cocteau' (Guest). Born near Paris, Cocteau (1889–1963) worked in almost every branch of the arts and was a dominant figure of the international avant-garde from World War One until his death. He directed films, his books and plays were filmed by others, he wrote passionately and with insight about the cinema. Among the finest accounts of the film-making process is the diary he kept during the production of *La Belle et la bête* (1946). He was honorary president of the Cannes Film Festival and in 1959 sent an urgent message to his friend Pablo Picasso, telling him to come to Cannes immediately to catch François Truffaut's *Les quatre cents coups*. (261)

'Losing Touch: In Memoriam George Cukor' (Harrison). Born in New York to Jewish immigrants from Hungary, Cukor (1899–1983) had a distinguished movie career lasting over fifty years following his arrival in Hollywood from Broadway to work as dialogue coach on *All Quiet on the Western Front* (1930). He was a celebrated director of women, especially Garbo and Katharine Hepburn, and his movies included *David Copperfield* (1935), *A Star is Born* (1954) and *My Fair Lady* (1964). His penultimate movie, *The Blue Bird* (1976), was the low point of his career – it appeared briefly in American cinemas and turned up in Britain for a daytime television screening. (261)

'Point of View' (Wallace-Crabbe). Born in Cheshire and educated at Cambridge, Christopher Isherwood (1904–1986) was passionately devoted to the cinema. He coined the phrase 'I am a camera' in his book *Goodbye to Berlin* (subsequently staged and filmed as both *I Am a Camera* and *Cabaret*). In 1934 he co-scripted Berthold Viertel's movie *Little Friend* and later wrote *Prater Violet* (1945), a novel inspired by the experience. In 1939 he and W. H. Auden emigrated to America. Auden settled in New York, Isherwood crossed the continent to Los Angeles, where he became involved in writing screenplays and the study of oriental religion. (263)

'The Fall of the House of Hitchcock' (Smith). The corpulent cockney Alfred Hitchcock (1899–1980) was the biggest frog in the small pond of British cinema when David O. Selznick encouraged him to leap into the great lake of Hollywood. His success was immediate and his brief personal appearances made him the one universally recognizable director in the history of cinema. French critics first probed the complexities of his art, and as directors they went on to acknowledge his influence. A generation of American 'movie brat' film-makers followed on. In Hitchcock's final movie *Family Plot* (1976) his personal signature is the silhouette behind frosted glass in a Californian municipal office. (263)

'Five Poems on Film Directors' (Morgan). Michelangelo Antonioni (born 1912, Ferrara) started out as a critic in Rome, then worked as a screenwriter and documentarist before directing features in the early 1950s. He became internationally famous through *L'Avventura* (1960), an oblique study of contemporary alienation in which the landscape and city streets are as dramatically significant as the characters who inhabit them. His key star was Monica Vitti and in *Deserto Rosso* (1964), his first colour movie, he painted the locations to contribute to the moods he sought.

The Glasgow-born and educated (a post-war degree in philosophy following World War One navy service) John Grierson (1898–1972) coined the term 'documentary' to describe the work of Robert Flaherty, and himself created the British documentary movement as director of *Drifters* (1929). Grierson ran the Empire Marketing Board Film Unit, the Film Department of the General Post Office, and launched the National Film Board of Canada.

The middle-west born son of Eastern-European immigrants, Andy Warhol (1927–87) established himself as a commercial designer and pop painter, then began making 'underground' movies with his so-called Factory in 1963. Before producing narrative movies featuring stars of his own creation (most of these pictures were co-directed by Paul Morrissey), he produced avant-garde movies, some several hours long, such as his six-hour *Sleep* and *Empire*, his endless contemplation of the Empire State Building.

Born in Tokyo in 1910, Akira Kurosawa brought Japanese cinema to a wide western audience through his masterly *Rashomon*, which won the Golden Lion at the 1951 Venice Festival, and *Seven Samurai* (1954), his three-hour epic about a band of chivalrous hired swordsmen defending a remote village imperilled by bandits in mediaeval Japan. He has created a cinematic world for occidental cinephiles.

Born in Paris in 1930 into a rich Swiss family, Jean-Luc Godard was a brilliant critic for *Cahiers du cinéma* and other journals, and the most innovative member of the French New Wave. He directed a series of seminal films – *A bout de souffle, Le Petit Soldat, Vivre sa vie* – that made him an international figure. But from the mid-1960s he became increasingly devoted to reconciling his love of popular cinema with an eccentric Marxist analysis of society. Morgan's poem describes his elegant late 1960s phase, exemplified by his Maoist *La Chinoise* (1967). Godard moved out of mainstream cinema, but has regularly found the money and engaged the interest of international stars to make handsome, large-scale movies to be shown at film festivals. (264)

'Flowers for Luis Buñuel' (Perkoff). Born into a well-off Spanish landowning family, a contemporary at Madrid University of Salvador Dali and Federico Garcia Lorca, Buñuel (1900–83) was celebrated for his European avant-garde movies, *Un chien andalou* (1928) and *L'Age d'or* (1930). He disappeared from the international moviemaking scene for nearly two decades, re-emerging with his Mexican masterpiece *Los Olvidados* at the 1951 Cannes Festival. Perkoff's poem was published in 1955 when Buñuel's other Mexican films were being discovered. The final, triumphant phase of his career began when he made *Viridiana* in Spain (1961) and four years later embarked on a series of movies in France that included *Belle de jour* and *The Discreet Charm of the Bourgeoisie*. (268)

'Ode to Fellini' (Carroll). Born in Rimini in 1920, Federico Fellini was an important writer in the Italian neo-realist movement and directed several films in that style, including *I Vitelloni* (1953) and *La Strada* (1954). With *La Dolce Vita* (1960) and *8½* (1963) he opened up a new kind of expansive personal cinema for Italy and the world. The Swedish actress Anita Ekberg became an iconic figure through *La Dolce Vita*, and nuns, priests and clowns are part of Fellini's memory bank of religion and popular culture. (269)

'Bresson's Movies' (Creeley). Born in 1907 in Bromont-Lamothe, Puy-de-Dôme, Bresson is among the cinema's most austere and revered talents, a Catholic writer-director working mostly with non-professional performers. His best known movies are his 1943 debut *Les Anges du péché*, *The Diary of a Country Priest* (1951) and *The Trial of Joan of Arc* (1962). The first movie invoked in this poem is *Le Diable probablement* (1977), in which a young couple watch a *bateau mouche* on the Seine and the man, disgusted by a corrupt, polluted world, persuades a drug addict to kill him in the Père Lachaise cemetery. The second is Bresson's preceding film, *Lancelot du Lac* (1974), a bleak view of the Arthurian knights of the Round Table as a group of etiolated losers. (270)

'Pasolini' (Schmidt). The Italian poet, novelist and film-maker Pier Paolo Pasolini (1922–75) was born in Bologna, the son of a dedicated fascist. After World War Two he became a member of the Communist Party and a defiantly open homosexual. He worked as a screenwriter before embarking on a prolific and controversial career as a director in 1961 with *Accattone*, a portrait of a Roman pimp. Numerous films followed, as apparently different from each other as his austere 1964 *The Gospel According to St Matthew*, and the posthumously released *Salò*, a calculatedly emetic World War Two allegory about the sado-masochistic orgies in the last weeks of Italian fascism's aristocratic élite. In November 1975 Pasolini was murdered on the outskirts of Rome by a teenage rent-boy, who was subsequently arrested driving the film-maker's Alfa Romeo. (271)

'Godard's Women' (Lance). The cool, detached heroines of Jean-Luc Godard's New Wave movies were Jean Seberg (*A bout de souffle*, 1960), Anna Karina (*Le Petit Soldat, Une Femme est une femme, Vivre sa vie, Bande à part, Alphaville, Pierrot le fou, Made in USA*), Macha Méril (*Une Femme mariée*), Chantal Goya (*Masculin féminin*), Marina Vlady (*Deux ou trois choses que je sais d'elle*) and Anne Wiazemsky (*La Chinoise*). (274)

VI

Films and Genres

Kameradschaft

When you are blind with comfort to your soul's
Essential debit of blood and bone,
May this thought wake your nerves and needle through
Your inactivity; of bodies like your own,
Red in a counterfeit morning, with a sheen of sweat
Like metal, and the whole
Earth ominous over them, never forgetting
The ghosts of tappings in the long galleries
Hopelessly blocked and no one to come: of cries
Hungering through emptiness: and bridges won
To that other country, built with bloodletting
And steel imperishable; and never known.

Randall Swingler*

The Undead

Even as children they were late sleepers,
Preferring their dreams, even when quick with monsters,
To the world with all its breakable toys,
Its compacts with the dying;

From the stretched arms of withered trees
They turned, fearing contagion of the mortal,
And even under the plums of summer
Drifted like winter moons.

Secret, unfriendly, pale, possessed
Of the one wish, the thirst for mere survival,
They came, as all extremists do
In time, to a sort of grandeur:

Now, to their Balkan battlements
Above the vulgar town of their first lives,

They rise at the moon's rising. Strange
 That their utter self-concern

Should, in the end, have left them selfless:
Mirrors fail to perceive them as they float
 Through the great hall and up the staircase;
 Nor are the cobwebs broken.

Into the pallid night emerging,
Wrapped in their flapping capes, routinely maddened
 By a wolf's cry, they stand for a moment
 Stoking the mind's eye

With lewd thoughts of the pressed flowers
And bric-a-brac of rooms with something to lose, –
 Of love-dismembered dolls, and children
 Buried in quilted sleep.

Then they are off in a negative frenzy,
Their black shapes cropped into sudden bats
 That swarm, burst, and are gone. Thinking
 Of a thrush cold in the leaves

Who has sung his few summers truly,
Or an old scholar resting his eyes at last,
 We cannot be much impressed with vampires,
 Colorful though they are;

Nevertheless, their pain is real,
And requires our pity. Think how sad it must be
 To thirst always for a scorned elixir,
 The salt quotidian blood

Which, if mistrusted, has no savor;
To prey on life forever and not possess it,
 As rock-hollows, tide after tide,
 glassily strand the sea.

Richard Wilbur*

In Defense of Poetry

Childhood taught us illusion. When I saw
On Fredric March's hands the fierce black hair
And long sharp nails of Mr Hyde, I ran
Screaming from the theater, his twisted face
Demonic behind me brighter than the day;
Then begged to stay up past bedtime, for fear
Boris Karloff wake me and, near despair,
I run to consolation through the dark.
And while Miss Hinton taught us spelling, grammar,
Multiplication – all like loving guides
To bring us safely from the labyrinth
Of self and self's intelligence – it seemed
I heard the voice that mocked them. 'There is no
Language,' it whispered, 'no A on tests, no trust
To keep you from the presence of my face.
Parents and children die, anguish will be
Greater than its hard sum and no familiar
Voices deliver you from Mr Hyde,
However Dr Jekyll seem secure.'

Now in a bright room in a building named
For one who taught the art of politics,
Three days a week I listen to the stories
My young friends write, remembering that my father
Loved stories and especially those he told.
Intelligent and brave, they risk their way
By speech from childhood anguish, formal candor
An old light shining new within a world
Confusing and confused, although their teachers
Deny the worth of writing – my latest colleagues,
Who hope to find a letter in the mail,
Are happy if their children study Shakespeare
At Harvard, Penn or Yale, write articles
To prove all writing writers' self-deception,
Drive Camrys, drink good wines, play Shostakovich
Or TV news before they go to bed,
And when their sleeping or their waking dream

Is fearful, think it merely cinema,
Trite spectacle that later will amuse.
But when my mind remembers, unamused
It pictures Korczak going with his children
Through Warsaw to the too substantial train.

Edgar Bowers*

Scar-Face

By Lake Erie, Al Capone could set
his price on the moonshine that enflamed Chicago –
'Funny thing, in this our thing, a man
in this line of business has too much company.'
He watched black and white men walk the tightrope,
and felt a high contempt for them all – poor fish,
sweating themselves to death for a starvation wage.
Little Caesar, like Julius Caesar, a rich man
knifed by richer. A true king serves the realm,
when he's equal to the man who serves his meal;
a gentleman is an aristocrat on bail . . .
Splendor spread like gold leaf in your hand, Al,
made in the morning and by midday hard,
pushed by your fellow convicts to the wall.

Robert Lowell*

Good Times

Once good times meant
a grand hotel,
                where John Barrymore,
in the luckless role
of a penniless aristocrat,

[286]

lay, one evening,
with a wound deep in his skull,

his celebrated profile
steeped in blood

and Greta Garbo,
a divine ballerina
and the love of his life,

kept struggling
valiantly to rearrange
her phantasmagorical chain
of misery and magic,

her face, in her boudoir,
silvery in its fever,
her throat luminous

and Joan Crawford,
a bouncy stenographer,
with a cigarette idly dangling
out of the corner of her sultry mouth,

kept appealing
to yet another wry twist of fate,
or, at least, the sympathetic care
of a common clerk,
                    Lionel Barrymore,
an old gentleman near to death

whose employer, Wallace Beery,
an industrial magnate
with the soul of a Junker
and the head of a bull,

spat on the floor
of our Art Deco bar, at our grand hotel,
in a righteous disgust . . .

All this, of course, was late in Berlin,
that oddly cosmopolitan city,
shortly before the arrival of Hitler,

and was the rosy
underside of the Threepenny Opera,

full of the bottomless glitter
of the Weimar Republic

and, maybe, as well,
of the swan song of a playboy,
svelte among the greenery
over by the Tiergarten,

and grown deaf to history . . .

   The good times
   we none of us
   shall ever know again

like the limo
at the end of the tale

carrying away Garbo
to a horizon of ashes

her eyes as grievous and fearful
as her heart was cold and eternal

                   Robert Mazzocco*

Fay Wray to the King

Dear Kong
Some have slurred our relationship
Some have called it unnatural;
Some have said I'm a tart;
Some have said you're an ape.
Dear Kong
Rumor, and rumormongers, old farts.
It's what you say that hurts.
It's when you criticize your little Fay that hurts.
Not rumor, rumormongers, and good taste.
When you speak of splitting, instead of loving,

When you talk of hating, instead of copulating,
When you rant of not relating, instead of knowing,
That's what hurts
Your little Fay,
Your own sweet flirt,
Your tiny Miss Wray.

They have been wrong –
As if miscegenetic pleasure was a freak of nature,
As if I was not easily satisfied or well supplied;
If only they could touch your hairy rump and tool –
They'd realize I wasn't such a fool.

Dear Kong
You are my beast;
Devour my nice white body if you please;
Don't act like a cowardly golliwog
Or use philosophical doublespeak;
Save me from the terrible pterodactyl;
I'm agog at your marvelous soul
And adore the hairs on your toes
And cylinder which towers above
The Empire State, though they say
You have torn four sexes to shreds
And had other women in bed.

Dear Kong
Save your adorable Fay;
Miss Wray who adores you
And loves you, is true to you.
                    Affectionately, YOUR QUEEN

                              Judith Rechter*

King Kong Meets Wallace Stevens

Take two photographs –
Wallace Stevens and King Kong
(Is it significant that I eat bananas as I write this?)

[289]

Stevens is portly, benign, a white brush cut
striped tie. Businessman but
for the dark thick hands, the naked brain
the thought in him.

Kong is staggering
lost in New York streets again
a spawn of annoyed cars at his toes.
The mind is nowhere.
Fingers are plastic, electric under the skin.
He's at the call of Metro-Goldwyn-Mayer.

Meanwhile W. S. in his suit
is thinking chaos is thinking fences.
In his head – the seeds of fresh pain
his exorcising,
the bellow of locked blood.

The hands drain from his jacket,
pose in the murderer's shadow.

Michael Ondaatje*

Kong Was King

Sae far awa, the insch whaur Kong was King
    And fancied Fay
    Was wan and wae
To watch thon apish etin dunt and ding.

Gane gyte wi love, he loundered yett and waa
    For Gowdenhair
    That sabbit sair,
She'd seen hou chairms o hers had fand his flaw.

Her blondie beauty, eftir quines o colour,
    Had brunt sae bricht
    As blind his sicht
Til aa but the ae fair heid, his doom and dolour.

To rax sae far, he rived his warld apairt,
    Thon ferlie earth
    O' monster birth
Owre wee to haud the swirl that swaulled his hert.

But muckler ferlies, born o the Nineteen-Hunders,
    Had band him fast,
    A beast frae the past
Nae maik for modren pouer that fanks and funders.

A keekin-shaw til crouds in mirk Manhattan
    (A jungle jyle
    On a coorser isle),
His leddy fair anither 'sicht,' in satin –

He bruke his bands, he grippit his queen o glamour
    And sclimmit hie
    To win them free
O' fikey fowk that deaved the warld wi yammer.

On tap o the haichmaist biggin (the Empire State)
    He fand a den
    Whaur midgie men
Micht gawp ablow but never gang thon gait.

The Lord o the lift, he blattered neives til breist
    Wi rair on rair
    That flegged the air
Wi micht that made him King owre ilka beast.

Alexander Scott

A Toast

here's to nick and nora charles,
pioneer hedonists who brightened the way
out of our grim cotton mather past.

they won where many stout revelers succumbed:
f. scott, zelda, hemingway, and crews gallantly

pursued the gin-filled grail until
john calvin, not john barleycorn, completely broke them.

but the pox of collective guilt and depraved man
could not daunt the thin man and his wife.
she, in genuine liberation, poured as they drank
for breakfast, lunch, and supper
without a single belch of shame.
nor did they ever start the day
stabbed with remorse or headache pledges.
nick usually set the morning tone:
'how about a drop to cut the phlegm?'

they loved life, each other, all the pleasures
of the flesh, despite Salem's fire and brimstone,
and Asta stands as wagging proof that
they were just alive, and not rebelling.
nora always slept with nick, not the dog,
and all three remained completely non-neurotic.

Charles Stetler*

Walker Evans' Atlanta

That Cherokee Parts Store photographed in 1936
By Walker Evans, chalet-style houses
On stilts with hoardings advertising Anne Shirley
In *Chatterbox*, Carole Lombard at the Paramount –
We nose past garage fronts with rubber tyres
Festooning them like wreaths, up Ponce de Leon,
West Peachtree, the driver getting lost
On Pine and Hunnicutt in a blizzard
Suddenly melting to canals rouged by sunshine.

And looking at those Evans pictures
In the Library of Congress, the tubercular driver,
Snowed-up boulevards of Old Atlanta
Edged out by highways, colonial mansions
Cut off at roof level by flyovers,

Is returning to a city gone underground,
Lost to us. Becalmed here, alone
In enforced idleness, I sit up drinking
At the Domino and Inter-Sex-Shun,
Charlie Prose 'telling it like it is',
Topless dancers relentlessly cavorting
Above tired faces of oral surgeons
And numismatists released from conventions.

Walking back up Edgewood and Alabama
Through snowpiles like marshmallows,
It was not through Evans' version
Of a paradise blighted by poverty,
The genteel run to seed –
What was imposed on it was glitter
Anonymous in its pretension,
Snow thawing over suburbs whose lone lights
Burned on like the bulbs
In rooms of suicides awaiting discovery.
Now it is Evans' memory that is real to me.

Alan Ross*

On Seeing the Leni Riefenstahl Film of the 1936 Olympic Games

The nation's face above the human shape,
Sunlight on leaf, gloved skin and water pearled
– No art can hide the shocking gulfs that gape
Even between such bodies and their world.

Art merely lets these tenants of a star
Run once again with legendary ease
Across the screen and years towards that war
Which lay in wait for them like a disease.

Roy Fuller*

[293]

Les Enfants de Thalia

At summer's end, Colditz or Wintersborn
Flies its Oflag from icy battlements
Above the stifling balcony where Perce
And I, a farewell party, watch alone
And early one hot matin, the dead march
Of Rauffenstein, de Boeldieu, Maréchal,
And Rosenthal through black night and white day
In search of honor and/or freedom, pure
In word and deed as only the pre-war
Was. They don't make them like that any more.
Especially not Perce and I as we,
Shortened and shadowed by the midday sun,
Say terse adieux aboard Pier 83.

                                    L. E. Sissman*

Claudette Colbert by Billy Wilder

run, do not walk, to the nearest exit
spain, or is democracy doomed
we regret that due to circumstances beyond our control
we are unable to bring you the cambridge crew trials

if you're counting my eyebrows
i can tell you there are two
i took your letter out and read it to the rabbits

describe the sinking ship
describe the sea at night
he lived happily ever after in the café magenta

how to preserve peaches
they're counting on you for intimate
personal stuff about hitler and his gang
it's a chance i wouldn't miss for anything in the
wait in holland for

instance watching the windmills
that's more than flash gordon ever did

all those bugles blowing
in the ears of a confused liberal
so long
pretty woman
wake me up at the part where he claims milwaukee

Tom Raworth*

Miss Scarlett, Mr Rhett and Other Latter-Day Saints

Novitiates sing Ave
Before the whipping posts,
Criss-crossing their breasts and
tear-stained robes
in the yielding dark.

Animated by the human sacrifice
(Golgotha in black-face)
Priests glow purely white on the
bas-relief of a plantation shrine.

(O Sing)
You are gone but not forgotten
Hail, Scarlett. Requiescat in pace.

God-Makers smear brushes in
blood/gall
to etch frescoes on your
ceilinged tomb.

(O Sing)
Hosanna, King Kotton.

Shadowed couplings of infidels
tempt stigmata from the nipples
of your true-believers.

(Chant Maternoster)
Hallowed Little Eva.

Ministers make novena with the
charred bones of four
very small
very black
very young children

(Intone DIXIE)

And guard the relics
of your intact hymen
daily putting to death,
into eternity,
The stud, his seed,
His seed
His seed.

(O Sing)
Hallelujah, pure Scarlett
Blessed Rhett, the Martyr.

Maya Angelou*

'Why don't you get transferred, Dad?'

One of Jimmy's friends comes by in his car,
and Jimmy goes out. 'Be careful,'
Mom says. He has to learn to drive,
but it makes her nervous thinking about it.

Darlene goes over to see Marion
whose father is being transferred
to a new branch of the company
in Houston. 'Why don't you get transferred, Dad?'

'I'd like to,' he replies.
'I'd also like a million dollars.'

This is a constant topic in the family:
where else you would like to live.
Darlene likes California –
'It has beautiful scenery
and you get to meet all the stars.'
Mom prefers Arizona, because of a picture
she saw once, in *Good Housekeeping*.
Jimmy doesn't care,
and Dad likes it here. 'You can find anything
you want right where you are.'
He reminds them of *The Wizard of Oz*,
about happiness, how it is found
right in your own backyard.

Dad's right, Mom always says.
The Wizard of Oz is a tradition
in the family. They see it every year.

Louis Simpson

Dream Song 9

Deprived of his enemy, shrugged to a standstill
horrible Henry, foaming. Fan their way
toward him who will
in the high wood: the officers, their rest,
with p. a. echoing: his girl comes, say,
conned in to test

if he's still human, see: she love him, see,
therefore she get on the Sheriff's mike & howl
'Come down, come down'.
Therefore he un-budge, furious. He'd flee
but only Heaven hangs over him foul.
At the crossways, downtown,

he dreams the folks are buying parsnips & suds
and paying rent to foes. He slipt & fell.
It's golden here in the snow.

A mild crack: a far rifle. Bogart's duds
truck back to Wardrobe. Fancy the brain from hell
held out so long. Let go.

John Berryman*

Rosebud

Paul Stewart's death — the valet in *Citizen Kane* —
Arrives soon after his master quit our scene.

How bored must be such readers as I've kept
At finding in my verse another death.

It's said the universe at its tiniest
Was somehow simply formed from nothingness.

And then the 'cosmic egg' exploded, with
The curious consequence of human life —

To say nothing of the fleeing galaxies,
Or mad proliferation of deities.

But if one could play through the thing again —
And again — some meaning might at last be seen.

'He just said Rosebud, then he dropped that glass
Ball and it broke on the floor.' The end, alas!

Roy Fuller*

Charley's Aunt

Can you think of any
Reason why Jack Benny
Should play Charley's Aunt?
I can't.

C. A. Lejeune*

[298]

Aloma of the South Seas

Extensive tour
of D. Lamour.
Nearly all
Of J. Hall.
Sudden panic,
Cause volcanic,
And a torso
Or so.

C. A. Lejeune*

Johnny Wayne and Randy Scott

Johnny Wayne and Randy Scott
They fought and fought and fought and fought
With joy they shed each other's gore,
And then they paused and shed some more.
To bust each other's blocks they strove;
They wrecked the bar and crashed the stove.
Then with a heave big Johnny Wayne
Hurled Randy through the window pane.
So in the street and down the lot
They fought and fought and fought and fought.
So fierce they mixed it up I'll bet
Them galoots might be fighting yet.

Robert Service*

Casablanca

In spite of the box-office conventions:
The lyrics awash with sentiment –

[299]

'A sigh is still a sigh';
The hero reluctant,
Doing good despite his worst nature:
The heart-rent heroine –
Husband or lover? one will have to go;
And the necessary soft-centred police chief,
Beyond these dollar-obligated fictions
There is a reality,
A fine feeling for the ephemeral.
'Here's looking at you kid'
The present is all we have
No matter now often we rerun the film,
So we know why that famous line
Is never spoken; 'Play it again Sam',
Because he can't, because he can't,
Because he can't – never quite the same.

John Cotton

You Were Wearing Blue

the explosions are nearer this evening
the last train leaves for the south
at six   tomorrow
the announcements will be in a different language

i chew the end of a match
the tips of my finger and thumb are sticky

i will wait at the station and you
will send a note, i
will read it
                it will be raining

                our shadows in the electric light

when i was eight they taught me *real*
writing
                to join up the letters

listen you said i
preferred to look

      at the sea. everything stops there at strange angles

only the boats spoil it
making you focus further

                      Tom Raworth*

Fantasy

Dedicated to the health of Allen Ginsberg

How do you like the music of Adolph
                    Deutsch? I like
it, I like it better than Max Steiner's. Take his
score for *Northern Pursuit*, the Helmut Dantine theme
was . . .
      and then the window fell on my hand. Errol
Flynn was skiing by. Down
            down down went the grim
grey submarine under the 'cold' ice.
                Helmut was
safely ashore, on the ice.
            What dreams, what incredible
fantasies of snow farts will this all lead to?
                  I
don't know, I have stopped thinking like a sled dog.
The main thing is to tell a story.
            It is almost
very important. Imagine
            throwing away the avalanche
so early in the movie. I am the only spy left
in Canada,
      but just because I'm alone in the snow
doesn't necessarily mean I'm a Nazi.
            Let's see,
two aspirins a vitamin C tablet and some baking soda

should do the trick, that's practically an
                                        Alka
Seltzer. Allen come out of the bathroom
                                        and take it.
I think someone put butter on my skis instead
of wax.
            Ouch. The leanto is falling over in the
firs, and there is another fatter spy here. They
didn't tell me they sent
                        him. Well, that takes care
of him, boy were those huskies hungry.
                                    Allen,
are you feeling any better? Yes, I'm crazy about
Helmut Dantine
                but I'm glad that Canada will remain
free. Just free, that's all, never argue with the movies.

                                        Frank O'Hara*

A Gothic Gesture

For Paul Violi

Is this the movie in which James Mason
Slams his cane down on Ann Todd's fingers?

Because she is playing piano? Yes, it was
A gothic gesture and made Mason a matinee idol

Overnight. One night, nights
Passed, we see him first

Meditating on a record by the Troggs, then groggy
Putting his fist through the ballroom window

In a sudden frog-like fit of Angst, his features
A concentrated form of melancholy, green . . .

Green and lumpy landscaping, brooding
Piano, parodistic Weltschmerz.

                                        Steve Levine*

Heart Failure

Our Hearts Were Growing Up

About this successor to *Our Hearts Were Young and Gay*,
There's only one thing to say.
It's a good thing our hearts were growing up because
Nothing else was.

C. A. Lejeune*

Humoresque

In this long rapture of pretence
There is one moment of good sense,
When Crawford (J), a female souse,
Displays a modicum of *nous*.

On hearing Wagner's *Liebestod*
Performed the way it wasn't wrote,
She proves her musical devotion
By walking straight into the ocean.

C. A. Lejeune*

Forties Flick

The shadow of the Venetian blind on the painted wall,
Shadows of the snake-plant and cacti, the plaster animals,
Focus the tragic melancholy of the bright stare
Into nowhere, a hole like the black holes in space.
In bra and panties she sidles to the window:
Zip! Up with the blind. A fragile street scene offers itself,
With wafer-thin pedestrians who know where they are going.
The blind comes down slowly, the slats are slowly tilted up.

[303]

Why must it always end this way?
A dais with woman reading, with the ruckus of her hair
And all that is unsaid about her pulling us back to her, with her
Into the silence that night alone can't explain.
Silence of the library, of the telephone with its pad,
But we didn't have to reinvent these either:
They had gone away into the plot of a story,
The 'art' part – knowing what important details to leave out
And the way character is developed. Things too real
To be of much concern, hence artificial, yet now all over the page;
The indoors with the outside becoming part of you
As you find you have never left off laughing at death,
The background, dark vine at the edge of the porch.

John Ashbery

The Red Shoes

It all comes back to me, *The Red Shoes*,
that film and the evening we saw it
and you a dancer – you had danced
on that very stage, the high school
renting the theatre and me feeling myself
blush as you lifted your legs like the Degas
dancer, your little fluff skirt light
as moth wings. Everyone a dancer
or composer! 'Lermontov says you can dance,
so you can go to Paris, on tour.' Did he add,
My dear? And after that film, the rush
of wings, the disappointment – Did someone die,
fall off the rocks at Monte Carlo? Damned
if I can remember. All I know for sure
is that the arts were so easy, so wonderful,
just being lifted like balloons into the wind,
fame and fortune, the gambling tables,
immortality like stars. We drove up the mountain
and you were aflame with desire to keep
dancing, and your blouse was quickly undone,

breast in my hand, and our kiss. Then down
to earth not so firm, inquisitions for both
of us, witches and wizards, beatings
sustained for our love. Not all who danced
were so beautiful as you, who entered
the film when I lost you, the vast room
of fantasy, nothing else ever. And the chorus
of cactus watched, still there perhaps
for the lovers, for those who have left
the film, the vast room of fantasy, returned
to the crust of the desert or the back seat
of the car, real enough to make love in.
And sometimes that's what love needs –
hard reality, though what whirls on in the head
is real enough too, constellation of freckles,
red hair whipped round in the wind
year after year touching my face. And blossoms
of stone, petal of heartwood, eyes of agate.

David Ray*

Dédée d'Anvers

Around the iron bed the camera moves
Or follows where, across the fog-wet stone
She and her life, like one automaton,
Run to exhaustion down the usual grooves.

Quick with desire to glimpse the unobsessed,
It switches restlessly from view to view,
Pauses an instant on a seeming clue;
Rejects it; and resumes its nervous quest.

Till in that trajectory of fear and boredom,
Letting the iron twilight slip and slough,
Life burns through briefly to its inch of freedom

And in the flicker of a lens or eye
Forms to one microcosm of all love
A woman's body and her fantasy.

Robert Conquest*

The Cinematographers, West Cedar Street

For Michael Roemer

There is a lion in the streets as I
Run from the travelling camera framing me
In its long eye. Under a sulphur sky
I lead my flight from men I cannot see:

The chase to be shot later. Quarrying
Down through crevasses in the baking brick,
I register a maze. The scurrying
Perspectives shuttle at the double quick

To vanishing points in chattering culs-de-sac.
Winded, I put my back to the brick wall,
The toes of my white bucks toward the pack
Baying my trail with a fearfully close call

Around the corner of the labyrinth.
Nothing can stop their tantara now but
A death. I climb up on the dinky plinth
Of a stone urn and wait to face them. Cut.

Take two. Take ten. At Sally Sayward's house
In the cool shoulder of West Cedar Street,
We seize iced Moxie from the set tubs, douse
Our heads with water, and sweat out the heat

Till Leo calls us back. The afternoon
Throws a long shadow into Louisburg Square,
Leading me on to evening as I run
Away again from the long lenses' glare.

L. E. Sissman*

Film Revival: *Tales of Hoffman*

Occasionally obsession
Comes to its flower, grip and shine
From the soundtrack and screen.

Light sheer to the glazed dark limbs and the smooth pool.

Integrities of the automatic voice.

Florid, impenetrable Venice.

In superfluity of magic a single note
Shatters the glass jewels. A dancer's arm
Makes a gesture that is love: and art.

                              Robert Conquest*

The Prisoner of Zenda

At the end a
The Prisoner of Zenda,
The King being out of danger,
Stewart Granger
(As Rudolph Rassendyll)
Must swallow a bitter pill
By renouncing his co-star,
Deborah Kerr.

It would be poor behavia
In him and in Princess Flavia
Were they to put their own
Concerns before those of the Throne.
Deborah Kerr must wed
The King instead.

Rassendyll turns to go.
Must it be so?
Why can't they have their cake
And eat it, for heaven's sake?

Please let them have it both ways,
The audience prays.
And yet it is hard to quarrel
With a plot so moral.

One redeeming factor,
However, is that the actor
Who plays the once-dissolute King
(Who has learned through suffering
Not to drink or be mean
To his future Queen),
Far from being a stranger,
Is *also* Stewart Granger.

Richard Wilbur*

Stakeout on High Street

For Richard Widmark and Samuel Fuller

bright lights on the jukebox
strings swoon into my favourite teenage popsong

again, this couldn't happen again . . .

his hard, cruel lips meet her full red ones
the blond sneering hoodlum
the brunette in the lownecked dress

streetlamps over the railwaybridge
tasting her lipstick all the way home

this is that once in a lifetime,
this is the thrill divine . . .

he slaps her hard across the face
black eyes gleam in the darkness
kisses her viciously again
resistance softens into passion

in a shelterhouse on the promenade
inexplicable soft shapes under the sweater

[308]

we'll have this moment for ever . . .

up the gangplank to his boat-house hideout
raincoat belted defiantly to the final shoot-out
cold eyes shadowed by his fedora

but never, never again

home, followed by the smell of cheap perfume
and the final showdown with tomorrow's homework.

Adrian Henri*

I Mean

all these americans here writing about america it's time to give
   something back, after all
our heroes were always the gangster the outlaw why
surprised you act like it
now, a place
the simplest man was always the most complex you gave me
the usual things, comics,
music, royal blue drape suits &
what *they* ever give me but unreadable books?

i don't know where i am now my face seems exposed
touching it   touching it

as i walk this evening no
tenderness   mad laughter from the rooms   what
do i know of my friends, they are always
showing small kind parts of themselves

no pacifist i am capable of murder
               the decision is not
this, but not
to sic on the official   the paid
extension of self   to react at the moment

oh, this ain't no town for a girl like dallas

jean peters to widmark 'how'd
you get to be this way?
how'd i get this way?   things
happen, that's all'   but

we ain't never gonna say goodbye

follow me into the garden at night
i have my own orchestra

Tom Raworth*

Double Sonnet for Mickey

In *Kiss Me Deadly* Cloris Leachman asks Mike Hammer in the car Do
you read poetry? He doesn't even answer but just looks at her. The plot
may be said to turn on a book of Christina Rossetti poems but to
me it is that pause, a careless sneer on Meeker's face as he not
only does not answer but sees no reason to get mad. She has no right
to ask the question in the first place of a tough guy whose hair,
just longer than a brush cut, is stiffened by something bryllish that might
ten years before have been brilliantine and he marine rather than air
force straight, chin tending to plumpness suggesting a tight military collar
forsworn. His girlfriend whose chin likewise etcetera gets evidence on
     johns
in ways not admirable. On the walls of his hideous apartment are camera
     cases, statues and two-dollar
framed people, everyone's limbs pointlessly extended, plasticman fixed
     for a decade in bronze,
none of this inadvertent. She asked him knowing he would look at her as if
     a bad
smell in the car were hers and she, producing it, would know he knew she
     had.
That look is not eternal. It is a product of the late fifties like *Bucket of
     Blood*, rude look
at art, snapshot of The Thinker with your sweetheart on his lap and I
     prefer
another photo of one of its castings blown half apart by terrorists who
     took

[310]

monument for establishment, ecriture for prefecture (how do you deface
 an Anselm Kiefer,
already glued up with straw and so on?) It's probably the locution, *a*
 Rodin
that maddened them, one of an oeuvre, thing valued as one of a series of
 makings
but then it's also celebritous, like the Sphinx now falling to bits, another
 endangered Man
as Hammer is, in the film made because there first were novels about his
 undertakings
but then one doesn't recognize a Hammer from sketchiest drawing or
 collage
the way a sphinx or thinker's fair game for cartoon or cover art. A taste for
 him is more
like going to the fights, choosing to smell of something that goes with
 Gillette, massages
a jaw wider than its forehead and thinks of kicking in a green door
behind which shuttered Experience waits, twirling a trilby, trying on a
 smile
above the angled shoulders built up from folded gauze we thought, then, a
 masculine style.

                                                        Gerald Burns*

In Memoriam

> In the novel he marries Victoria but in the movie he dies.
>
>   caption in *Life*

Fate lifts us up so she can hurl
  Us down from heights of pride,
Viz.: in the book he got the girl
  But in the movie, died.

The author, seeing he was brave
  And good, rewarded him,
Then, greedy, sold him as a slave
  To savage M-G-M.

He perished on the screen, but thrives
  In print, where serifs keep
Watch o'er the happier of his lives:
  Say, Does he wake, or sleep?

        John Updike*

Tarantula

Time, from my burrow, was a string of beads,
alternating black-and-cold, white-and-hot,
before you came. I was one of a trillion

growing tips of the spider-vine already
thriving when your ancestors wriggled
from the surf. Then one dawn, a rumbling

in the desert; a glow like the sun on a hot
day. I started growing. My burrow couldn't
hold me, so I found a cave. I didn't mean

to kill the driver of that scurrying black
Ford. My web was spun, my fangs slick
with blood before I could think. Yes, I could

think. My brain was growing with my body,
senses heightened until I looked down
on you like a God. I saw it all:

your frantic phone calls, the screaming
blonde with her tight shorts and pretty
legs, the square-jawed hero who believed

her, the old sheriff who scolded
'Talk sense!' To make him believe in me,
I sacrificed a farmer and his wife,

the way your old God used to do. I pitied
you the way He must have as you quailed
before the monsters you always create.

I understood why He died. Who could live
with such knowledge? Your National Guard
were soft and helpless as ant-larvae against me.

I found the square-jawed one the others
followed because he was handsome, and placed
the word 'electrocution' in his brain.

I didn't die the way you thought,
guarding my eggs in that dark cave already
grown too small for me. I led you there.

Charles Webb*

Popular Revivals, 1956

The thylacine, long thought to be extinct,
Is not. The ancient dog-like creature, linked
To kangaroos and platypi, still pounces
On his Tasmanian prey, the *Times* announces.

The tarpan (stumpy, prehistoric horse)
Has been rebred – in Germany, of course.
Herr Heinz Heck, by striking genetic chords,
Has out of plowmares beat his tiny wards.

The California fur seal, a refined
And gullible amphibian consigned
By profit-seeking sealers to perdition,
Barked at the recent Gilmore expedition.

The bison, butchered on our Western prairie,
Took refuge in our coinage. Now, contrary
To what was feared, the herds are out of danger
And in the films, co-starred with Stewart Granger.

John Updike*

Ingmar Bergman's *Seventh Seal*

This is the way it is. We see
three ages in one: the child Jesus
innocent of Jerusalem and Rome
– magically at home in joy –
that's the year from which
our inner persistence has its force.

The second, Bergman shows us,
carries forward image after image
of anguish, of the Christ crossd
and sends up from open sores of the plague
(shown as wounds upon His corpse)
from lacerations in the course of love
(the crown of whose kingdom tears the flesh)

. . . There is so much suffering!
What possibly protects us
from the emptiness, the forsaken cry,
the utter dependence, the vertigo?
Why do so many come to love's edge
only to be stranded there?

The second face of Christ, his
evil, his Other, emaciated, pain and sin.
Christ, what a contagion!
What a stink it spreads round

our age! It's our age!
and the rage of the storm is abroad.
The malignant stupidity of statesmen rules.
The old riders thru the forests race
    shouting: the wind! the wind!
Now the black horror cometh again.

And I'll throw myself down
as the clown does in Bergman's *Seventh Seal*
to cower as if asleep with his wife and child,
hid in the caravan under the storm.

Let the Angel of Wrath pass over.
Let the end come.
War, stupidity and fear are powerful.
We are only children. To bed! to bed!
    To play safe!

To throw ourselves down
helplessly, into happiness,
    into an age of our own, into
    our own days.
There where the Pestilence roars,
where the empty riders of the horror go.

                                    Robert Duncan*

Vertigo, A Sequel

When Alfred Hitchcock traveled underground
And settled his famous bulk in Charon's boat
('A star vehicle at last!'), and heard the sound
Of oars, and felt the deathship float,

He turned for one last framing glance
At the cool blondes, the shapely auburn-haired,
Whose shades whirled about him in a bawdy dance,
Lifting their crimson dresses, bosoms bared.

His fingers trembled toward Grace
Who modeled once more the postures of sin.
He read the brazen line on her painted face:
'I don't like cold things touching my skin.'

He would kill her, again, for saying that.
Strangle or stab, in living room and shower . . .
Hell swung into view like a Hollywood matte;
Kim and Tippi spun beyond his power.

At the helm, some likeness of their leading men
Directed his freight toward the *paysage triste*,

[315]

But their king-sized genius, scissors in hand,
Gazed backward till their movement ceased.

Laurence Goldstein*

Two Deaths

It was only a film,
Perhaps I shall say later
Forgetting the story, left only
With bright images – the blazing dawn
Over the European ravaged plain,
And a white unsaddled horse, the only calm
Living creature. Will only such pictures remain?

Or shall I see
The shot boy running, running
Clutching the white sheet on the washing line,
Looking at his own blood like a child
Who never saw blood before and feels defiled,
A boy dying without dignity
Yet brave still, trying to stop himself from falling
And screaming – his white girl waiting just out of calling?

I am ashamed
Not to have seen anyone dead,
Anyone I know I mean;
Odd that yesterday also
I saw a broken cat stretched on a path,
Not quite finished. Its gentle head
Showed one eye staring, mutely beseeching
Death, it seemed. All day
I have thought of death, of violence and death,
Of the blazing Polish light, of the cat's eye:
I am ashamed I have never seen anyone die.

Elizabeth Jennings*

The Blob Speaks to its Mother

just to have held one clear memory of shape.
not always to be approaching some limit other
than can be derived from me. not to be possessed by your voice.
not defined by any voice factored out of my voicelessness.
not to leave remainders of myself each place
i pass over.
      not constantly to find fractions, hardly ingested,
of alien minds worked into my bubbling mass.
not to be forced to race
to feel like an integer
         to get there in one piece.

i swear to you i'd shave away
even my infinitely minute
        variable
           hypothetical
              disappearing
center for this

and leave myself no more than a function from outside space.

                     Judith E. Johnson*

Shapes of Things

We are living in the long shadow of the Bomb –
a fat Greenpeace whale, simplified and schematic
like the sign 'lavatories for the handicapped',
its whirling genitals a small outboard swastika . . .

I saw the rare Ava Gardner, the last woman alive,
modelling her check workshirts in *On the Beach*.
As the wind drove the heavy clouds of fallout
towards them, there were no ugly scenes of anarchy –

only revivalist preachers and the Salvation Army band . . .
She admired the *esprit de corps* of her husband

[317]

as he went down in the last living submarine –
an obsolete nuclear cigar, doused in the bay.

Michael Hofmann*

Turkish Delight

On a day that's already dark
and sensuous with murmurs, unwrappings of sweets,

El Cid is strapped up on his horse
and sent galloping off. His enemies don't know

he's dead, but we do, but the wistful,
almost playful tremolos of the music

fading and the final pan
across silky dunes suggest an afterlife

of sorts to which late, as usual, but dressed
as instructed in black and white, we arrive

with our glib excuses. Your head bent
as you rummage inside your handbag

for the Visa card that'll prove we're who
we say we are, you're exactly the height

of the row of coloured ribbons
on the doorman's uniform; while in fits and starts,

through waiting rooms inlaid with travel
posters and back-issue weeklies, comes the buzz

of conversation, its troughs
of lost ground occasionally lit up

by a flash on the ramparts of Saracen shields.

Charles Boyle*

The Hustler de Paris

Notre-Dame, Sainte-Chapelle, Sacré-Cœur by foot –
deep in the Louvre the Mona Lisa smirks
at the good tourist who grants her a minute
for each star in the Michelin, then soldiers on.
So all of Paris could be mine?

Quel est le prix d'entrée?
For the price of admission, I can sit in defeat
and view an *arrondissement* from home:
a small-town main street, a gas station
somewhere on a studio back lot. A car

like a loaf of bread pulls up. Two men get out.
One's the young god, Paul Newman,
about to step into a pool hall's gloom
undubbed, only the picket fence
of French subtitles between him and us.

Like a sleepy sexton, the janitor performs
uncalled-for miracles, raising the blinds
to flood the hall with daylight
so dirty it must be divine.
'Like a church,' Newman says.

'Church of the Good Hustler.'
Even in black-and-white his eyes are blue.
The fair Savior of Western art,
devil too handsome for his own good.
The fat man with a carnation in his lapel

opens his great, soft palms
to receive the ritual talcum,
his the hands of a priest, so dainty, so mechanical.
At midnight he intones the litany of his shots.
Gray bills rain down on the gray felt.

To the gargoyles who watch, it's the old story –
boy hustles anything that moves, even pain.
La petite escourgette to mortify the flesh,

[319]

the Crown of Thorns, the Holy Sponge,
un morceau considérable of the True Cross –

that is the smell of money,
of nights just a few thousand old.
Now the saint of the broken thumbs.
'I came to play pool, Fats.'
Très bien, Eddie Vite. Combien?

How much the things of this world
have darkened while we were inside.
Even the late light hurts,
the old stone cleaned of the centuries
that we sat through, until it glows.

Just ahead of a last sweep by *les flics*,
street sellers roll up their rugs,
their little 'Winged Victories',
and weave into the nearest throng,
saints without permit passing among us.

                                        Debora Greger*

Shades of Grey

Over my head, you drift round the bedroom.
I'm glued to the late film, *Marienbad*,

compelled by what I once thought 'pseud'.
Beyond a vast hotel the vistas freeze.

Frames shot in black and white yield shades of grey,
this riddling couple . . .

He says they met last year, had an affair.
She tests him, *Tell me the rest of our story.*

Winters ago we strolled home, arm in arm,
our verdict clear: 'The man trumped up the past.'

But soon, beside you, I'll dream of a maze
where shapes, our doubles, trace and retrace steps

– or so I conceive when subtitles claim:
Again I walked down these same corridors.

Michael O'Neill*

Ride the High Country

The long red underwear of Randolph Scott,
the gold-rimmed spectacles of Joel McCrea,
underscore age, and through the reverend plot
the old gunfighters ride for one more day.
And Ladd was old in *Shane*, and in *High Noon*
old Coop had all his wrinkles emphasized
(with visible distaste he drew his gun).
The ritual of honor is disguised
and is an act of memory and will.
The pistol packing, popcorn eating child
feels the pretended stubble on his chin
and imagines his bones weary after the kill.
Even the movies' west is no longer wild,
its *virtu* now a trail bum, a has-been.
That's the first part. Here's part two:
Odysseus, safe at home, can be our friend.
Orestes and the Furies come to terms
– our terms: we, craven, crave the tamest end,
the fireside remembrances of storms,
the hero's diminution. The old hand
is slower on the draw, the eyes are gone.
We may admire, but we understand
that nerve is all McCrea is working on,
that aged manliness becomes absurd.
He makes mistakes out on the trail, he has
fallen into their obvious trap, is hit,
and crumples with gun blazing. On the hard
ground he shakes our comfort as he dies,
affirming the agelessness of what is fit.

David Slavitt*

[321]

Working for Dr No

What sort of man could inspire fear
like that?

Perhaps it was the beautiful efficiency
of the Doctor's organization,
or the attraction of strict discipline,
or the fact that everyone else was doing it –
the little luxuries that those on the payroll let show
like hints: a silk shirt, a bracelet, old wine
in unaccustomed, shaking hands . . .

Awake each morning at dawn, tossing
searching his rum-soaked brain
for details of the evening before:
the chance word slipped at the Club;
sweating under the sheets,
with always the image of two steel hands,
the round room, the echoing dark voice . . .

Does Professor Dent remember the days
before he worked for Doctor No?
Does he dream of leaving the island
retiring with his nest egg
to pursue geological research?

He would still waken sweating, trying
to remember where he slipped up . . .
And could he ever be sure?
He is safer staying where terror
becomes a way of life
as well-oiled as any other,
where there's no need to wonder what he fears.

Now his days are rigidly prescribed.
The order at Crab Key:

> There.
> On the table.
> Pick it up.

Has the tarantula
reached through its cage to his skin?
Or is it his nerves dancing?

Valery Nash*

A night out

Friends recommended the new Polish film
at the Academy in Oxford Street.
So we joined the ever melancholy queue
of cinemas. A wind blew faint suggestions
of rain towards us, and an accordion.
Later, uneasy, in the velvet dark
we peered through the cut-out, oblong window
at the spotlit drama of our nightmares:
images of Auschwitz almost authentic,
the human obscenity in close-up.
Certainly we could imagine the stench.

Resenting it, we forgot the barbed wire
was but a prop, and could not scratch an eye:
those striped victims merely actors, like us.
We saw the Camp orchestra assembled,
we heard the solemn gaiety of Bach,
scored by the loud arrival of an engine,
its impotent cry, and its guttural trucks.
We watched, as we munched milk chocolate,
trustful children, no older than our own,
strolling into the chambers without fuss,
whilst smoke, black and curly, oozed from chimneys.

Afterwards, at a loss, we sipped coffee
in a bored espresso bar near by
saying very little. You took off one glove.
Then to the comfortable suburb swiftly
where, arriving home, we garaged the car.
We asked the au pair girl from Germany
if anyone had phoned at all, or called,

and, of course, if the children had woken.
Reassured, together we climbed the stairs,
undressed together, and naked together,
in the dark, in the marital bed, made love.

Dannie Abse*

Alphaville and after

— Savez-vous ce qui transforme la nuit en lumières?
— La poésie.
Lemmy Caution interrogated by computer in Jean-Luc Godard's *Alphaville*

we never did
get to Paris
but yes
in Usclas
the days opened
like blue shutters
on fictions of other cities

a bed
wide as the sea
the pomegranate
that Persephone-tree,
like a fire in the field

these minutes
we were married to
nights
in the underworld
believing
we ate people
possibly
we were gods

just another love poem
your fruit
mine
the light
seeded in our thighs

[324]

unstable bargains
which end like Alphaville:
Paris snowbound
under a swaying bare light-bulb
words of love
reflections of night trains
nowhere to go

Alison Fell*

On Pasolini's *Teorema*

Glimpsed in a courtyard, a gallery, a cloister, a garden –
yes, we know him all too well,
that plausible young male demon,
unscrupulous messenger of hell, fair angel of our fate,
handsome, mysterious, understanding,
and inexplicably loving,
who comes one day from nowhere
and takes our hearts, our minds, our souls,
in exchange for – what?

For loneliness and desolation worse than anything we knew
before his coming; for a persistent sense of loss,
an ache of separation, a bitter, loveless isolation
in a world to which he brought
a temporary joy, a passing sweetness.
– But was it worth it? A brief time
of unforgettable pleasure in a life of pain?

For now the pain grows worse,
the isolation more intense,
and he who came and took our souls
when we least needed him
does not come now, now that we need him most.

Instead, a hollow shadow walks beside us
and haunts us day and and night
with visions, madness, dreams

of impossible and unimaginable love
that, even if we knew it once again,
we should reject, knowing it untrue
and foul: and unavailing, hollow
as the words and smiles with which
he first approached us, come from nowhere,
to take us back there with him, and leave us there alone.

James Kirkup*

The Shirt

For years
we called it Paul's shirt,
wine-dark, with one torn
tail and a deadly collar
pointed at any fainting heart in sight.
He left it at my place
in Paris after one of those
nights he brought the girls.
In twenty years I wore it
twice – once in sartorial
emergency, once
in a fit of nostalgia.
'Why do you keep this horror?'
After three moves
it disappeared.

Yesterday,
in one of the film books I read now,
a lurid frame enlargement pounced from hiding.
Naked and frowning, Paul
lounges in bed with a high-tensile,
fully clothed doll. She's
his wife off and on
the screen, the caption says, and calls
his self-fulfilling script
'an incisive description of bourgeois

marriage conventions.'
Jesus.
The New Wave.
He made it
or helped.

We should have stuffed
that shirt.

Roger Shattuck*

He's a Nice Guy, But Always Worrying

What if he touched a leper? Got bit by a rabid squirrel?
What if a pregnant burglar tripped over his barbells,
     miscarried, and sued?
What if his car quit in a blizzard on a mountain pass, and
     mafiosi picked him up, smashed in his face, stole his wallet
     and gold Seiko watch, and kicked him out to freeze to death,
     ugly and broke?

He can't have ten straight seconds of good time
     without worry rushing in to squeeze the fun out,
     the way water squeezed the air out in *The Poseidon Adventure*,
     that disaster movie where a tidal wave flips an ocean-
     liner upside down, but it floats long enough
     to let the heroes scurry room to room –
     always just beating the sea –
     as they search for the ship-bottom (now on top),
     knowing there's no way they can pierce the thick steel
     hull unless Greeks bearing blowtorches happen to be
     standing there waiting for optimists to pound.
     Which of course happens.

See, I told him, if they'd sat around and fretted,
     they'd be dead.
You think he'd listen? No – he was too busy bashing

escape hatches in his daughter's plastic pool-boat,
and building a blowtorch in the shape of worry-beads.

Charles Webb*

Homage to Walter Hill's *Hard Times*

Lonely men in lonely rooms
City men   on the

Cutting edge   of the fringe

       Down town

Shades
on the dark horizon –
Romantics
    in Buddha's palm
    of no vision

Alone   with the consciousness
of

    how it smells
    where men de-gut oysters
    for a wage

    foghorns in the Southern rivers of America night

    Cajun caged bears
    & neon cafés on the backroads

A woman's haunted eyes look out upon the scene
    But it does not take her in.

William David Sherman*

The Mirror Crack'd

It was days of filming in the warm sun –
a stately home in Kent – the grass was shorn short
under small fruit trees, the green broken with
heraldic bursts of red clover, self-heal
and yellow bird's foot trefoil. Some cows
looked on across a fence.

One time the locals descended, spoiling
shot after shot, standing in the foreground
in their non-Fifties polyester frocks,
before they got down to the autographs.

'Please sign my book for me, Miss Taylor.'
Five minutes later they were round again.
'Can't remember if I asked you,' one woman said.
'I've just done Angela Lansbury. If not,
please sign.'

The woman called her husband up to look.
'Ooh, isn't she beautiful?' They peered closely.
She sat motionless on a wooden bench,
her violet chiffon dress caught on splinters.

The man stood thinking. His belly peeped
from a small tear in his orange nylon shirt
close by her face. 'Nah!' he said. 'Take off
all that powder and paint and she'd be just
like you or me.' He rammed his cap down hard
on his oiled hair and went off comforted.

Fiona Pitt-Kethley*

Final Farewell

Great moment in *Blade Runner* where Roy
Batty is expiring, and talks about how everything
he's seen will die with him –
ships on fire off the shoulder of Orion
sea-beams glittering before the Tannhauser gates.

Memory is like molten gold
   burning its way through the skin
it stops there.
      There is no transfer
Nothing I have seen
will be remembered
beyond me
That merciful cleaning
of the windows of creation
will be an excellent thing
my interests notwithstanding.

But then again I've never been
   near Orion, or the Tannhauser
gates,

I've only been here.

Tom Clark*

Firestarter

I don't want to set the world
on fire, I just want to burn
a hole in the wall.
And when Daddy hugs me
I'm inspired to burn up
bad men all around us. They flee
to the trees, so the trees
burn as well. I can wish

water to flames, and my skin
is unscorched though I blow
buildings sky-high. If I reach
puberty's age I become
atomic (and a sequel, they say),
my rage all held in, then let
out where it flames.
When you flick
your plastic, disposable Bic
you are worshipping me, young
goddess of fire. When they touched
soldiers in caves
with a flamethrower's tongue,
when the dragons of old spat
tongue-lashing fire, they were mine,
helots of Helios, servants
whose flambeaux joined ancient
candles, light playful at orgies.
And the slow embers burn
like fireflies on fingers, in homage
to me, on your millions
of hands. Rings glow
like my jewels, like my eyes, amber
as beach agate hit by the sun,
or topaz when my anger heats up.
And for Daddy I dance
till I'm wed with the sun,
give up my career, travel
forever, like retired movie stars.

David Ray*

Movies

For Jane Goodall

We watch *Gorillas in the Mist*.
Evidently it is nicer

[331]

to be gorillas
than to be people like us.
The lady was at war with the bad people.
She loved the good gorillas
who beat their chests,
fought for their children,
died trying – but she was no match
of course for the bad people,
which seems to be the case in all
the bad places
that were once paradise. One sees
how hard it is to save anything –
a tree, a tusk, an infant gorilla.
I'm surprised if I can save
from the fire of time one poem,
one shard of the jug we drank from.
The lady flies into a rage –
for they've attacked again,
those with the law on their side.
The grieving babe is carried off
in a crate, another theft
off her sacred mountain.
The bad men want heads for trophies,
babies for zoos, hands for ashtrays –
the hand she held, feeling that touch,
that flow of one being into another –
what Michelangelo painted on the ceiling,
scene we must still look up to, something
of the divine. She found it
there in the jungle,
but then the movie is over
and a wise one among us tells us
the lady was not such a nice person.
The lover in the movie was not
her lover. The man that part
was based on said he didn't
even like her and her hair
was always unkempt. She was irrational,
you might say, warring with the locals,
who had to make a living off gorillas.

She had smoked herself so close
to death that her murder was merciful,
a blessing, and so on. It seems
that only in movies heroes
and heroines are perfect. Swift
loved the horses and she
the gorillas we say, and leave it at that.

David Ray*

Kid

Batman, big shot, when you gave the order
to grow up, then let me loose to wander
leeward, freely through the wild blue yonder
as you liked to say, or ditched me, rather,
in the gutter . . . well, I turned the corner.
Now I've scotched that 'he was like a father
to me' rumour, sacked it, blown the cover
on that 'he was like an elder brother'
story, let the cat out on that caper
with the married woman, how you took her
downtown on expenses in the motor.
Holy robin-redbreast-nest-egg-shocker!
Holy roll-me-over-in-the-clover,
I'm not playing ball boy any longer
Batman, now I've doffed that off-the-shoulder
Sherwood-Forest-green and scarlet number
for a pair of jeans and crew-neck jumper;
now I'm taller, harder, stronger, older.
Batman, it makes a marvellous picture:
you without a shadow, stewing over
chicken giblets in the pressure cooker,
next to nothing in the walk-in larder,
punching the palm of your hand all winter,
you baby, now I'm the real boy wonder.

Simon Armitage*

The Monster Karloff

As an undergraduate I read Kafka, the *Journals, Letters to Milena,*
  Dearest Father
bought in Schocken shocked-green bindings from Gordon Cairnie, Nova
Scotian proprietor of Grolier, brick walks with staggers from Adams
  House to it.
Together they looked boxy, one octavo height except *Great Wall of*
  China, short.
These taught me merchant speech, BBC German, It has come to our
  attention
and so on, what's called the Corporate Veil, a voice behind like Isis.
At the film I watched Jeremy Irons all through as if he were Kafka,
pleased and disappointed that Alec Guinness played the Head Clerk
  unintelligent,
cheeks a continuation of the bald head, a stranger nothing like *Kind*
  Hearts.
It was odd, to be 'looking at' Kafka for a whole film, hero of my youth
with Samuel Johnson, magnificent Czech posters on the hoardings,
  newspapers
of the period on desks and cafe tables. I thought I saw, on the way out, a
need not to break into speech, as if the film asked it (my friend Searcy who
saw it said on the phone ultimately color's OK, that kind of thing). We've
  offices
like *Ikiru*, wads of paper, typewriters, the horror of office marble, that *no*
  surface
looks natural indoors. Clio said outside, with infinite apology, what
  struck her was
how much Irons could play Boris Karloff in a filmed bio. Those eyelids, his
  mouth,
ear to jaw relation adequate. Though his life, she said, was so quiet,
  raising flowers.
I could see it, Karloff on his knees with a trowel, dibble, looking up at a
  messenger
from Universal with a new script, *The Mummy* not yet made, Anne Rice in
  limbo.
That look would be the film, so kind but distant, the voice (perhaps better
  for having

been held back in his good one) a fourth-rate castle on the Rhein, 'Won't
   you come in.'
His hands, holding digging tools, wouldn't move at all. Both his pauses
   and static
postures would become trademarks, and as film layers onto film we see
   him sorting
out, with a kind of balance, a *general* mode of wickedness on film, wide-
   eyed
expostulation in the later ones is 'innocence,' his early scientists wind-up
Pasteur, Bichat, that science you went to Heidelberg to master.
It has its dignity people rushing down halls at night in country houses,
and funny reporter, don't disturb. But all of it would always be there
like meeting Dickens or Henry Irving. Imagine Karloff handing you a
   business card.
A studio head takes it, looks down at it, looks up. The question is how
   much
weight, how much humanity, can be put in that simple act of looking up.

                                                      Gerald Burns*

Hoppy

When Mary pulled the sorrel's reins from Stephen
The stunt man's hands, swung her buckskin squaw's skirt
Over, leaned up into his neck and, by God,
Was gone, Morris began screaming: 'What are
You doing? Is she ruining me? Cut!
Hey, sweetheart! Somebody grab that woman. Cut!
She shouldn't be galloping in it here! Cut!'
I was the camera jockey on this series.
I got her last frames going over the rise.
Guitars were to volume up there for *The End*
With boys back here all lithe as cats, leaning
Against the fence and singing 'Tumbleweed'
While Hoppy turned, waved, and rode away.

[335]

It was his riding off like that that took her,
I guess. It must have made the girl forget
Hoppy was phony. It's hard to understand, though.
She'd been around. She knew the camera angles.
You would say this one had quit pulling taffy.
One time I took her out myself. Just once.
She was OK – a little hard is all.
But that was back before they disappeared.
Way back before the war. You never know
About a person. Some people get mixed up.

I could have used a Hoppy, Oh, my God,
At Anzio. Oh, you'd have been great, Hoppy,
The way you jingle-jumped from boulders, bullets
Whining in ricochet but plugged your ten
And came out clean ('Move in for the close-up, William.')
And gee-whiz coursed the outlaws through the hills,
Leaped on them horseback, rolled into the gulches
And whipped them silly in the sound effects.

Maybe she thought it was the real thing or
Something like that. It's hard to understand –
The Conestoga wagons, whiskey brawls,
Gold miners, Sioux with smuggled Winchesters –
They'd take your scalp – the gunfights at high noon.
But in that wild land she was safe with Hoppy.

It's interesting to think what they said when
She caught up with them. Hoppy would grin and nod:
'You keep a sharp eye out for Indians, Ma'am.'
And she, 'At last I've found you, Hoppy. Hoppy,
I love you.' 'But Ma'am,' he'd say, 'no epic heroes
Have time for love – I mean, the family kind.
I can't be different. It's mostly killing here.
A hard country, here, to live in.' 'Better,'
She'd say. And he, 'But this is no place for a
Woman or child.' 'Why it's a good place, Hoppy,
A good place. We'll have sons – trust me – more than
The sands of the desert. Every one a hero.
I've seen the signs.' 'We ought to make camp soon . . .'
(What could he say?) 'You understand you'll have

To keep a sharp eye out.' They'd build a campfire,
Drink coffee, eat sourdough hotcakes, and hear coyotes.
It wouldn't be as easy as a motel.

So all in buckskin went love riding on
Somewhere. At least they never reappeared.
Old actors say they ride the desert still
(At times they see a faint family resemblance
In one of the young crew but never so soft-
Spoken or beautiful as Hoppy was) –
She and the hero with the tall black Stetson
And easy grin of a boy, on the white steed.
They say they ride toward sunset by the mesquite,
Through the arroyos and beneath saguaros
That stand like giants in the land: Clip-clop,
Clippity, clippity, clippity, where the dust
Splashes like pools of water from those hoofs,
And twilight coming on in El Dorado.
It's nice to think like that, but what I think is
They ran into trouble at Los Alamos
Back in the forties, and needed to move fast
('Ma'am, what in hell is that?') and didn't make it –
And lost the way I lost at Anzio.

Edwin S. Godsey*

The Westerners

Were they the real Protestant heroes,
Those Westerners of the screen,
Tall in the saddle and journeying
Into the far country,
Alone and seeking their own salvation,
Owing allegiance to none of the big outfits:
All the trappings of hagiology were theirs:
The stern unwritten code;
The self-denial of the long nights
In the wilderness of the Californian Desert;

The Magdalenes of the saloons,
In their frills and high-heeled boots
And the Hays permitted daring
of décolletage,
For whom they would stand
With backs to the long bar mirror
Waiting for him who would cast the first stone,
As quick on the draw
As the angel that arrested Abraham.
Theirs, too, the hair-splitting theology
Of murder and self-defence;
Though at the end there was no casuistry,
On the day of the inevitable
Long walk down Main Street
Where good and evil
Shot it out.

John Cotton*

Beasts

Beasts in their major freedom
Slumber in peace tonight. The gull on his ledge
Dreams in the guts of himself the moon-plucked waves below,
And the sunfish leans on a stone, slept
By the lyric water,

In which the spotless feet
Of deer make dulcet splashes, and to which
The ripped mouse, safe in the owl's talon, cries
Concordance. Here there is no such harm
And no such darkness

As the selfsame moon observes
Where, warped in window-glass, it sponsors now
The werewolf's painful change. Turning his head away
On the sweaty bolster, he tries to remember
The mood of manhood,

But lies at last, as always,
Letting it happen, the fierce fur soft to his face,
Hearing with sharper ears the wind's exciting minors,
The leaves' panic, and the degradation
Of the heavy streams.

Meantime, at high windows
Far from thicket and pad-fall, suitors of excellence
Sigh and turn from their work to construe again the painful
Beauty of heaven, the lucid moon
And the risen hunter,

Making such dreams for me
As told will break their hearts as always, bringing
Monsters into the city, crows on the public statues,
Navies fed to the fish in the dark
Unbridled waters.

Richard Wilbur

Werewolf Movies

Men who imagine themselves covered with fur and sprouting
fangs, why do they do that? Padding among wet
moonstruck treetrunks crouched on all fours, sniffing
the mulch of sodden leaves, or knuckling
their brambly way, arms dangling like outsized
pajamas, hair all over them, noses and lips
sucked back into their faces, nothing left of their kindly
smiles but yellow eyes and a muzzle. This gives them
pleasure, they think they'd be
more animal. Could then freely growl, and tackle
women carrying groceries, opening
their doors with keys. Freedom would be
bared ankles, the din of tearing: rubber, cloth,
whatever. Getting down to basics. Peel, they say
to strippers, meaning: take off the skin.
A guzzle of flesh
dogfood, ears in the bowl. But

no animal does that: couple and kill,
or kill first: rip up its egg, its future.
No animal eats its mate's throat, except
spiders and certain insects, when it's the protein
male who's gobbled. Why do they have this dream then?
Dress-ups for boys, some last escape
from having to be lawyers? Or a
rebellion against the mute
resistance of objects: reproach of the
pillowcase big with pillow, the tea-
cosy swollen with its warm
pot, not soft as it looks but hard
as it feels, round tummies of saved string in the top
drawer tethering them down. What joy, to smash the
tyranny of the doorknob, sink your teeth
into the inert defiant eiderdown with matching
spring-print queensized sheets and listen to her
scream. Surrender.

Margaret Atwood

Horror Movie

Dr Unlikely, we love you so,
You who made the double-headed rabbits grow
From a single hare. Mutation's friend,
Who could have prophecied the end
When the Spider Woman deftly snared the fly
And the monsters strangled in a monstrous kiss
And somebody hissed, 'You'll hang for this!'?

Dear Dracula, sleeping on your native soil,
(Any other kind makes him spoil),
How we clapped when you broke the French door down
And surprised the bride in the overwrought bed.
Perfectly dressed for lunar research,
Your evening cape added much,

Though the bride, inexplicably dressed in furs,
Was a study in jaded jugulars.

Poor, tortured Leopard Man, you changed your spots
In the debauched village of the Pin-Head Tots;
How we wrung our hands, how we wept
When the eighteenth murder proved inept,
And, caught in the Phosphorous Cave of Sea,
Dangling the last of synthetic flesh,
You said, 'There's something wrong with me.'

The Wolf Man knew when he prowled at dawn
Beginnings spin a web where endings spawn.
The bat who lived on shaving cream,
A household pet of Dr Dream,
Unfortunately, maddened by the bedlam,
Turned on the Doc, bit the hand that fed him.

And you, Dr X, who killed by moonlight,
We loved your scream in the laboratory
When the panel slid and the night was starry
And you threw the inventor in the crocodile pit
(An obscure point: Did he deserve it?)
And you took the gold to Transylvania
Where no one guessed how insane you were.

We thank you for the moral and the mood,
Dear Dr Cliché, Nurse Platitude.
When we meet again by the Overturned Grave,
Near the Sunken City of the Twisted Mind,
(In *The Son of the Son of Frankenstein*),
Make the blood flow, make the motive muddy:
There's a little death in every body.

Howard Moss

St Agnes' Eve

The settings include a fly-specked Monday evening,
A cigar store with stagnant windows,
Two crooked streets;
The characters: six policemen and Louie Glatz.

Subways rumble and mutter a remote portent
As Louie Glatz holds up the cigar store and backs out with

$14.92.

Officer Dolan noticed something suspicious, it is supposed,
And ordered him to halt,
But dangerous, handsome, cross-eyed Louie the rat

Spoke with his gat
Rat-a-tat-tat
Rat-a-tat-tat
And Dolan was buried as quickly as possible.

But Louie didn't give a good God damn,
He ran like a crazy shadow on a shadowy street,
With five policemen called to that beat
Hot on his trail, going Blam! Blam! Blam!

While rat-a-tat-tat
Rat-a-tat-tat
Said Louie's gat,

So loud that Peter Wendotti rolled away from his wife,
Got out of bed to scratch his stomach and shiver on the cold floor
Listening to the stammering syllables of instant death met on
    secret floors in the big vacant galleries of night.

Then Louie sagged and fell and ran.
With seven bullets through his caved-in skull and those feeble
    brains spilling out like soup,
He crawled behind a water hydrant and stood them off for an-
    other half minute.

'I'm not shot,' he yelled. 'I'm not shot,' he screamed. 'It isn't
    me they've shot in the head,' he laughed. 'Oh,
I don't give a damn!'

And rat-a-tat-tat
Rat-a-tat-tat
Stuttered the gat
Of Louie the rat,
While the officers of the law went Blam! Blam! Blam!

Soft music, as the wind moans at curtained windows and shut-
    tered doors.
The vibrant throats of steamships hoot a sad defiance at distance
    and nothing.
Space lays its arm across the flat roofs and dreary streets.
Bricks bulge and sag.

Louie's soul arose through his mouth in the form of a derby hat
    that danced with cigarette butts and burned matches and
    specks of dust where Louie sprawled.
Close-up of Dolan's widow. Of Louie's mother.
Picture of the fly-specked Monday evening, and fade out slow.

                                        Kenneth Fearing

Two Figures from the Movies

I

The papers that clear him tucked in his inside pocket
And the grip of the plucky blond light on his bicep,
He holds the gang covered now, and backs for the door
That gives on the daylit street and the yare police.
But the regular customers know that before the end
With its kissing and money and adequate explanation,
He has still to back into the arms of the baldheaded man
With the huge signet-ring and the favorable odds of surprise,
Somehow to outface the impossible arrogant stare,
And will his luck hold, they wonder, and has he the skill?

II

PERICLES: This is the rarest dream that e'er dull sleep
    Did mock sad fools withal: this cannot be.
    My daughter's buried . . .

O Helicanus!
Down on thy knees, thank the holy gods as loud
As thunder threatens us: this is Marina . . .
Mine own, Helicanus;
She is not dead at Tarsus, as she should have been . . .

They wouldn't dare to let it end like this:
Her lying still and silver on the screen.
Surely some recog recog recognition scene
Will cornily restore our stone-dead child,
Her who for reels beguiled us and who lies
Now mirror-undetected and called cold.

William Meredith

War Movie: Last Leave, 1944

Then. No. Now.
A long silk scarf of voice, pulled through the loop of throat –
Jo Stafford singing on the radio.
He wants so much to hear a voice like that, and it exists,
as simply as creation, the way the world provides
an image for the feeling
that's richer than the feeling, so that part of the satisfaction
is possession, part the perfection of the longing.
The way you know through flowers what perfect human flesh is,
the way the wife perfects the dim maternity she somehow flowered from,
and you derive the gold circles on your hands
from the sun's blinding ultimate wedding band.

There's a hotel room with a key that fits the door,
and inside, drinking coffee, arguing
or sleeping, the two of them keep marrying.
The arch of every nine-to-five is Notre Dame
where, strangely, you don't need ever to have been.
On Lexington, walking with his arm around her,
out of the earshot of that mother-in-law, the war,
he sees a man lunching on a roll and a cold beer,
and he's so goddamned grateful that he has to swear.

Love is good work, but they stagger sometimes
like a pair of stevedores beneath all the thinking
that it takes to feel, and strange to know precisely
how young on Bleecker and who you are at three-fifteen is:
bronze and sculpture.
And they've got tickets left for the Lombard picture.

The quivering caged canaries of the houselights dim;
the audience, cashmered in theme and shadow, dreams
the accumulating story as it snows on them.
The pilot is at peace, living in the film,
but his young wife only watches him, an afterlife
of movie changing his right cheek. She's swept under fire,
sensing all alone the dark as inexhaustible.
She's in love and terror; and it's hers now, the world's parure,
the legendary suite of matched black jewels.
And she watches the angle of her husband's head
cresting from his shoulders, and she swears
that if it's asked of her, she'll care
for his death as tenderly as any child his body gives her.
The screen swastika flickers in his wire rims.
She strokes his hair, he turns; she takes the cross from him.
Their young night comes toward them outside like a daughter,
wearing city lights like white gardenias in her hair.
Effortlessly, unlike Christ's disciples, they stay awake
with her, the fifth of their five nights, the brunette girl
that history – older, experienced, irresistible – is about to take.

Patricia Storace

War Movie Veteran

You can't tell me a thing that I don't know
About combat, son. I reckon I've seen them all
On the big screen or TV, the late-night show
Or Sunday matinee. I'm what you'd call
An old campaigner; some of them I've seen
Four-five times maybe. I've got so's I

Can tell for sure which ones among that green
Platoon of rookies are the guys to die.
You know the sensitive and quiet kid
Who can't stand rough stuff, says his prayers at night
And never cusses? He's got to wind up dead
But not before we've seen that he can fight
And he's got guts. He ain't afraid to kill
Once the chips are down. The one to see
Turn really yellow is the loud-mouthed mother
That talks like he ain't scared of nothing; he
Will go, expendable. So will the other,
The black guy who's as good as you or me,
And the Jew that's seeking vengeance for his brother.
The comedian – the hero's buddy – could
Come through the battle in one piece or not:
He's only there for laughs, that's understood
By veterans like me. The hero's got
To be alive and kicking at the end.
The one I really like – you know the guy –
The tough top-sergeant, nobody's best friend,
His favourite meal is bullets, blood and rye;
The Krauts he's killed is anybody's guess.
He's made of steel and leather, but you'll find
That he can be the soul of gentleness
With scared old ladies, babies and the blind
Pooch whose master's been knocked off. But never
Think the guy's gone soft: back under fire
He's just as cold and murderous as ever,
He's everything a General could desire.
He'll come through safe okay.
                              I tell you, son,
I could write out the list of casualties
Long before the battle has begun.
I've seen it all. I know the way it is
And got to be. Well, that's what you could call
The human side, psychology I guess.
The other stuff – a cinch to learn it all
In half-a-dozen battles, maybe less.
It takes no time to get the different ranks:
Enlisted men and noncoms, officers,

The names of hardware, ammunition, tanks
And how the thing is planned. You'll think at first
That war is chaos, howl of bullet, shell
And bomb; flashes and thunder as they burst,
Flying shit, hot jig-saw bits of hell.
Not so. It's all worked out before the start.
It's choreographed, like in a dance, okay?
You get to know the pattern. War's an art,
It's one I understand. There ain't no way
That you'll find anyone to tell you more
Than me about realities of war.

Vernon Scannell

Film Shooting

See how they fall, how many ways there are:
Operatic in their own embrace,
Back-flipping over table-top or bar
With gargling yell, disintegrating face,
Arms conducting great finales, or,
Like joke mendacious anglers, wide apart,
Or clutching belly with both hands before
Making deep obeisance as they start
The slow collapsing journey to the floor.

Their costumes alter with the changing scene:
In desert, prairie, on the dusty track
That snakes through scrub towards the dark ravine
They wear the Western villain's garments – black
And battered stetson, shirt and neckerchief.
They need a shave. On modern battlefield,
In Europe or the East, they come to grief
In khaki, grey or green, the face concealed
By helmet-shade and camouflaging leaf.

The urban victims' dress may vary more,
But snappy suits and tipped fedoras are
The usual gear; they croak in liquor store,

In sidewalk filth or, like a blackened star,
Might power-dive from the sky. They could, instead,
Be drilled in restaurant or while at stool,
In some broad's swell apartment on the bed,
Outside a movie-house or by the pool;
There's plenty of locales for getting dead.

Whenever shooting happens we see red
Expressed from neat-punched wound, a signet set
In flesh, soft sealing-wax that runs. The head
Stays more or less intact. That pirouette
Is fake, rehearsed; take it from one who knows.
I was myself once shot, though thank the Lord
Not fatally, as you might well suppose
Could camera objectively record
My cadaverous appearance in repose.

                                   Vernon Scannell

A Day with the Foreign Legion

On one of those days with the Legion
When everyone sticks to sofas
And itches and bitches – a day
For gin and bitters and the plague –
Down by Mount Tessala, under the plane trees,
Seated at iron tables, cursing the country,
Cursing the times and the natives, cursing the drinks,
Cursing the food and the bugs, cursing the Legion,
Were Kim and Bim and all those brave
Heroes of all those books and plays and movies
The remorseless desert serves.
And as they sat at the iron tables cursing the country,
Cursing the food and the bugs, cursing the Legion,
Some Sergeant or other rushed in from The Fort
Gallantly bearing the news
From which all those the remorseless desert serves
Take their cues:

'Sir!'
    'What is it, Sergeant?'
        'Sir, the hordes
March e'en now across the desert swards.'

Just like the movies.

Now in the movies
The Sergeant's arrival touches off bugles and bells,
Emptying bunks and showers, frightening horses,
Pushing up flags and standards, hardening lines
Of unsoldierly softness, and putting farewells
Hastily in the post so two weeks hence
A perfectly lovely lovely in far-off Canada
Will go pale and bite buttons and stare at the air in Canada.
And in the movies,
Almost before the audience spills its popcorn,
The company's formed and away, with Bim or Kim
Solemnly leading them out into a sandstorm,
Getting them into what is quite clearly a trap,
Posting a double guard,
Sending messengers frantic to Marrakech,
Inadvertently pouring the water away,
Losing the ammunition, horses and food,
And generally carrying on in the great tradition
By making speeches
Which bring back to mind the glorious name of the Legion,
And serve as the turning point,
After which the Arabs seem doped and perfectly helpless,
Water springs up from the ground, the horses come back,
Plenty of food is discovered in some old cave,
And reinforcements arrive led by the girl
From Canada.

But in this instance nothing from *Beau Geste*
Or the Paramount lot was attempted,
It being too hot, too terribly hot, for dramatics
Even from Kim and Bim
Aging under the plane trees,
Cursing the food and the bugs, cursing the Sergeant
Who gallantly bore the news because he was young,

Full of oats and ignorance, so damned young
In his pretty khaki; nothing at all,
So late in the day, with everyone crocked
And bitten to death and sweaty and all,
Was attempted despite the Sergeant,
Who whirled on his heel, his mission accomplished, and marched,
Hip hip,
Out of the bar, a true trooper, as if to the wars.

So the lights went on and the audience,
Pleasantly stupid, whistled and clapped at the rarity
Of a film breaking down in this late year of Our Lord.

But of course it was not the film; it was not the projector;
Nor was it the man in the booth, who hastened away
As soon as the feature was over, leaving the heroes
Cursing the food and the bugs, cursing the Legion
As heathendom marched and the Sergeant whirled, hip hip;
But some other, darker cause having to do
With the script perhaps, or the art.
Or not art —
None of these but still deeper, deeper and darker,
Rooted in Culture or . . . Culture, or . . .

Or none of these things. Or all.
What was it?

None of these things, or all. It was the time.
The time and the place, and how could one blame them,
Seated at iron tables cursing the country?
What could they do,
Seated under the plane trees watching the Sergeant
Whirl on his heel, hip hip, in his pretty khaki?
What could they say,
Drinking their gin and bitters by Mount Tessala,
What could they say?

For what after all *could* be said,
After all was said,
But that the feature had merely run out, and the lights had gone on
Because it was time for the lights to go on, and time
For them not to dash out in the desert,

But to rage
As befitted their age
At the drinks and the country, letting their audience
Clap, stamp, whistle and hoot as the darkness
Settled on Mount Tessala, and the lights went on,
The enemy roamed the desert, and everyone itched.

Reed Whittemore

Paradise Lost

'One step beyond *Star Wars*
and *Close Encounters of the Third Kind*,
based on the book by John Milton
from an original idea by God,
Chaos Films proudly present . . .'

It never reached production. Finance
fell through, the Writers' Guild
wrangled over credits
and casting was always a problem.

Pandemonium really set in
when the director, a stickler for detail
and playing devil's advocate,
suggested Latin dialogue.
The poet would have approved, he said.
Why else did the guy write in English
if not to alienate
the international audience of his day?

Paul Munden*

B Movie

Eyes glowing like headlights
   move through the trees
poking holes in darkness
   in search of you and me.

Where shall we hide? The last plane
   succumbs to black vines, its tires
eaten by ants. We send a radio message
   and the static snickers.

Clutching a little column of noon
   surrounded by spanish moss
we shiver in the violence of our sweat:
   flesh squeaks against flesh.

'Darling,' I say to my shadow in your eye
   and point to the sawtooth mountains
where we may just escape the light
   that burns like acid.

The sun falls, a murdered grape.
   We hear only our echoes
gallop through the canyon,
   then far below

a dim signal
   followed by another.
Remote-controlled they come
   swaying sensitive apparatus.

We wake where robot faces
   lean in a circle above,
choosing surgical instruments.
   I ease out of one sleeve

and lunge at the laser eye –
   glass – blue sparks – metal groans!
I grab you and crawl through the smoke.
   Incredibly, help comes.

*

Later, where the moon foams like lather
    on the wet cheek of the sand,
we two, new-pressed, clean-shaven,
    clinch . . . fade out . . . THE END.

                                    Robert Siegel

Cultural Exchange

in the garment factory where I work
all the young Chinese guys are
kung-fu freaks
they're always kicking at each other
punching boxes & hissing & spitting
moving sideways like crabs
showing me Chinese movie magazines
pictures of kung-fu heroes
smeared with blood
kicking their front legs up
seven feet or more.

they take in two or three movies a week
& the plot is almost always the same:
there is a small Chinese village
it looks somehow like an old western town
& the place is being terrorized
by some Japanese villains
they go around grimacing, making ugly faces
killing women & children
like marauding Indians
until a slim hipped hero emerges &
kicks the shit out of hundreds of
fat Japs
& he never has to worry about
running out of bullets.

most of these guys are students
they study business or accounting
have their hair done

so it doesn't look so straight
go to ball games when they
run out of kung-fu movies.

their young anglo co-workers come in
carrying Lao-tzu & talking of
buddhism & last night's opium.

Al Masarik*

A New Reality is Better than a New Movie!

How will it go, crumbling earthquake, towering inferno, juggernaut, volcano, smashup,

in reality, other than the feverish nearreal fantasy of the capitalist flunky film hacks

tho they sense its reality breathing a quake inferno scar on their throat even snorts of

100% pure cocaine cant cancel the cold cut of impending death to this society. On all the

screens of america, the joint blows up every hour and a half for two dollars an fifty cents.

They have taken the niggers out to lunch, for a minute, made us partners (nigger charlie) or

surrogates (boss nigger) for their horror. But just as superafrikan mobutu cannot leop ardskinhat his

way out of responsibility for lumumba's death, nor even with his incredible billions rockefeller

cannot even save his pale ho's titties in the crushing weight of things as they really are.

How will it go, does it reach you, getting up, sitting on the side of the bed, getting ready

to go to work. Hypnotized by the machine, and the cement floor, the jungle treachery of trying

to survive with no money in a money world, of making the boss 100,000 for every 200 dollars

you get, and then having his brother get you for the rent, and if you want to buy the car you

helped build, your downpayment paid for it, the rest goes to buy his old
    lady a foam rubber
rhinestone set of boobies for special occasions when kissinger drunkenly
    fumbles with
her blouse, forgetting himself.
If you dont like it, what you gonna do about it. That was the question we
    asked each other, &
still right regularly need to ask. You dont like it? Whatcha gonna do,
    about it??
The real terror of nature is humanity enraged, the true technicolor
    spectacle that hollywood
cant record. They cant even show you how you look when you go to
    work, or when you come back.
They cant even show you thinking or demanding the new socialist reality,
    its the ultimate tidal
wave. When all over the planet, men and women with heat in their hands,
    demand that society
be planned to include the lives and self determination of all the people ever
    to live. That is
the scalding scenario with a cast of just under two billion that they dare
    not even whisper.
Its called, 'We Want It All . . . The Whole World!'

Amiri Baraka*

Blue Films

These aficionados so dramatically at it –
angling their carrots, their bossy boobs,
twiddling frantic nipples, wiping tongue on tongue –
these topsy-turvy bareback braves
quirting the bedsprings, scalping each other's moans –
from climax to head-squirmed suffocating climax
where do they live, apart from this?

Why do they never show the rest of it –
post triumphant coasting its quiet level
with surrendered skis, no more plying to impress?

Never the mindful details that make love –
shifting the weight to propped elbows,
sorting the duvet so that feet aren't cold,
doodling filigree edges, squeezing a sleepy thigh –
giving the dovetailed miracle its ark?

Geoffrey Holloway

Saturday Afternoon at the Movies

Movies are badder
                 than ever
in San Francisco.
Man, if you wish to go,
then perhaps you should listen
to what a midwestern
buff has to say:
They
      showed nude girls before
(crotch shots looming up near)
and, usually on alternate days,
they showed nude guys.
Next they let the naked fellow pretend to ball
(rather softly)
              the wildly
frenzied, faking girl.
But some of these
                 amateurs could
not help taking their scenes
harder than they were told.
So now there's no pretense –
and, hence, this melancholy singing.
Frisco's dirty flicks are really into something!
Fucking, blowing, sixty-nine.
               And, *che sera*
                    sera
let whatever comes, come.

Trouble is
    I'm not at all at ease
with the technicolored sur-
           facing of sperm,
sentimental music piped
        behind.
Trouble is
the patterning of pubic hairs
is not
   abstract.
Trouble is inside the cunt
I see more than a hint
of a human face
hooded, primitive, unfinished.
And there's a face in the head
of the erect
cock. A changing face rolls
in the balls
      as they make a further thrust.
Also a face at the breast
that will
    gather
round the eye or
the little
tough nose of the nipple.
There's another, more hairy face
in the man's chest.
Or in the back of the cares-
sing hand,
      the hollows of the thighs.
And
   always there is this
face
   in the *face*.
For our conscience views itself
in the mirror of the flesh.
Satur-
    day after-
       noon at the
movies. A far cry from the

[357]

Grande Theatre in Red Oak, Iowa.
Shit. With the porn
there's not even any popcorn.
So what should a boy from the Iowa farm
do when
        he finds himself in San
Francisco at a pornographic film?
Well, I guess
        he should just face the facts
and get his ass home.

                John Logan

A Report from the Chairman

Pornography comes from the stars:
The Emperor Ming chose this week's bill
For planet Earth; Miss Thrill
Meets Honeyfunnel, Rapists of Mars,
The Galactic Grope Show.
These are the films to make your senses glow.

See how Deep Throat engulfs deep space,
A masque in which all vice appears
Like latent virtue. Years
In the movie archive lend it grace,
Uplift replaces shock
As frigid Linda gobbles Johnny's cock

And finds redemption. Strange but true.
Resolve your doubts, only connect
Says the computer, checked
On the hour to keep its gospel new.
Love is an alien here, but lust
Homesteads beyond the rocket's furthest thrust.

Can we do less? The satellites
That wobble through the stratosphere
Shed like a panacea

Their aspirin for the soul; dead beats
From Vegas, women versus
Whatever, a froth of soaps, the tame fuss

Of chat shows, sumo grapplers, a quiz
To which the world plays grinning host.
No longer coast to coast,
But vaulting black holes, this is the biz
Which, given time, will bleach
All men, all minds, from Maine to Bondi Beach.

Homage to Ming! The pirate plank
He bids us walk is perilous
And yet, the worst he shows
Is better than our best. On a blank
Screen the next programme sets
Like jelly, silicones dole out their treats.

There are no takers. The switch-off
Is complete. The emperor's yo-yo
Climbs its string, then lets go.
Nobody cares. Enough
Is better than the feast
Which, offering all, delivers least.

The skies are silent. Channel Ming
Talks to itself. The greed game beats
Its drum. No-one competes.
Out there the next voice you hear will bring
The music of the spheres,
Divinely sponsored, cleansing like tears.

Is this how the story will end,
With alleluias, heavenly choirs?
The franchise waits. Buyers
Perceive the bottom line. Demand
Is up, intermission
Is over and the industry grinds on.

In plexi-domes by Saturn's rim
Controllers calculate the mix
Of coming schedules, flicks
For the horny astronaut, the prim

Banker, the teenage bride.
All prayers are answered, fantasies supplied.

Culture turns up its toes, plays dead;
Critics coin the all-purpose puff.
Production booms to stuff
Each empty, aching heart and head.
                    History descends

Like dust, publicists fake legends
To mimic tradition.
While actors in the feature coming soon
Fellate the Creature from the Black Lagoon.

                              Philip Oakes*

Cahiers du Cinéma, 1956

Dissolve from a proscenium arch of 'L'
In Flushing to a matching arch of mike
Booms, light stands, Fearless dollies, blimps inside
The building in its shade, where thirty-two
Souls stiffen at the sound of 'Speed!' and clap
Of clapsticks clapping on the set. In dream,
A blond wife ambulates across a room
Built out of flats, her back lit by a Con
Edison evening sun. She's carrying
An insubstantial crown of peach ice cream
To her peach-featured, immaterial
Young holy family. She muffs a line.
Cut. Take two. Outside, by the Optimo
Cigar Store, a live, dirty, dying man
Dives for the Daily News in a trash can.

                              L. E. Sissman

Documentary

Bring the camera closer in. Focus
On the burning *ghat*. They've finished
The ceremony around the body, and are torching
The wooden pyre. See how the tongues of flame
Rise from the limbs. Zero in on the head –
I want you to catch the skull when it bursts.
Pan down the torso, the spine in ashes, the hips
Crumbling. Then dolly back for the scenic shot –
The Ganges flowing past. But keep the tension
Sharp, you might catch the silhouette
Of a river dolphin. Filter the lens
To bring the blue out of the mud-silt.
Now zoom down to the middle of the river,
That small boat, the boatman dumping a child
Overboard. Get his flex of muscle
As he struggles with the stone tied to the corpse.
Then back to the panorama, the vista. The storm
Rushing in. The lightning flashing far off
Over the river palace. The silver drizzle
Of rain. The quiet glow on the water.

Joseph Stroud

Soundstage

US Signal Corps Photographic Center: 1945

I

Catwalk, backdrop, cable, girder, fly –
A schooner capsized:

Sea-fans of artifice
Buoyed in the middle currents; gelatin and foil;
Baskets of radiant cordage, geysers of frost,
Miraculous canvas in the glowing levels, glazed,
The backdrops weedy, like oil:

> The ropes plunge and are lost;

Are parted like hair,
Where, at the summit, among crucibles of light,
Equilibrist Gulliver
Calls to the carpenters in a tightwire vertigo,
At the Archimedean center of deception, unamazed.

And all that is, is film; film is
The serpent in Eden Garden, the cord in the chrysalis,
The bough in the dove's beak trying the deluge,
The thread in the labyrinth,
The great wall of China spanning the dynasties
Like a calligraphic symbol; meridians, staves,
Between the upper and nether icecaps; trajectory
Of shell and tracer-bullet, phosphor and satchel-charge;
The looped 'I' given to the paper poorly on the burning tripod

And the victory over horror in an image.

2

The boy in the uniform of Oberleutnant, the demoniac flier,
Will not bleed humanly from the papier-mâché doorway.

> The door

Will not close truly on the plausible flight,
With leisure for vanity, vacancy, mania, the stunned recognition.
And mocking the human wish for asylum,
Spray-gun and saw, the jaw of the plier,
Have outpaced fable.

It is divertissement, after all.
What is stilted in canvas, jailed to the plywood wall,
Stabbed to the floor
With wing-screws and metal angles,
Melts into vaudeville in a whirr of velocipedes
And a yelping of trained poodles,
A swindle of spangles.
Only the scaffold gives stress to the weightless interior
On the wrong side of the pattern: the artisan's touch of the actual.

Yet teased out of thought,
The smiling divination of the Spool
Whirls forever in the large eye of Keats, heavy with film.
For even that Attic shape,
The bride of quietness brought to bed on the urn,
Was not more actual than this.
                                And, in equivocal distance,
Necessitous armies close, image and spectacle wait,
And beat on the canvas door;
The fiction
Calls in the ripening crystal to existence,
Loud as myself –
                        in deed, in ghost –
And bleeds in Agamemnon's color,
And is articulate.

                                                Ben Belitt

Travel Film, in Technicolor

We take you to Pendragonia, oldest of countries.
It is full of ruins and rivers and wind-blown cypress.
Here people are happy, they sing, in their peasant costumes
They dance through the hayfields on Sunday. This village stalwart
Is courting his love in a meadow. See how she blushes.
See in this close-up how tightly he holds the girl to him.

This panorama
Reveals beyond the haycocks the guardian mountains,
With their attendant glaciers, their bustling torrents
That flow to the flourishing plains. Notice the shepherd
Standing beside that furious fall of water.
He is playing a pipe, but the notes, alas, are not heard.

This long shot
Shows us an antique temple, a sacred precinct
For the sun-worshipping ancestors of the lad

Who was kissing the girl much earlier in the reel.
A careless world has let the moss surround it;
Ages of rain have worn its stones away.

This close shot
Presents a policeman in the busy metropolis.
Behind him we see the cathedral, the white façade
Of the modern city hall, and behind that, rearing
Ionian columns to the sky, we find
The palaces of government, wherein are Ministers.

And with these monstrous columns we must take
A sad farewell of Pendragonia, land of
Peace, fruition, conception, intelligence, art.
The cameraman's hands are tired, his feeling for angles
Strained, his provisionary visa quite expired,
The producer's budget exhausted, the lenses blurred.

We had wanted to show you the barracks, the latest tanks
Engaged in manœuvers, the handsome soldiers in battle
Dress, but you must understand it was not felt
That these expressed the spirit of this land.
We had wanted to show you the faces of the people,
But when we looked at them they turned away.

We had wanted to show you truth, but truth photographs badly.
We had wanted to show you hope, but we could not find it.

Harry Brown

Reservation Special

The man with the camera comes,
whirling black metal knobs, while
yelling chief commands, unanointed.
Aiming his one-eyed magic
he frames headroaches and cockroaches.
Separating houses from the land,
he plots Indian plight
with pre-answered questions.

Then he stuffs his black bag
with our lives and is gone
in his alphabet auto.

Lew Blockcolski

Flower of *The Living Desert*

It is too sudden
For our sluggard sight
This unfolding flower:
The time compressed,
The blossom magnified,
By cunning lens.

Too swift the petals
Come unshuttered;
The huddled stamens quivering
Pale creatures of the dark
Exposed to a fierce light.

Watching a crimson bud
Flare to a fiery disk,
Its beauty bursting like a cry –
We came too close to hidden marvel
Uncovered by a cold and convex eye.

Mary Winter*

First News Reel: September 1939

It was my war, though it ended
When I was ten: could I know or guess
What the talking really said?
– 'Over the top. At the front.
Sealed-with-a-loving-kiss.

Train-loads of wounded men
At the old seaside station.
Two million dead' –
Child of the nightmare-crying 'Never again'.

The same 'I' sits here now
In this silent throng
Watching with dull surprise
Guns limbering to the line
Through umber sheaves,
Guns topped with dappled boys
And crowned with beckoning leaves,
Like floats for some harvest home
Of corn or wine;

A self removed and null
Doubting the eye that sees
The gun in its green bower,
Yet meticulously records
At each load, discharge, recoil,
How the leaves spin from the trees
In an untimely shower
Over the sunlit fields, and are whirled away
To the edge of the sky.

No mud. No wounds. No tears.
No nightmare cries. Is it possible
It could be different this time?
Far-off that passing bell
Tolls 'Different.
Yes always different. Always the same':
As the guns roar and recoil
And the leaves that spin from the trees
Deck boys for a festival.

Joan Barton

Newsreel in Wartime

Flame-thrower Attacking Dugout

The red persuasion of the flames
Poured in on him and he came out
From his blind dungeon, routed by
A furnace coughing in his face.
His eyes held neither hope nor fear,
But swam in animal surprise;
He grew a coat of boiling hair
Before our eyes.
            A popcorn sack
Split wide and crashed. A seat sighed down
Upon its hinge. The usher's light
Surprised the dark where boys-with-girls
Kissed, murmuring.
            He slowly burned
And burning crawled and crawling died.

The scream was censored. What was left
Were less lugubrious events:
A close-up of Mount Erebus,
And babies kissing presidents.

                        Adrien Stoutenburg

Newsreel

This would not be the war we fought in. See, the foliage is
heavier, there were no hills of that size there.

But I find it impossible not to look for actual persons known to me
and not seen since; impossible not to look for myself.

The scenery angers me, I know there is something wrong, the sun
is too high, the grass too trampled, the peasants' faces too broad,
and the main square of the capital had no arcades like those.

Yet the dead look right, and the roofs of the huts, and the crashed fuselage burning among the ferns.

But this is not the war I came to see, buying my ticket, stumbling through the darkness, finding my place among the sleepers and masturbators in the dark.

I thought of seeing the General who cursed us, whose name they gave to an expressway; I wanted to see the faces of the dead when they were living.

Once I know they filmed us, back at the camp behind the lines, taking showers under the trees and showing pictures of our girls.

Somewhere there is a film of the war we fought in, and it must contain the flares, the souvenirs, the shadows of the netted brush the standing in line of the innocent, the hills that were not of this size.

Somewhere my body goes taut under the deluge, somewhere I am naked behind the lines, washing my body in the water of that war.

Someone has that war stored up in metal canisters, a memory he cannot use, somewhere my innocence is proven with my guilt, but this would not be the war I fought in.

Adrienne Rich

Home Movies

How the children have changed! Rapt we stare
   At flickering lost Edens where
    Pale infants, squinting, seem to hark
To their older selves laughing in the dark.

And then, by the trellis in some old Spring –
   The seasons are unaltering –
    We gather, smoother and less bald,
Innocently clowning, having been called

By the cruelly invisible cameraman.
How silently time ran!
We cannot climb back, nor can our friends,
To that calm light. The brief film ends.

John Updike

Movies for the Home

I see the map of summer, lying still,
Its edges under water, blue, fragile,
You cannot hear, of course, from here
The Pacific's portable orchestra –
A kind of shimmery marimba music –
But if you follow all those lines of light,
The nerve-nets of connection, coast to coast,
That screened the days and nights from east to west,
You'll come upon their visions and their sounds:
The dawn's fine print when ink has leaked away,
And a radio turned off still tuned to play
Invisible music. Riding in that car,
I think that where we were is where we are.

The towns the distance fired into being
(By dint of light diagonally drawn
Downward to strike a steeple with a star)
Became fool's gold the closer we came near,
Assembling into lassitudes of palms,
The fresh rot of the wharfs, the hunchbacked hills,
But none of those visions we were driving for.
They drained away, strip cities come and gone,
As if we stayed while we went driving on,
Or they remained where they had never been,
Before us and behind us. They disappeared,
And what at first was flame at last was char.
One wheel turns or another, and there you are.

By supple deviations, twisting on,
The Snake River bent its shapely mail

[369]

In moonlight, enlarged and palpable.
The Tetons capped by a display of snow
Refreshed four lakes of summer far below
(Thimblefuls of a barbarian sky);
We dipped our fingers in their sunburnt water
To dribble waterdrops back into blue.
Telegraph wires stitched themselves to trees,
Then dropped away, somewhere in the Rockies.
The pictures pass. We are what we need.
If I remember rightly, we were lost.
We lost the way, being the way we are.

A beautifully painted abstract speed
Lacquered the windshield's cemetery
Of wing and smear so factually there
It seemed the factual was arbitrary
But natural. In those swift ends we saw
The wreckage of ourselves, our wheels in air . . .
Transparent vacancies attack the brain
At one point or another, as if a train
Should smash into a moving mirror of itself
Point-blank high up upon a mountain pass,
And the snow, not even disturbed, give back
Its glacial white indifference to the wreck.
And there, where imagination ends, we are.

Where are we? In a country of lakes?
A Switzerland of Self through which we ski,
Dropping down a lighted scoop of valley
That soon transforms itself into the sea?
(And thus we might arrive at the Impossible:
That place where there is nothing left to see.)
Now we are standing on a wooden pier
Watching the Pacific stun itself on rocks;
If the camera stopped, if you could stare
Out far enough, the Orient, over there,
Might have the excitement of intense boredom.
Our house in Berkeley? You turn the corner there,
Go left and down the hill, and there you are.

Alongside water all the afternoon,
The sea so far below we could not fall,
What threatened ending rose from its abyss
To rattle in the tin can of the car?
Was it the blue that flaked away to cloud,
The green that flew away on either side,
The white-lined serpent of the road ahead,
Intense as distance in its silences,
That colored what we thought until we thought:
The color of the distance is the color bled
Out of the time it takes to get us there?
The pictures pass. We are the way we were.
Being here and there is what we are.

By going forward we were coming back.
When the film rewinds, you'll see what I mean.
In the woods, that lipsticked drinking cup,
Stuck in the drying margins of the stream,
Turns up again in the desert coming up
Quite soon in malignant iodine and green.
Now we are looking at an estuary
Whose waters gently poach an evening star
Whose spidery edges are collapsing down
As far as the eye can see, but just so far.
I wonder if you can go as far as far
And still not see things as they really are,
Only as they were, if that is where you are.

Howard Moss

NOTES

Kameradschaft' (Swingler). In G. W. Pabst's great 1931 movie *Kameradschaft* ('Comradeship'), German and French coal miners in Alsace-Lorraine shortly after the end of World War One overcome their recent enmity and assert a comradeship that transcends national borders by collaborating during a colliery disaster to rescue their fellow workers trapped underground. (283)

'The Undead' (Wilbur). In an essay called 'A Poet at the Movies' in *Man and the Movies*, ed. W. R. Robinson, 1957, Wilbur writes – of two poems published in this section – that 'Beasts' draws in its third and fourth stanzas on the 1943 Universal horror film *Frankenstein Meets the Wolf Man* and that 'The Undead' was influenced by the original 1931 *Dracula* starring Bela Lugosi. (283)

'In Defense of Poetry' (Bowers). The first of numerous sound movies inspired by Robert Louis Stevenson's *Dr Jekyll and Mr Hyde* was directed by Rouben Mamoulian in 1931 and starred Fredric March. Dr Janusz Korczak, the Polish physician, writer and educator, cared for his school of orphans in the Warsaw ghetto and accompanied them to Treblinka, a story told in Andrzej Wajda's *Korczak* (1990). (285)

'Scar-Face' (Lowell). The career of Al Capone (1899–1947), czar of Chicago's underworld in the Prohibition era, has inspired numerous gangster films, starting with Edward G. Robinson in *Little Caesar* (1931, director Mervyn LeRoy) and Paul Muni in *Scarface* (1932, director Howard Hawks). (286)

'Good Times' (Mazzocco). The 1932 MGM movie *Grand Hotel*, adapted from Vicki Baum's novel and directed by Edmund Goulding, concerned the interrelated lives of a variety of guests at a Berlin hotel in the days of the Weimar Republic. It features Greta Garbo's line 'I want to be alone', and won an Academy Award as the year's best film. (286)

'Fay Wray to the King' (Rechter). Although Fay Wray (b. 1907) appeared in a number of other notable films (including Erich von Stroheim's *The Wedding March* and Ernest Schoedsack's *The Most Dangerous Game*), her claim to immortality is her role as beauty to the beast in *King Kong* (1933). (288)

'King Kong Meets Wallace Stevens' (Ondaatje). The eponymous giant ape of the monster movie *King Kong* (1933, directed by Merian C. Cooper and Ernest Schoedsack) was brought back from Skull Island to be exhibited in New York and died after being machine-gunned off the top of the Empire State Building. (In the 1976 remake he falls from the roof of the World Trade Center.) The American poet Wallace Stevens (1879–1955), after graduating from Yale, worked briefly as a journalist, then as a lawyer, before joining the Hartford Accident and Indemnity Company in 1916, combining the roles of insurance executive and prominent modernist poet until the end of his life. (289)

'A Toast' (Stetler). Starting with *The Thin Man* (1934, director W. S. Van Dyke), William Powell and Myrna Loy appeared in a series of MGM comedy thrillers as the sophisticated, hard-drinking upper-class husband-and-wife detective team, Nick and Nora Charles. They were usually accompanied by the fox terrier Asta. Their creator, Dashiell Hammett, modelled Nick and Nora on himself and Lillian Hellman. (291)

'Walker Evans' Atlanta' (Ross). Numerous photographs of the 1930s contrast the grim reality of daily life in the Depression with the cheerful images on advertising hoardings. One of the most notable is 'Atlanta, Georgia, 1936' by Walker Evans, in which two vast rectangular movie posters are plastered on a fence beneath some seedy three-storey clapboard houses. The movies that owe their present fame to Evans's photograph are the RKO comedy *Chatterbox*, starring Ann Shirley and Margaret Hamilton (the wicked witch in *The Wizard of Oz*) and the Universal comedy *Love Before Breakfast*, starring Carole Lombard and Preston Foster. (292)

'On Seeing the Leni Riefenstahl Film of the 1936 Olympic Games' (Fuller). Leni Riefenstahl (born Berlin, 1902), after working as an actress and director of feature films, was chosen by Adolf Hitler to make *Triumph of the Will* (1935), the notorious documentary of the Nazi Party's Nuremberg Rally. The following year she was provided with a vast team of technicians and assistants to make her controversial masterpiece, a two-part documentary on the 1936 Berlin Olympic Games designed as 'a song of praise to the ideals of National Socialism'. It was released in 1938 as *Olympische Spiele 1936* (aka *Olympia*). (293)

'Les Enfants de Thalia' (Sissman). The Thalia, one of Manhattan's best-loved art houses, is memorialized in John Hollander's 'Moviegoing'. The film being watched in Sissman's poem is Jean Renoir's 1937 classic *La Grande Illusion*, a story of World War One prison-camp life starring Erich von Stroheim (Captain von Rauffenstein), Pierre Fresnay (Captain de Boeldieu), Jean Gabin (Lieutenant Maréchal), Dalio (Rosenthal). (294)

'Claudette Colbert by Billy Wilder' (Raworth). Claudette Colbert played in two sophisticated comedies, both set in Europe, co-scripted by Wilder and Charles Brackett and directed by Mitchell Leisen. In *Midnight* (1939) she plays an American stranded in Paris and hired by an elderly aristocrat to impersonate a Hungarian countess. In *Arise My Love* (1940) Colbert and Ray Milland are American foreign correspondents covering the Spanish Civil War and the outbreak of World War Two. (294)

'Miss Scarlett, Mr Rhett and other Latter-Day Saints' (Angelou). Starting with D. W. Griffith's *Birth of a Nation* (1915), Hollywood has all too frequently celebrated the chivalry of the aristocratic Old South, never more so than in the 1939 film of Margaret Mitchell's novel *Gone with the Wind* starring Clark Gable as Rhett Butler and Vivien Leigh as Scarlett O'Hara. (295)

'Dream Song 9' (Berryman). In *High Sierra* (1941, director Raoul Walsh), the film that made him a fully fledged star, Humphrey Bogart plays the gangster Roy 'Mad Dog' Earle, who dies in the Californian mountains after being surrounded by the police. (297)

'Rosebud' (Fuller). As a radio producer in the 1930s, the actor and director Paul Stewart (1908–85) introduced Orson Welles to broadcasting and along with other members of Welles's Mercury Company made his movie debut in *Citizen Kane* (1941). Stewart played the smarmy European valet at Xanadu who claims to have the key to the meaning of Kane's dying word, 'Rosebud'. (298)

'*Charley's Aunt*' (Lejeune). American critics thought more highly of this 1941 movie of Brandon Thomas's classic farce (directed by Archie Mayo) than Miss Lejeune did. (298)

'*Aloma of the South Seas*' (Lejeune). One of numerous South Sea adventure films featuring Dorothy Lamour as an island beauty dressed in a sarong. Four years earlier she and her co-star Jon Hall featured in John Ford's Polynesian story, *The Hurricane* (1937). (299)

'Johnny Wayne and Randy Scott' (Service). In *The Spoilers* (1942, director Ray Enright), the second of three sound versions of Rex Beach's 1906 novel about honest gold prospectors, claim-jumpers, crooked businessmen and saloon owners in turn-of-the-century Alaska, John Wayne and Randolph Scott engage in one of the screen's most protracted and destructive fist-fights. Robert Service must have seen similar fights during his years in the Yukon.

   Service's poem 'The Spell of the Yukon' is quoted by Gene Hackman as Jack McCann, the prospector-hero of Nicolas Roeg's film *Eureka* (1983), who strikes gold, becomes a multimillionaire and subsequently leads a disappointing, anti-climactic life that concludes with his bizarre death in the West Indies during World War Two. The character of McCann was closely based on the real-life tycoon Sir Harry Oakes, who struck it rich in Canada; his still unsolved murder in the Bahamas in 1943 remains the subject of considerable speculation. (299)

'You Were Wearing Blue' (Raworth): In Michael Curtiz's *Casablanca* (1942), when Rick and Ilse meet again in North Africa he recalls the day the Germans marched into Paris: 'I remember every detail. The Germans wore grey, you wore blue.' Later, in a flashback, he recollects the gunfire getting nearer to Paris and how, about to take a train bound for Marseille, he received her letter, informing him that she wouldn't be coming. (300)

'Fantasy' (O'Hara). Adolph Deutsch (1897–1980), the London-born composer and arranger, worked on major productions at Warner Brothers and MGM. At

Warners in the 1940s he was in competition with Max Steiner and wrote the music for Raoul Walsh's *Northern Pursuit* (1943), a World War Two thriller set in Canada where North-West Mounted Policeman Errol Flynn chases Nazi intruder Helmut Dantine. (301)

'A Gothic Gesture' (Levine). In the British psychological drama *The Seventh Veil* (1945, director Compton Bennett) concert pianist Ann Todd is browbeaten (and worse) by her crippled guardian James Mason and comforted by psychiatrist Herbert Lom. (302)

'Heart Failure' (Lejeune). The escapist Paramount comedies *Our Hearts Were Young and Gay* (1944) and *Our Hearts Were Growing Up* (1946), based on an autobiographical novel by Cornelia Otis Skinner, star Gail Russell and Diana Lynn as upper middle-class flappers in Paris and at university in the 1920s. (303)

'*Humoresque*' (Lejeune). The Warner Brothers weepie (1946, director Jean Negulesco) stars Joan Crawford as a hard-drinking socialite agonizing over her poor protégé, John Garfield, a violin virtuoso. Isaac Stern plays an anthology of snatches from popular classics on the soundtrack. (303)

'*The Red Shoes*' (Ray). Written and directed by Michael Powell and Emeric Pressburger, *The Red Shoes* (1948) is the most popular classic dance movie ever made, and probably responsible (as cited in *A Chorus Line*) for more vocations in the ballet than any other picture. It features Moira Shearer, Robert Helpmann, Ludmilla Tcherina, Leonide Massine and Frederick Ashton. (304)

'*Dédée d'Anvers*' (Conquest). Made in 1948 between the high period of French poetic realism and the coming of the New Wave, *Dédée d'Anvers* was directed by Yves Allégret and starred his then wife Simone Signoret (1921–85) as a prostitute on the Antwerp waterfront with Bernard Blier as her pimp. The critic of *Paris-Presse* wrote: 'With *Dédée d'Anvers*, Simone Signoret has finally found the part she was looking for, which immediately raises her up to the first rank of French screen actresses.' (305)

'The Cinematographers, West Cedar Street' (Sissman). Michael Roemer (born Berlin, 1928) came to Britain as a refugee in the 1930s and moved on to the United States in 1945. He enrolled at Harvard University and between 1947 and 1949 made the fantasy-documentary *A Touch of the Times*. This low-budget film, claimed as the first feature-length production shot on a university campus, included in its cast the poet L. E. Sissman, who here memorializes this legendary, pioneer venture of independent American cinema. Roemer subsequently worked in various capacities on liberal documentaries before making his feature debut with *Nothing But a Man* (1964), a film widely praised for its sympathetic approach to black life – it won prizes at the 1965 Venice Festival and elsewhere. *The Plot Against Harry* (1969), his low-budget, monochrome, pre-*Godfather* satire on the Mafia, ran into post-production problems and was shelved. Roemer retreated into producing documentaries and film teaching. Twenty years later, *The Plot Against Harry* resurfaced at the Cannes Festival to considerable acclaim. (306)

'Film Revival' (Conquest). An extravagant opera and ballet movie based on Offenbach, *Tales of Hoffman* (1951) was the last masterpiece from the team of Michael Powell and Emeric Pressburger. Sir Thomas Beecham conducted the Royal Philharmonic Orchestra. (307)

'*The Prisoner of Zenda*' (Wilbur). Anthony Hope's Ruritanian adventure was filmed twice in the silent era and three times after the coming of sound: starring Ronald Colman in 1937 (the classic treatment), Stewart Granger in 1952 (the opulent Technicolor version) and Peter Sellers in 1979 (the parodic embarrassment). (307)

'Stakeout on High Street' (Henri). In Samuel Fuller's cult thriller *Pickup on South Street* (1953), one of a cycle of anti-Communist movies from the McCarthy era, Richard Widmark plays a New York pickpocket who becomes involved with a Communist spy ring and confronts them with the help of a brunette prostitute (Jean Peters) at a shack on the Manhattan waterfront. The song running through the poem, 'Again', was a hit of the late 1940s and was written by Dorcas Cochran and Lionel Newman for an earlier Richard Widmark movie at 20th Century-Fox, *Road House* (1948), in which it was sung by Ida Lupino. (308)

'I mean' (Raworth). The exchange between Richard Widmark and Jean Peters is from Fuller's *Pickup on South Street*. The reference in the preceding line is to Dallas, the prostitute played by Claire Trevor in John Ford's *Stagecoach* (1939), who is driven out of Tonto by the Ladies of the Law and Order League. (309)

'Double Sonnet for Mickey' (Burns). In the Robert Aldrich thriller *Kiss Me Deadly* (1955), based on the sensational Mickey Spillane novel, Ralph Meeker plays the seedy private eye Mike Hammer. In the opening scene he gives a lift to a stranded woman (Cloris Leachman) who passes on a clue in the form of a quotation from Christina Rossetti's sonnet 'Remember', which reverberates through the film. (310)

'In Memoriam' (Updike). In George Cukor's 1956 film version of the John Masters novel *Bhowani Junction*, the Anglo-Indian heroine Victoria Jones (Ava Gardner) – in post-War, pre-partition India – is torn between British army officer Rodney Savage (Stewart Granger) and her Anglo-Indian fiancé Patrick Taylor (Bill Travers), a railway engineer. She finally marries the latter. The film was tested in 1955 on a student audience in UCLA who were horrified by the idea of Ava Gardner ending up with a half-caste, even though she was playing one herself. As a result the film was extensively re-edited and the fiancé is killed off. (311)

'*Tarantula*' (Webb). In Jack Arnold's low-budget horror flick *Tarantula* (1955), a giant spider developed by scientist Leo G. Carroll terrorizes the desert. One of the

US air force pilots assigned to destroy the creature was played by Clint Eastwood during his first year at Universal. In *Back to the Future III, Tarantula* is showing with another early Eastwood film in a double-bill at a 1955 drive-in cinema. (312)

'Popular Revivals, 1956' (Updike). In the Richard Brooks Western *The Last Hunt* (1956), Stewart Granger plays a decent frontiersman concerned over the extinction of the bison who comes into conflict with the Indian-hating buffalo hunter Robert Taylor. (313)

'Ingmar Bergman's *Seventh Seal*' (Duncan). In *Det Sjunde Inseglet*, a knight (Max von Sydow) returns from the Crusades to a plague-ridden mediaeval Sweden and plays a game of chess with Death (Bengt Ekerot) to win a respite on earth in an attempt to prove the inherent goodness of man. Shown at the 1957 Cannes Festival, it decisively established Ingmar Bergman's international reputation. (314)

'*Vertigo*, A Sequel' (Goldstein). This elegy for Alfred Hitchcock (1899–1980) is named for the 1958 film that many consider his masterpiece. Its hero is a San Francisco detective (James Stewart) who becomes obsessed with a blonde (Kim Novak) whom he is hired to shadow. The other blonde Hitchcock heroines invoked are Grace Kelly and Tippi Hedren. '*Vertigo*, A Sequel' is modelled on Baudelaire's poem on Don Juan. (315)

'Two Deaths' (Jennings). In *Ashes and Diamonds* (1958), the concluding film in Andrzej Wajda's classic trilogy about anti-Nazi partisans in World War Two Poland, the charismatic Zbigniew Cybulski plays a doomed young man charged with assassinating a newly arrived Communist functionary in a provincial town in the last days of the war. He ends up mortally wounded, hiding between sheets on a washing line through which his blood appears, and finally dies on a rubbish dump. (316)

'The Blob Speaks to its Mother' (Johnson). In the low-budget horror movie *The Blob* (1958, director Irwin S. Yeaworth Jr), Steve McQueen as a rather elderly teenager turns up trumps when a carnivorous, ever-growing ball of jelly descends upon his middle-American small town. The apparently irresistible Blob invades the local cinema but turns out to be defenceless against cold temperatures. There was a 1971 sequel and a big budget 1988 remake. (317)

'Shapes of Things' (Hofmann). Based on the Nevil Shute novel and one of numerous films at that time dealing with nuclear angst, Stanley Kramer's *On the Beach* (1959) proposes a nuclear war in 1964 that wipes out the Northern Hemisphere and leaves the Southern Hemisphere with a mere four final months. Gregory Peck plays the commander of an American submarine who heads to Melbourne, Australia, where the last vestiges of civilization are to be found, and has a meaningful affair with hard-drinking local Ava Gardner. (317)

'Turkish Delight' (Boyle). *El Cid* (1961), one of the great epic movies, was directed on location in Spain by Anthony Mann in the 70mm Super Technirama process. Charlton Heston, giving what many critics consider his finest costume performance, plays Rodrigo Diaz (c.1043–99), the Spanish hero known as El Cid who led his Christian followers against the Moorish invaders, winning the respect of the enemy's leader. In the final sequence El Cid is strapped into his saddle and though dead he inspires his troops to their ultimate victory. It might also be noted, apropos of the eighth couplet of this poem, that up until the mid-1960s it was customary for the uniformed employees of British cinemas to wear on the left breast of their tunics the ribbons of the campaign medals and other awards they had received from wartime service, in some cases reaching back beyond World War Two to the Great War, the Boer War and various imperial campaigns. (318)

'The Hustler de Paris' (Greger). In *The Hustler* (1961), Robert Rossen's classic moral fable set in the subculture of professional pool, Paul Newman plays the callow 'Fast Eddie' Felson, an ace of the green-baize world. He works the bars and small pool-halls of Middle America with his manager (Myron McCormick), conning local players to raise the money to challenge the reigning pool champion Minnesota Fats (Jackie Gleason). Through his arrogant over-confidence, Eddie is defeated and proceeds to lose his manager, the use (temporarily) of his thumbs, and his girlfriend on the way to gaining character and achieving a final bitter victory. Twenty-five years later, Newman played 'Fast Eddie' again in Martin Scorsese's *The Colour of Money* (1986), and at last won the Oscar he should have received for *The Hustler*. (319)

'Shades of Grey' (O'Neill). Directed by Alain Resnais from a screenplay by novelist Alain Robbe-Grillet, *L'Année dernière à Marienbad* (1961) was, and has remained, the ultimate art-house puzzle movie, centre of enduring controversy and conversation. Delphine Seyrig and Giorgio Albertazzi play a pair of aristocrats, staying at a grand middle-European country house, who may or may not have met and had an affair the previous year in Marienbad. (320)

'*Ride the High Country*' (Slavitt). Sam Peckinpah's second movie for the cinema, *Ride the High Country* (1962, released in Britain as *Guns in the Afternoon*) is ranked among the best Westerns ever made. Randolph Scott (in his final screen appearance) and Joel McCrea (in his last sizeable role) play a pair of ageing ex-marshals reduced to delivering a small consignment of gold from a mining camp in the Sierras to a Californian bank at the turn of the century when the horseless carriage is arriving and times are changing. (321)

'Working for Dr No' (Nash). *Dr No* (1962, director Terence Young) was the first of Ian Fleming's James Bond novels to be filmed. Fleming (1908–64) approved the casting of Sean Connery but only lived to see two movies. In *Dr No* a tarantula crawls over the sleeping 007; in the novel the creature is a deadly poisonous six-inch centipede. The edgy Professor Dent is played by Anthony Dawson, the would-be hitman in Hitchcock's *Dial M for Murder*. (322)

'A night out' (Abse). Left uncompleted when its Polish director Andrzej Munk (1921–61) died in a car crash, the black-and-white widescreen *Passenger* was edited into a presentable 63-minute form by his colleague Witold Liesewicz and released in 1963. Some years after World War Two on a transatlantic liner a former prison guard at Auschwitz believes she recognizes a fellow passenger as a Jewish prisoner from the camp and recalls their wartime relationship. The shipboard scenes are presented in the form of stills with voice-over narration. *Passenger* was shown in 1964 at the now defunct Academy Cinema, Oxford Street, then London's most prestigious art house. (323)

'*Alphaville* and after' (Fell). In Jean-Luc Godard's Kafkaesque SF movie *Alphaville* (1965), Lemmy Caution (the tough private eye created by British novelist Peter Cheyney) is despatched on a mission through space to the planet Alphaville. The film was shot largely at night in black and white in present-day Paris and starred the expatriate American Eddie Constantine, who had played Caution in a series of low-budget French crime movies. (324)

'On Pasolini's *Teorema*' (Kirkup). Distributed in English-speaking countries as *Theorem*, Pier Paolo Pasolini's 1968 movie *Teorema* was adapted from his own novel and starred Terence Stamp as a beguiling stranger (called 'The Visitor') who charms his way into the bourgeois household of a rich Italian industrialist and seduces everyone within it – the father (Massimo Girotti), the mother (Sylvana Mangano), their daughter (Anne Wiazemsky), their son (Andrès José Cruz) and the family maid (Laura Betti) – transforming their lives. The film was unsuccessfully charged with obscenity (almost a routine procedure for Italian films of any consequence in the 1960s and 70s) before going on to become one of Pasolini's biggest international successes, opening in London in April 1969, the same week as his *Oedipus Rex*, which starred Sylvana Mangano as Jocasta. Of the Terence Stamp character, Pasolini remarked in a 1969 BBC television interview: 'I adapted my character to the physical and psychological person of the actor. Originally, I intended this visitor to be a fertility god, the typical god of pre-industrial religion . . . Naturally when confronted with things as they were, I had to abandon my original idea and so I made Terence Stamp into a generically ultra-terrestrial and metaphysical apparition: he could be the Devil, or a mixture of God and the Devil. The important thing is that he is something authentic and unstoppable'. (325)

'The Shirt' (Shattuck). Paul Gégauff scripted numerous films directed by Claude Chabrol, starting with the key New Wave movie *Les Cousins* (1959). In 1975 Gégauff (1922–83) wrote and acted alongside his ex-wife Danielle in *Une partie de plaisir*, a frank account of the breakdown of their marriage, directed by Chabrol. (326)

'He's a Nice Guy' (Webb). One of the most successful of the 1970s cycle of Disaster movies, *The Poseidon Adventure* (1972, director Ronald Neame) concerns the fight for survival of the passengers in a luxury liner hit by a freak

wave and submerged upside down in the eastern Mediterranean. The Reverend
Gene Hackman leads a party on a journey to the section of the hull most accessible
to rescuers. (327)

'Homage to Walter Hill's *Hard Times*' (Sherman). Walter Hill's directorial debut
of 1975 (released in Great Britain as *The Streetfighter*) is set around New Orleans
in the 1930s at the height of the Great Depression and draws for its visual style on
the paintings of Edward Hopper. Charles Bronson plays Chaney, a taciturn,
itinerant loner who makes a living as a 'hitter' in illegal bare knuckle fights staged
on ships, in warehouses and at outdoor parties in the bayou. James Coburn
appears as the fast-talking gambler who arranges his fights and Jill Ireland is the
lonely woman Chaney meets in a café and befriends, before she rejects him and his
drifting, uncommitted life. (328)

'*The Mirror Crack'd*' (Pitt-Kethley). The least exotic of the period Agatha Christie
movies produced by John Brabourne and Richard Goodwin, *The Mirror Crack'd*
(1980, director Guy Hamilton) has Angela Lansbury as Miss Marple investigating
a murder during the shooting of a movie in a Home Counties village in the 1950s.
The suspects include Elizabeth Taylor, Rock Hudson and Tony Curtis. The title
comes from Tennyson's 'The Lady of Shalott'. (329)

'Final Farewell' (Clark). In Ridley Scott's SF thriller *Blade Runner* (1982),
Harrison Ford is officially charged with pursuing renegade androids in a dystopian
AD 2019 Los Angeles. In the climax he has a rooftop fight with the proud android
Roy Batty (the name suggesting a mad king), played by Rutger Hauer. (330)

'*Firestarter*' (Ray). Based on the Stephen King novel, *Firestarter* (1984, director
Mark L. Lester) is an SF horror movie starring Drew Barrymore (her first film after
E.T.) as a child whose pyrokinetic powers make her the object of government
interest as a potential secret weapon. (330)

'Movies' (Ray). In *Gorillas in the Mist* (1988, director Michael Apted), Sigourney
Weaver plays the American ethologist Dian Fossey chosen by Louis Leakey to
study the disappearing mountain gorillas in Central Africa. She wrote several
bestselling books and was the victim of a still unsolved murder in 1985. The
poem's dedicatee Jane Goodall conducted similar studies in Africa. (331)

'Kid' (Armitage). The *Batman* comic strip was created in 1939 by Bob Kane and
featured Bruce Wayne, the millionaire playboy who swore as a child that he would
avenge the murder of his parents by Gotham City hoodlums. As an adult he
disguised himself as Batman to become the nemesis of the underworld. Wayne
took as his ward a fellow orphan, Dick Grayson, who joined the Caped Crusader
in his mission against crime as Robin the Boy Wonder. The pair appeared in two
fifteen-part movie serials (*Batman*, 1943, impersonated by Lewis Wilson and
Douglas Croft; *Batman and Robin*, 1948, featuring Robert Lowery and John

Duncan), and in a tongue-in-cheek 1965 TV series starring Adam West and Burt Ward, who in 1966 also starred in the big-screen spin-off *Batman*. When Tim Burton came to make the 1989 *Batman* and its sequel *Batman Returns* (1992), starring Michael Keaton, he not only rejected the camp tone of the TV series but also (following some recent, deeply serious, *Batman* books) dispensed with Dick Grayson, whose relationship with Bruce Wayne had long been thought to have homoerotic undertones – a canard first popularized by the scourge of the horror comics, Dr Frederic Wertham, in his 1955 book *Seduction of the Innocent* ('It is like a wish dream of two homosexuals living together', he wrote). Hence the Boy Wonder's angry, Browningesque address in Simon Armitage's poem, responding to the publicity attendant upon the launch of the Tim Burton film. (333)

'The Monster Karloff' (Burns). Steven Soderbergh's film *Kafka* (1991) is set in post-World War One Prague with Jeremy Irons in the title role heading a cast that includes Alec Guinness, Armin Mueller-Stahl and Theresa Russell. In the 1932 horror classic, *The Mummy* (directed at Universal Studios by the great German cinematographer Karl Freund), Boris Karloff plays an Egyptian mummy who is restored to life after thousands of years in his tomb and takes on the identity of a Cairo archaeologist. Akira Kurosawa's *Ikiru* (1952) centres on an ageing civil servant working in a cluttered office in Tokyo who learns that he has terminal cancer. After going through a brief period of despair he dedicates the remainder of his life to cutting through bureaucratic red tape to create a children's playground in a rundown working-class area. (334)

'Hoppy' (Godsey). After a variety of jobs as itinerant labourer, William (Bill) Boyd (1895–1972) played in various Cecil B. DeMille movies of the 1920s. He came into his own as the heroic cowboy Hopalong Cassidy in a series of low-budget Westerns that began in 1935. In 1943 Boyd became his own producer and after the war sold his films to television and made a new series for the small screen, becoming one of the first Western stars of the new medium. (335)

'The Westerners' (Cotton). The Hays referred to in line 13 is not George 'Gabby' Hayes (1885–1969), the bearded, toothless comic sidekick or 'pardner' of endless heroes (William Boyd, Roy Rogers, John Wayne and Randolph Scott among them) in some 200 Westerns, but the jug-eared Indiana lawyer and Republican politician, Will H. Hays (1879–1954). Hays left President Warren Harding's cabinet in 1922 (he was Postmaster General) to become Hollywood's 'czar' and put the movie industry in order as head of the Motion Picture Producers and Distributors of America Inc. (MPPDA), a post he held until 1945. The highly detailed Motion Picture Production Code, a rigorous form of movie censorship, was introduced in 1930, strictly enforced from 1934 onwards, and not finally abandoned until President Johnson's former aide Jack Valenti became head of the MPAA (Motion Picture Association of America). It was known informally as the Hays Office Code. (337)

[381]

'*Paradise Lost*' (Munden). Oddly enough the British novelist and short story writer John Collier wrote a screen treatment of *Paradise Lost* that was never made (though it was later published), and in his essay 'A Poet at the Movies' (op. cit.) Richard Wilbur wrote: 'Knowing how far my mind's eye must have been conditioned by motion pictures, I venture with diffidence the opinion that certain pre-Edison poetry was genuinely cinematic. Whenever, for example, I read *Paradise Lost*, 1 44–58 (the long shot of Satan's fall from Heaven to Hell, the panorama of the rebels rolling in the lake of fire, the sudden close-up of Satan's afflicted eyes), I feel that I am experiencing a passage which, though its effects may have been suggested by the spatial surprises of Baroque architecture, is facilitated for me, and not misleadingly, by my familiarity with screen techniques.' (351)

'Cultural Exchange' (Masarik). Though from time to time oriental martial arts were featured in the cinema, the international craze for kung-fu and martial arts movies began in the 1970s owing to the brief but immense success of the San Francisco-born Bruce Lee (1941–73) in *Fist of Fury* and *Enter the Dragon*, produced in Hong Kong. (353)

'A New Reality is Better than a New Movie!' (Baraka). In the early 1970s there were two cycles of movies in America, Disaster (or Group Jeopardy) films (like *Earthquake* and *Towering Inferno*) and so-called Blaxploitation movies, such as the action movies starring black actor-director Fred Williamson (e.g. *The Legend of Nigger Charley*, 1972, and *Boss Nigger*, 1975). The 'mobutu' referred to in the poem is Joseph Mobutu, the African politician who became President of Zaïre in 1965 and its increasingly dictatorial ruler. He was implicated in the deposition and assassination of the socialist statesman Patrice Lumumba (1925–61), first prime minister of the Democratic Republic of the Congo (later Zaïre). (354)

'A Report from the Chairman' (Oakes). The evil Ming the Merciless, Emperor of the planet Mongo, was the principal enemy of Flash Gordon in the science-fiction comic strip created in 1934, the low-budget serials starring Buster Crabbe that it inspired in the 1930s and 40s, and the big-budget Dino De Laurentiis *Flash Gordon* (1980, director Mike Hodges) where Max von Sydow played Ming. In the 1974 soft-porn comedy *Flesh Gordon* the character became Emperor Wang. Linda Lovelace starred in *Deep Throat* and other hard-core pornographic movies of the 1970s. (358)

'Flower of *The Living Desert*' (Winter). In 1953 the Disney Studio began making the 'True Life Adventures', natural-history documentaries for the cinema using concealed camera and stop-motion photography. The first was the 72-minute *The Living Desert*, which was followed by, among others, *Prowlers of the Everglades* and *The Vanishing Prairie*. (365)

VII

Movies as Metaphor

The news-reel

Since Munich, what? A tangle of black film
Squirming like bait upon the floor of my mind
And scissors clicking daily. I am inclined
To pick these pictures now but will hold back
Till memory has elicited from this blind
Drama its threads of vision, the intrusions
Of value upon fact, that sudden unconfined
Wind of understanding that blew out
From people's hands and faces, undesigned
Evidence of design, that change of climate
Which did not last but happens often enough
To give us hope that fact is a façade
And that there is an organism behind
Its brittle littleness, a rhythm and a meaning,
Something half-conjectured and half-divined,
Something to give way to and so find.

Louis MacNeice

I Am Not a Camera

The photographable life is always either trivial or already sterilised.
Eugen Rosenstock-Huessy

To call our sight Vision
implies that, to us,
all objects are subjects.

What we have not named
or beheld as a symbol
escapes our notice.

We never look at two people
or one person twice
in the same way.

[385]

It is very rude to take close-ups and, except
when enraged, we don't:
lovers, approaching to kiss,
instinctively shut their eyes before their faces
can be reduced to
anatomical data.

Instructive it may be to peer through lenses:
each time we do, though, we should apologise
to the remote or the small for intruding
    upon their quiddities.

The camera records
visual facts: i.e.,
all may be fictions.

Flash-backs falsify the Past:
they forget
the remembering Present.

On the screen we can only
witness human behavior:
Choice is for camera-crews.

The camera may
do justice to laughter, but must
degrade sorrow.

W. H. Auden

I Am a Cameraman

They suffer, and I catch only the surface.
The rest is inexpressible, beyond
What can be recorded. You can't be them.
If they'd talk to you, you might guess
What pain is like though they might spit on you.

Film is just a reflection
Of the matchless despair of the century.
There have been twenty centuries since charity began.
Indignation is day-to-day stuff;
It keeps us off the streets, it keeps us watching.

Film has no words of its own.
It is a silent waste of things happening
Without us, when it is too late to help.
What of the dignity of those caught suffering?
It hurts me. I robbed them of privacy.

My young friends think Film will be all of Art.
It will be revolutionary proof.
Their films will not guess wrongly and will not lie.
They'll film what is happening behind barbed wire.
They'll always know the truth and be famous.

Politics softens everything.
Truth is known only to its victims.
All else is photographs – a documentary
The starving and the playboys perish in.
Life disguises itself with professionalism.

Life tells the biggest lies of all,
And draws wages from itself.
Truth is a landscape the saintly tribes live on,
And all the lenses of Japan and Germany
Wouldn't know how to focus on it.

Life flickers on the frame like beautiful hummingbirds.
That is the film that always comes out blank.
The painting the artist can't get shapes to fit.
The poem that shrugs off every word you try.
The music no one has ever heard.

Douglas Dunn

A Shooting Script

They are riding away from whatever might have been
Towards what will never be, in a held shot:
Teachers on bicycles, saluting native speakers,
Treading the nineteen-twenties like the future.

Still pedalling out at the end of the lens,
Not getting anywhere and not getting away.
Mix to fuchsia that 'follows the language.'
A long soundless sequence. Pan and fade.

Then voices over, in different Irishes,
Discussing translation jobs and rates per line;
Like nineteenth century milestones in grass verges,
Occurrence of names like R. M. Ballantyne.

A close-up on the cat's eye of a button
Pulling back wide to the cape of a soutane,
Biretta, Roman collar, Adam's apple.
Freeze his blank face. Let the credits run

And just when it looks as if it is all over –
Tracking shots of a long wave up a strand
That breaks towards the point of a stick writing and writing
Words in the old script in the running sand.

Seamus Heaney

Dream Song 363

I cast as feminine Miss Shirley Jones
as she was in *Oklahoma!* and for male
George C. Scott
as he was in *The Hustler:* off stage moans,
we begin with them in bed: if this relation should fail,
if it should not prove hot,

God bless our fate in the West & do me down
a potent Communist – as we all know,
the peoples in the East
have no sexual problems, have no problems
but housing & food & ideology:
all lesser problems ceased

when criminal attractive Lenin, bald,
went over the frontier in a sealed train

to take over the Revolution.
We know the issue of that, it has been told.
But the issue of Miss Jones & Mr Scott
comes at us, lovely & sane.

John Berryman

The death of John Berryman in slow motion

We open on a frozen river
(the spot where the poet has arranged to meet death).
The whiteness is blinding.
The glare hurts our eyes.

From somewhere above he jumps.
We see the shadow first
seeping into the ice
like a bruise. Thickening.

There is no sound but the wind
skulking beneath the bridge.

Now the body comes into shot.
Falling, blurred, a ragged bearskin.
The shadow opens its arms to greet it.

The wind is holding its breath.

We freeze frame at the moment of impact
(noting the look of surprise on the poet's face).
We then pan slowly upwards
to the grey Minnesota sky.

Fade to black.

Roger McGough*

One Picture is Worth a Thousand Words

Books have never been the same
since dinosaurs stopped popping up
from behind cardboard trees
and the lines of text, once found only
in the very top or bottom margin,
began to scamper all over the page.

Two moon-faces chortle
through the froth of their beer,
glued to a juicy page three.
(.)(.) News
is squeezed into the wings.

Don't underestimate a literate script.
One blockbuster's wordage grosses as much
as all those art-house flops
I could cite as *auteur*.
Personally, I don't even have a TV.
That? Oh, the VDU – receives only
my signals, nothing from the outside world.

Paul Munden*

Movie

Spotlight her face   her face has no light in it
touch the cheek with light   inform the eyes
press meanings on those lips.

               See cities from the air,
fix a cloud in the sky, one bird in the bright air,
one perfect mechanical flower in her hair.

Make your young men ride over the mesquite plains;
produce our country on film : here are the flaming shrubs,
the Negroes put up their hands in Hallelujahs,
the young men balance at the penthouse door.

We focus on the screen : look   they tell us
you are a nation of similar whores   remember the Maine
remember you have a democracy of champagne –

And slowly the female face kisses the young man,
over his face the twelve-foot female head
the yard-long mouth enlarges and yawns
                           The End

Here is a city   here the village grows
here are the rich men standing rows on rows,
but the crowd seeps behind the cowboy the lover the king,
past the constructed sets America rises
the bevelled classic doorways   the alleys of trees are witness
America rises in a wave a mass
pushing away the rot.

              The Director cries Cut!
hoarsely CUT   and the people send pistons of force
crashing against the CUT! CUT! of the straw men.

Light is superfluous upon these eyes,
across our minds push new portents of strength
destroying the sets, the flat faces, the mock skies.

                            Muriel Rukeyser

They Were All Like Geniuses

The lunchroom bus boy who looked like Orson Welles,
Romeo, Brutus, and a man from Mars in his two eyes,
the bellhop who was Joe Louis to the life,
the Greek fruit peddler who in church on Sundays
was a lightning-struck dead image of J. P. Morgan,
the Italian barber who in a mirror was more like
John Barrymore than Barrymore himself,
the Woolworth demonstration cold-cream girl
who was Garbo at a glance, only more real,
the shoe clerk who in midnight rain outside of Lindy's
should have been Clark Gable,

the Second Avenue ex-Baptist minister
who was born to have a face like Cordell Hull's –
why do they look at me like that,
why do they stare,
                    sleepwalking through my dreams?
What was the big mistake?

They looked like power and fame,
like love, like everything you need;
and you would think their looks would put them where
they could dictate a letter or run a bank
or kiss a microphone or float a yacht or sleep in
a genuine imitation Marie Antoinette bed
or get somewhere before they die
instead of dropping into dreams too deep
to tell themselves who, what, or where they are
until a fire turns them out into the street
or a shot is heard and the police are at the door.

                                        Horace Gregory

Poison Light

For J. Overstreet

Last night
I played Kirk Douglas to
Your Burt Lancaster. Reflecting
20 years of tough guys I
Saw at the Plaza Theatre in
Buffalo, New York. I can
Roll an L like Bogart
You swagger like Wayne

Ours was a bad performance
The audience, our friends
Panned it. The box office
Hocked the producers

We must stop behaving like
The poison light we grew on

Ancient loas are stranded
They want artfare home
Our friends watch us. They
Want to hear what we say

Let's face it
My eye has come a long way
So has your tongue
They belong on a pyramid wall
Not in a slum
(*Dead End*; 1937)

Ishmael Reed

Motion Picture Show

Can this, the world we see today, be real?
Oh, sleeper, turn and dream a dream more true
to faith in God's design and manhood's due
Than this shrill fever-fantasy of steel
With men too rushed to think, too massed to feel!
Could Life deprive so many, bless so few?
Our lives are but a shadowplay that you
Need never fear our wakening will heal.

And now when music drowns the slumland din,
Evolves a world not destitution-racked,
I know, while Something Greater looms and yearns,
The curtain that is consciousness grown thin,
The silver screen on which our passions act
The photoplays from which the Spirit learns.

Ralph Cheyney

The Legend of Gaucho

Gaucho had three brothers:

Harpo, the Silent One, who honked his horn like a taxi
or a goose, his favorite gesture

Chico, who was never one of us

and Zeppo, the beautiful, who died old.

Gaucho wore a short bolero and a wide flat hat
like Senora Stanwyck wears
in *El Big Valley*

his weapon was a thong with three iron balls
State, Church and Family, the Trinity
that Gaucho loved

so we get a witch as President
and a renegade doctor killed by the CIA

and we get a dope as President
and a film in which the renegade doctor

is played by Jack Palance
the CIA is played by itself

and the witch is played on Broadway
by Patty Lupone (*the wolf*)

and the wolf stalks the pampas
and Gaucho doesn't sleep

walk out through the pampa door
and all you see in all directions
is grass, Senor

the cattle here are scrawny

I'm a cow-muchacho and I tell you
it is tough, the meat
the border war

toughened up the young men
lean meat, meester
heat my beans in pampa dusk

At night there are three colors in the sky.

Overhead, it's black as mud.
In the west, a faint glow from the Christ
of the Andes

further west, the Andes and the stars.

I want to be a gaucho star.
I want to be the man with the bolero
and the fake moustache.

When Basil Rathbone as Sherlock Holmes
figured out that Dr Moriarty was about to steal
the crown jewels, a gaucho
was sent to murder Ida Lupino's brother
to throw the great detective off the scent.

The scent I like is on the pampas.
Damp grass, with a thousand miles
of air to breathe.

Here in the interior, the junta
is a thousand miles away.

I love a man in uniform. The uniform scent
of the pampas goes on for a thousand miles.

Tim Dlugos

The Cutting Room Floor

You had your life
shot on location

Now you lean back in the dark
humming softly and smiling

But where are the best shots?
the bone face that rose among trees
the fast river in the empty park
where snow fell, covering the baby
the President and his assistant
struggling in the swimming pool
the distant banjos on the soundtrack
that rabbit black against the sky
and the effigy, dancing alone
at night in the wet meadow . . .

Back there
on the cutting room floor

David Young

In the Cutting Room

Working together (this
late) & below us with its
carchases
its sirens & sex
symbols the real
city flickers.
The Ramrod all-male cinema
and the twentyfive cent peepshow girls.

Here mister moviola you share
your high strange place
of stacked flat cans & numbered
glistening strips like pegged
filmy stockings on a bathroom line
you are at work on them
in your small corner,
I in mine.

Chaste on Broadway, we moved
our privacy through the public streets.

The Brill elevator clanked us up through forty floors,
a water beetle big as a man's fist
scrabbling its corner.

You run it
over & over
forward back – one
dizzy whirr her scream shuts
& the woman in the white
night gown jerks herself backward
to the bed the nicely
glossed over
bad black sex.
Under the light of the
anglepoise I am
(beauty & the beast) at my business
of putting new twists
to old stories.

Working together & we seem
to love each other (but
that too is an old story)
yet not one of those fine few skills
(loops of language
spliced syllables of movement) we
have learned to curse but labour at
together   separate

No love is not a Steenbeck
a heart is not
an editing machine – we can cut
out nothing   ignore everything
except what we want to see.
Ribbon of dreams,
have we put together too much
from scanty footage?

                                        Liz Lochhead

Continuous Performance

The place seems strange, more strange than ever, and the times are still
    more out of joint;
Perhaps there has been some slight mistake?

It is like arriving at the movies late, as usual, just as the story ends:
There is a carnival on the screen. It is a village in springtime, that much is
    clear. But why has the heroine suddenly slapped his face? And what
    does it mean, the sequence with the limousine and the packed valise?
    Very strange.
Then love wins. Fine. And it is the end. OK.
But how do we reach that carnival again? And when will that springtime
    we saw return once more? How, and when?

Now, where a moment ago there was a village square, with trees and
    laughter, the story resumes itself in arctic regions among blinding
    snows. How can this be?
What began in the long and shining limousine seems closing now,
    fantastically, in a hansom cab.
The amorous business that ended with happiness forever after is starting
    all over again, this time with a curse and a pistol shot. It is not so
    good.

Nevertheless, though we know it all and cannot be fooled, though we
    know the end and nothing deceives us,
Nevertheless we shall stay and see what it meant, the mystery of the
    packed valise,
Why curses change at last to kisses and to laughter in a limousine (for this
    is fixed, believe me, fixed),
How simply and how swiftly arctic blizzards melt into blowing trees and a
    village fair.

And stay to see the Hydra's head cut off, and grown again, and incredibly
    multiplied,
And observe how Sisyphus fares when he has once more almost reached
    the top,
How Tantalus again will nearly eat and drink.
And learn how Alph the sacred river flows, in Xanadu, forever to a sunless
    sea,

How, from the robes of simple flesh, fate emerges from new and always
  more fantastic fate.

Until again we have the village scene. (And now we know the meaning of
  the packed valise)
And it is a carnival again. In spring.

                                        Kenneth Fearing

Movies, Left to Right

    The action runs left to right,
    Cavalry, the water-skiers –
    Then a five-hour film, *The Sleeper*,
    A man sleeping for five hours
    (In fifteen sequences),
    Sleeping left to right, left to right,
    Cavalry, a love scene, elephants.
    Also, the world goes left to right,
    The moon and all the stars – sex, too,
    And newspapers, catastrophe.

    In bed, my wives are to my left.
    I embrace them, moving left to right.
    I have lived my life that way,
    Growing older, moving eastward –
    The speedometer, the bank balance,
    Architecture, good music.
    'All that is most real moves left to right,'
    Declares my friend the scenarist,
    Puffing on a white cigar, eating
    The *Herald Tribune*, the *New Republic*.

    My life is a vision, a mechanism
    That runs from left to right. I have lived badly.
    Water-skier, I was until recently
    In the US Cavalry. Following that,
    I played elephant to a lead by Tarzan.
    Later, I appeared in a film called *The Sleeper*.

Till today, standing on the edge of things,
Falling and about to fall asking 'Why?,'
I look back. Nowhere. Meanwhile, one or more wives
Go on stilts for the mail.

                                        Robert Sward

Not Where We Came In

'This is not where we came in,
The story has all gone wrong.
Don't you remember, we saw
Terraces, vistas, marble urns,
Magnolias of human skin, a tall
Carved door, and that low superb
Smooth car? Between the two
The perfect girl was poised, to lead
With the scent of her physical pride
A millionaire playboy wolf
And a polished, lecherous duke.
It was what we had paid to see –
An epic of processed tripe.

'But the story has all gone wrong,
Her castle was pastry, her diamonds dew,
Her glossy hair is withered,
Her shoe-heels are abraded.
Just look at the girl, would you know her?
A refugee drab, she's lugging
A suitcase full of grudges
That nobody wants to buy.
Look at her now, she's pointing
Straight at us. She's armed. She's speaking.
"It's *you*, and *you*, and *you*
To blame. Take *that*! and *that*! and *that*!"
My God, she's real! I'm shot! It's blood!'

                                        William Plomer

If Life's a Lousy Picture, Why Not Leave
Before the End

Don't worry
One night we'll find that deserted kinema
The torches extinguished
The cornish ripples locked away in the safe
The tornoff tickets chucked
In the tornoff shotbin
the projectionist gone home to his nightmare

Don't worry
that film will still be running
(the one about the sunset)
& we'll find two horses
tethered in the front stalls
& we'll mount
& we'll ride off
         into
            our
               happy
                   ending

               Roger McGough

Fin

I know it's the end
I can see it coming. I'm
like those women in the cinema who make you mad
fumbling for gloves
elbowing themselves into coats, buttoning up –
such a final snapping shut of handbags
the minute it looks like it's all over
but a change of mood and music.
So you demand response, do you,
right to the bitter end, you like

to see the credits roll?
I'm off.

Liz Lochhead

Notes for a Movie Script

Fade in the sound of summer music,
Picture a hand plunging through her hair,
Next his socked feet and her scuffed dance slippers
Close, as they kiss on the rug-stripped stair.

Catch now the taxi from the station,
Capture her shoulders' sudden sag;
Switch to him silent in the barracks
While the room roars at the corporal's gag.

Let the drums dwindle in the distance,
Pile the green sea above the land;
While she prepares a single breakfast,
Reading the V mail in her hand.

Ride a cold moonbeam to the pillbox,
Sidle the camera to his feet
Sprawled just outside in the gummy grasses,
Swollen like nightmare and not neat.

Now doorbell nudges the lazy morning:
She stills the sweeper for a while,
Twitches her dress, swings the screendoor open,
Cut – with no music – on her smile.

Carl Holman

The Fallen Star

My tipsy shadow propels the walls from lamp
To lamp, the pavements crawl beneath my feet, turn
Corners, stop at kerbs, take manholes
In their stride, and go down steps.
Treading a revolving stage, through sets
Of plaster, paper, glass, a thing on legs, myself,
Spectacular, fantastic, pans down the mammoth street.

In this divingbell of dark, both viewer and performer,
I move my wall of glass, gigantic double feature, through
The cinemas of night, against a gale that bears the tides of men
In close-up companies away. Their faces, from the black
Projection-room of time, tracking towards me, jostle, chatter,
Laugh, vanish along the edges of the screen.
I am the locomotion camera they all look into,

Waving and smiling like a snappy newsreel, each
Wanting to stand out a moment from the crowd,
Hoping for a build-up in the longshot of a life,
And in the cutting-room of fate, that fabulous two-timer.
But the soundtrack is crazy, and I cannot synchronize
Their actions with the words they speak; wisecracks and crosstalk
Are maybe screams and wailings, each laugh a shriek.

When everyone appears to be a star
No one can ever be the star again.
My deadpan director has mislaid me in the crowd's
Vast human panorama, the passionate, colossal
Mob-scene of unparalleled, stupendous violence.
A cast of millions, a galaxy, all talking, singing, dancing,
Has swept my name, my make-up, and my script away.

Night my dressing-room becomes a cold
Hangar, high and lonely, open at both ends.
I would read my comfort in the stars,
Dear Dietrich, Bette Davis, Charlie Chaplin,
Harpo, Garbo, Marlon Brando,
And in these other faces read
The words we once believed

Were true, the lines we learned
To follow-up on any cue, fit any situation.
But I am always told
What I dared never tell myself
Till now, fired by new wine:
All men are brothers, but
Not all the time.

Put sentiment away, and cruelty.
Keep upright for a comeback.
Walk straight on the terrific, staggering sets,
Preserve the face your fans will recognize
When it is once more magnified upon the screens
Of love, sensational, tremendous, three-dimensional.
And tirelessly accept, consent, say yes to what is harder to deny,

Forgiveness for yourself, your fall, and for those others
In the stadium, the cinema, the streets, all who have seen
Things you have never seen, who drank
In the local, too, a universal wine.
These are your fellow-creatures: if they displease you,
Look into yourself again, and see if you are pleased.
Be good yourself: they will be better then.

James Kirkup

The Border

We arrive at *Gare du Nord* in a snowstorm.
You are from my future life.
Everything has the grain
of old movies – the great wheels,
the collapsible ladder
from the Pullman. Your face
is flecked and wavering.

You follow me to the bookstand
where shadowy things happen,
where spies know each other

by their magazines.
We both are looking for stories
to keep us occupied
on a long trip,
for the right person
to drop a ticket.

The clerk is suspicious
exchanging your currency:
When did your beard turn silver?
What was your name in Budapest?
I take down my hair in the bathroom.
Marble amplifies steps,
I'm afraid to look
over my shoulder.
It is you

you take my arm at the Exit.
The sun is lost,
gray monuments surround us,
we are mysteries
in our wintercoats.
We shift our luggage
to keep from bumping.

You are thinking
black Irish
those slate eyes
twinkling in this blizzard.
You feel years of flight
rush your breathing.
Do my ruffles mean
I'm wrong
for your persuasions?
You regret packing the boxers
your mother sent.

Even the tick from your valise
sounds ominous.
I search your eyes
for a man who squeezes
too hard coming

[405]

or a man who expects women
to unpack for him
confusing his heart
with a suitcase.
The cut of your boots
is fastidious. I regret
all I gained in Florence.

The future comes
from behind us,
from the tiny projection room
and its hidden microphones.
It drives a black roadster;
we can shake it.
Any minute, rounding a corner,

trading the exact color
of our eyes
facing sideways – *aujourd'hui*
at noon in Paris –
we will speed
toward the border.

Kita Shantiris

Lead Star Lovers

We met on the cutting room floor
Examining one
Another's rushes
Frame by frame we went over
Actions designed to tell stories,
We screened each other,
Without makeup or lights
We went through our lines,
No blue pencils for our out-takes,
We attended the premieres
Of our life stories,
Carefully edited out,

Were the eggs on our chins,
Bruises that taught in blood,
And all the unflattering camera angles.
Every profile, a close up,
Smooth moves from rags to riches,
With never a hair out of place,
Auditions before corpses,
Whose only intentions were
Resolved in darkrooms,
With amber lights burning
Not quite bright enough
To see the EXIT sign,
Pinned to the locked door
Trays of fixer tipped over
In the hungry rush.
By the enlarger light,
Film school taught us,
To only show,
What must go on.

Israel Halpern

Silent Movie

I look at our life together
as one watches a movie without sound.
I hear others laugh and weep
and I don't know why;
children say, 'Why did she do that, daddy?'
and there is no answer.

I fall from balconies —
sometimes you push me, I think —
but always land in a hay cart.
Men with strange eyes leave bombs
that look like croquet balls,
but just as I lift my mallet to hit them
you wave from a window, and I go in.

Will you love me forever?
How did we get into this scrape?
I lean forward and try to lipread,
making out a few syllables,
liking just about everything I see,
not quite understanding the whole.

David Kirby

The Good Guy

Darling, you're predictable
as Bonaparte for the canvas.
Count all the times you've leaned forward,
the same arrangement of elbow and knee,
jaw set half-smiling. It leaves me uneasy,
like dark that's too quiet
or a long spell of unbroken dishes.

Our album could illustrate a story.
Mt Lassen, Las Vegas, the family graveyard –
your pose recurs like the white hat
in a cowboy movie. It reduces our vacations
to backdrops that move behind the actor.

We judged the hero by his hat.
I've ceased to notice the moods
around your mouth and eyes,
whether the down on your body is backlit.
I see a posture repeating itself.

Looking at photos of you is like staring
at Gene Autry for a long time.
When I close my eyes I see your stance
gone black
just as his stetson would turn villainous.

No, you didn't gallop into these pictures.
I put you there to have something

to focus on in the foreground.
Mountains diminish without you for scale.

I was looking for the innuendos of weather:
wedges of dusk on your forehead,
raspberry stained fingers,
gestures of wind through your cowlick.

You could have quivered.
I have fast film and perfect resolution.
I have a book on *All The Photo Tricks* –
Distortion, Ghosts and Doubles, Lazy Shutter –
all I need is a natural.

Kita Shantiris

After Not Winning the Yale Poetry Prize

He files the form-letter under REJECTIONS, and thinks, 'So many talents
   exceed mine.'
He writes to thank the judge for his expertise. (Since thousands lose for
   every winner, anger outweighs gratitude thousands to one.)
He files his poems under TO REVISE, and thinks, 'One pencil-stroke can
   change my life!'

He reads the paper, learning who bought a four million dollar home, who
   won the Oscars, who ascended to the Hall of Fame.
He picks the phone up and makes cold calls until dinner: Swiss Steak,
   steaming in its microwave box.
His wife leaves for ceramics class; he gulps a shot of Scotch, and falls in
   bed, reminding himself that he's blessed simply to breathe,

To get up on the coldest morning and take out the trash, his arms and legs
   working perfectly.
He shuts his eyes and barely hears his window creak open, barely sees the
   forms which slip outside:
Frankenstein's monster, the Mummy, Wolf Man, King Kong, Dracula,
   Blacula, the Blob, Macarbie, the Birds, It,

The Triffids, She, Tarantula, Giant Squid and Octopi, Piranha, Sharks,
   Cat Woman, Crocodiles, the Fog, the Blood Beast,
The Pod People, Aliens, Medusa and the Minotaur, Freddy Krueger,
   Leatherface, Mr Hyde, the Hideous Sun Demon, Evil Dead,
The Creature from the Black Lagoon, Zombies, Rodan, the Phantom of
   the Opera, The Wicked Witch of the West, Godzilla,

Mothra, The Thing That Couldn't Die, every ghost in Hell House, every
   Fiend that Came From Beyond,
Crawling, lumbering, oozing, flapping, wriggling, writhing toward a
   certain New Haven address,
A certain judge's hand-carved, solid oak, already-smoldering door.

Charles Webb

Revenge of the Pleasure Seekers

would make a great name
for a cheap movie
& would probably gross
over a $1,000,000
by continuing to fray
the moral fabric of our
impressionable & well dressed
youth. The moral of this is
immoral & escapes me, now
like James Earl Ray.

Jeffrey Cyphers Wright*

Subtitle

We present for you this evening
A movie of death: observe
These scenes chipped celluloid
Reveals unsponsored and tax-free.

[410]

We request these things only:
All gum must be placed beneath the seats
Or swallowed quickly, all popcorn sacks
Must be left in the foyer. The doors
Will remain closed throughout
The performance. Kindly consult
Your programs: observe that
There are no exits. This is
A necessary precaution.

Look for no dialogue, or for the
Sound of any human voice: we have seen fit
To synchronize this play with
Squealings of pigs, slow sound of guns,
The sharp dead click
Of empty chocolatebar machines.
We say again: there are
No exits here, no guards to bribe,
No washroom windows.

No finis to the film unless
The ending is your own.
Turn off the lights, remind
The operator of his union card:
Sit forward, let the screen reveal
Your heritage, the logic of your destiny.

                         Weldon Kees

NOTES

'The death of John Berryman in slow motion' (McGough). John Berryman committed suicide on 7 January 1972 by jumping from a bridge in Minneapolis, where he was a Professor of English at the University of Minnesota. (389)

'One Picture is Worth a Thousand Words' (Munden). The third line of the second stanza refers to the topless girls featured on the third page of the British tabloid newspaper, the *Sun*. (390)

'Revenge of the Pleasure Seekers' (Wright). The civil rights leader Martin Luther King was assassinated on 4 April 1968 in Memphis, Tennessee by James Earl Ray. (410)

VIII

TV and the Afterlife of Movies

Stars in an Oldie

They are all dead. These are vestiges
Remaining a little while longer
Of their existence.

Those who were their lovers and mistresses,
Do they want to know about
Such poor travesties?

Voices and certain tricks of speech
Yes. Mannerisms beloved of many
Perhaps. But the character each

Is playing only spoils the memorable
Smile, adulterates the pure
Bogie or Gable.

Still – something's recorded of them
Though it may not comfort
Any who loved them.

These are the stars, who are assured
Of a re-run when the time is ripe.
But we don't repeat our show.

Only a few traces last.
Impressions left lying about.
Or at a wedding breakfast

On a home-movie. Or holiday slide –
All fixed enjoyment and bosom
And grinning sky.

But fading like the after-image on
Your retina. If anything does linger
That's God's pigeon.

Just what's been drawn to His attention.
Old drama re-enacted. Goodies and baddies
Raising up dead passion.

[415]

Is it merely casual cruelty
That those who see ghosts from armchairs
May suffer more fully

In the gratuitous and random habit
Of this famous world, so loved,
As they roll the credits?

Please do not repeat me yet.
Anyway not too loud or
Bang, bang, I shall be dead.

John Normanton

Old Movie Stars

'O where are you going?' said farer to fearer.
'To the latest movie of Norma Shearer?'

Who until some months ago
Dreamt each night of Clara Bow,
Laura La Plante, or Jean Harlow?

Mooned about all day
Because of Fifi d'Orsay?

Cared to rekindle the passionate love
Felt for Bessie Love
Or Billie Dove?

Say anything sweet
Or incomplete
Or indiscreet
About Blanche Sweet?

Argue, agree or disagree,
About Pola Negri?

Most people naturally saw more in
Lollobrigida and Sophia Loren;

Practically nobody seemed to care a
Blessed thing about Theda Bara;

Few indeed found it rewarding
To discuss Ann Harding.

One would have been thought decidedly cranky
To babble on about Vilma Banki,

Or rather odd
To launch into a heated appraisal of Nancy Kelly and Thelma Todd.

But now that TV's
Reviving them all with Helen Twelvetrees
And Marion Davies,

The old movie stars like Gilda Gray,
Alice Faye,
Fay Wray,
And Renée Adorée
Are no longer *passées*.

And so tonight, parading under Memory's star-encrusted marquee,
They return to me –

More dazzling now than they were when first they gazed from
a long-since-faded silver screen
At a boy of thirteen –

With ropes of pearls and ostrich plumes and beaded skirts, through
  Night's revolving door –
Lily Damita, Janet Gaynor, Lupe Velez, Dolores del Rio, Norma
  Talmadge, Edwina Booth, Anna Q. Nilsson,
  Colleen Moore.

                                        William Jay Smith

Grenadine

The movies, she told me
ruined my life.
we were sitting there
drinking bourbon and soda
flavored by grenadine.

I in the leather chair
that engulfed me
carrying me back,
on the television
a late movie
we weren't watching,
its noise took up our silences.
she was fat from all her drinking
and her eyes darted
unfocused about the room
her voice jumped from deep
to high laughter.
Really, she said,
no kidding, she said,
I mean that,
the movies, she said
curling her lip
and looking meanly
at George Sanders
on the TV.
'They,' she said
pointing and accusing
'tell you things about life
that aren't true.'
she sat staring a long time
trying to focus on my eyes.
'Hello, sweetie,' she said
and smiled at me
like a cockeyed hula dancer
from inside a ukelele.
She put her glass
embellished with splashes of
gold on the metal TV tray
her feet on the leather stool.
She had it fixed
so she never had to move.

'Your father,' she said
'he was a good man,
do you know why

we di-
vorced?'
'No,'
I stared at the
grenadine in my bourbon.
'Because of the movies,'
she said.
I blinked past her eyes
heaved in the leather chair
trying to upright myself
trying to refill my glass,
the television
busily selling cars,
my step-father snoring on
the couch
like a giant vacuum cleaner.
she laughed
a high-pitched laugh and tried
her very best
to stare right at me.
'We would go to the movies
your father and I.'
I nodded at her.
'And I'd come out
being Carole Lombard,
only he refused
to be Humphrey Bogart.'
We stared at each other
the television
sticking to the sides of our faces
George Sanders pretending to be
evil pretending to be good
being unmasked by
Rosalind Russell pretending
to be a lady reporter
pretending in real life
all she really wanted was
a home and family she said
to Ladies Home Journal reporter but

job of acting and stardom
thrust upon her
never found right man.

'All the myths,' my mother
said. 'I saw a movie'
about, about
they made me think, she said
running off with another man
would be African jungle
beautiful in dark green
Don Ameche canoeing to
palace in wilderness
speaking mad poetry
of love
absolute lusty
freedom of it all
glorious spirit of man
kissing
in white bow tie
and unconquerable
white orchid
maraschino cherry red lips
she said
they made it look so glamorous
drinking her grenadine bourbon
and fell asleep,
my step-father snoring
on the couch,
while the dog
whined outside the screen door
to be let in.

Susan Griffin

Mousemeal

My son invites me to witness with him
a children's program, a series of cartoons,
on television. Addressing myself to share
his harmless pleasures, I am horrified
by the unbridled violence and hostility
of the imagined world he takes in stride,
where human beings dressed in the skins of mice
are eaten by portcullises and cowcatchers,
digested through the winding corridors
of organs, overshoes, boa constrictors
and locomotive boilers, to be excreted
in waters where shark and squid and abalone
wait to employ their tentacles and jaws.
It seems there is no object in this world
unable to become a gullet with great lonely teeth;
sometimes a set of teeth all by itself
comes clacking over an endless plain
after the moving mouse; and though the mouse
wins in the end, the tail of one cartoon
is spliced into the mouth of the next, where his
rapid and trivial agony repeats itself
in another form. My son has seen these things
a number of times, and knows what to expect;
he does not seem disturbed or anything more
than mildly amused. Maybe these old cartoons
refer to my childhood and not to his
(The ogres in them wear Mussolini's face),
so that when mice are swallowed by skeletons
or empty suits of armor, when a tribe
of savage Negro mice is put through a wringer
and stacked flat in the cellar, he can take
the objective and critical view, while I
am shaken to see the giant picassoid
parents eating and voiding their little mice
time and again. And when the cheery announcer
cries, 'Well, kids, that's the end,' my son gets up
obediently and runs outside to play.

I hope he will ride over this world as well,
and that his crudest and most terrifying dreams
will not return with such wide publicity.

Howard Nemerov

Goodbye, Old Paint, I'm Leaving Cheyenne

From the television set come shots and cries,
a hollow drum of hooves and then,
emerging from snowy chaos, the tall riders
plunging in a tumultuous surf of dust.
The Stage, it seems, is overdue.
My children, armed to the teeth, enchanted,
are, for the moment at least, quiet.
I see the Badmen riding for the Gulch,
all grins, not knowing as we do
('The rest of you guys follow me!')
the Hero's going to get there first.
And as the plot like a lariat spins out
a tricky noose, I shrink and become
a boy with a sweaty nickel in his palm
waiting to see two features and the serial
at the Rialto on a Saturday morning:
Buck Jones, the taciturn, Tom Mix
of silver spinning guns and a white horse,
and somebody left face to face with a buzz saw,
to writhe into next Saturday morning.

But how you have changed, my cavaliers,
how much we have had to grow up!
No Hero now is anything but cautious.
(We know the hole a .45 can make.)
No Badman's born that way.
('My mother loved me but she died.')
No buzz saw frightens like the whine
of a mind gone wild. No writhing's like
the spirit's on its bed of nails.

[422]

I clench my nickel tighter in my fist.
Children, this plot is new to me.
I watch the Hero take the wrong road
at the Fork and gallop away, grim-faced,
worn out from the exercise of choice.
I see the Badmen safely reach the Gulch,
then fight among themselves and die,
proving good luck is worse than any wound.
My spellbound children stare and couldn't care
less about my fit of raw nostalgia
or all the shabby ghosts I loved and lost.

George Garrett

Cowboys

The science-fiction movie on the telly in which the world, threatened by
   aliens with destruction,
is, as always, saved is really just a Western with rays and jets instead of
   pistols and horses.
The heroes crouch behind computers instead of rocks, but still mow down
   the endlessly expendable villains
who fire back but somehow always miss the stars, except one, the extra-
   lovable second lead,
nice guy, funny, a little too libidinal, who you know from minute one will
   teach us to die,
in his buddy's arms, stoical, never losing sight of our side's virtues:
   community and self-denial.
On the other channel, Pompeii: Christians, pagans, same story, them and
   us, another holy mission,
the actors resonating with deep conviction, voices of manly sanctity, like
   Reagan on the news.

C. K. Williams

Movies on TV: 1982

Watching old movies in the afternoon,
The light fades from the western winter sky;
Leaves all as grey and sable as the screen;
Girls prettier even than in memory.

Into the gloaming sometimes comes a shade,
The name remembered though the face forgot.
Today it's Lucille Bremer who has made
Time reappear with chiselled features, not

A scythe. I look her up in Halliwell –
Dancer, for stardom groomed by MGM;
The later Forties was her epoch. Hell!
I think: myself was not yet forty then.

'Retired', says the manual. How can that be?
Still thawing hearts of iced consistency.

Roy Fuller*

The Man Who Knew Too Much

I've finished with the listlessness
of snow on pine boughs, or the page's invitations,
also snow. That's why this morning
the pines shake it off in gusts,
why I'm tired of the ways we look at ourselves.
From the window I watch you
throwing pinecones for the dogs,
resin on your glove, their breath that rises
like the drastic lights of a winter city
and illustrates nothing. Before,
I thought our lives, these mornings,
could all be ennobling and abstract,
but the sky has whitened for days;
there are more than six sides to every question.

Last night you brushed your hair
a hundred strokes in the TV's light
that flickered thirties movies until dawn:
Hitchcock's *The Man Who Knew Too Much*,
who saved himself through irony
and fear. All these mazes of plot –
I can't let them go, as after those nights
we'd argue for hours, finally seeing
we'd come to nothing. We lived in a neighborhood
of blacks and Chicanos and I'd walk away
to the Mexican movies, though I'd lost
my Spanish years before. This is the way
it always seemed – someone talks and you know
you won't understand. The *hombre* puts a pleasant
on the kitchen table. The *mujer* begins to weep.
Abstract movement, where some feeling is trapped,
like the *hombre* frowning at a steamed-up mirror.
He cleans it and forgets what he was thinking.
And I'm leaving my seat, weary
of the dialogue, tired enough for home.

David Wojahn*

Big Sue and *Now Voyager*

Her face is a perfect miniature on wide, smooth flesh,
a tiny fossil in a slab of stone. Most evenings
Big Sue is Bette Davis. Alone. The curtains drawn.
The TV set an empty head which has the same
recurring dream. Mushrooms taste of kisses. Sherry trifle
is a honeymoon. *Be honest. Who'd love me?*

Paul Henreid. He lights two cigarettes and, gently,
puts one in her mouth. The little flat in Tooting
is a floating ship. Violins. Big Sue drawing deeply
on a chocolate stick. *Now Voyager depart. Much,
much for thee is yet in store.* Her eyes are wider,
bright. The previous video unspools the sea.

This is where she lives, the wrong side of the glass
in black-and-white. To press the rewind,
replay, is to know perfection. Certainty. The soundtrack
drowns out daytime echoes. *Size of her. Great cow.*
Love is never distanced into memory, persists
Unchanged. Oscar-winners looking at the sky.

Why wish for the moon? Outside the window night falls,
slender women rush to meet their dates. Men whistle
on the dark blue streets at shapes they want
or, in the pubs, light cigarettes for two. Big Sue
unwraps a Mars Bar, crying at her favourite scene.
The bit where Bette Davis says *We have the stars.*

Carol Ann Duffy*

Dependants

These specks of metal on my hands: gold dust,
or the lead we accumulate that kills us?
I have put off your visit this week, and watch
the late movie on TV, alone with my regrets . . .

The searchlight is a romantic theatre moon.
It makes the rounds of the prison, bathes it
in a blue glow, then swivels off across the bay . . .
The inmates wear denim and sleep six to a room.

They share a girl on a calendar, her pout
a vague ecstasy that recalls a wife or girlfriend
to each of them. In their interminable nights,
they climb the moonbeams and cross to the mainland

of their memories, the love that led them astray
with its dreams of mediocrity and comfort.
Her upturned face, framed by expensive furs . . .
Now they meet once a month, through a grille.

The initiative is with those on the outside:
a wife's assurances; a lawyer come to say
that divorce proceedings are being instituted;
the file slipped into a home-made birthday cake.

Michael Hofmann*

Late Movies with Skyler

All week since he's been home
he has watched late movies alone
terrible one star films and then staggering
through the dark house to his bed
waking at noon to work on the broken car
he has come home to fix.

21 years old and restless
back from logging on Vancouver Island
with men who get rid of crabs with Raid
        *2 minutes bending over in agony
        and then into the showers!*

Last night I joined him for *The Prisoner of Zenda*
a film I saw three times in my youth
and which no doubt influenced me morally.
Hot coffee bananas and cheese
we are ready at 11.30 for adventure.

At each commercial Sky
breaks into midnight guitar practice
head down playing loud and intensely
till the movie comes on and the music suddenly stops.
Skyler's favourite hours when he's usually alone
cooking huge meals of anything in the frying pan
thumbing through *Advanced Guitar* like a bible.
We talk during the film
and break into privacy during commercials
or get more coffee or push
the screen door open and urinate under the trees.

[427]

Laughing at the dilemmas of 1920 heroes
suggestive lines, cutaways to court officials
who raise their eyebrows at least 4 inches
when the lovers kiss . . .
only the anarchy of the evil Rupert of Hentzau
is appreciated.
                            And still somehow
by 1.30 we are moved
as Stewart Granger girl-less and countryless
rides into the sunset with his morals and his horse.
The perfect world is over. Banana peels
orange peels ashtrays guitar books.
2 a.m. We stagger through
into the slow black rooms of the house.

I lie in bed fully awake. The darkness
breathes to the pace of a dog's snoring.
The film is replayed to sounds
of an intricate blues guitar.
Skyler is Rupert then the hero.
He will leave in a couple of days
for Montreal or the Maritimes.
In the movies of my childhood the heroes
after skilled swordplay and moral victories
leave with absolutely nothing
to do for the rest of their lives.

                                    Michael Ondaatje

Sky Diving

'It's a good way to live and
A good way to die'
From a Frankenheimer video about
Sky diving
The hero telling why he liked to

        The following noon he leaped
        But his parachute wasn't with him

He spread out on the field like
Scrambled eggs

Life is not always
Hi-lifing inside
Archibald Motley's
'Chicken Shack'
You in your derby
Your honey in her beret
Styling before a small vintage
Car

Like too many of us
I am a man who never had much
Use for a real father
And so when I'm heading
For a crash
No one will catch me but
Me

The year is only five days old
Already a comet has glittered out
Its glow sandbagged by
The jealous sun

Happens to the best of us
Our brilliance falling off
Like hair from Berkeley's roving
Dogs

Even on Rose Bowl day
An otherwise joyous occasion
A float veered into the crowd
Somebody got bruised over the incident
Like a love affair on second ave.

It's a good lesson to us all
In these downhill days of a
Hard-hearted decade
Jetting through the world
Our tails on fire

You can't always count
On things opening up for you
Know when to let go
Learn how to fall

Ishmael Reed*

The Godfather Returns to Color TV

The lit night glares like a day-glo strawberry,
the stakeout car beside the hydrant is full of feds,
and the ikon of our secret hero(ine?), atop the
feckless funnypaper mesa we try to live in, is that
poor dumb indestructible super-loser Krazy Kat.

O Innocence, spoiled Guinea Brat! – after whose
fits of smashing and screaming, O Holy Mother,
All-American Girl, I need you, I want
to protect you: after that one sunstruck
glimpse, on a Sicilian mountainside,

of virgin stupidity, its sensual lockbox
so charged with possibilities of being
that we too tremble at the thought of nakedness,
of marriage, we too burn to build a shrine for,
raise armies to protect a property that history

godfathered dumb. I told you: DON'T ASK
QUESTIONS ABOUT MY BUSINESS! While the old
bull in a new world, who's lost respect,
too-big pants bunched underneath the belly, stumbles
expiring past the staked tomato vines,

and the grandchild thinks for a minute he's
only playing, we *know* he is, admiring
Marlon Brando in a show of weakness. But the blood
isn't all ketchup, or the weekend all football, nor
do all commodities survive in lighted shrines.

Amy Clampitt*

The End of The Late Show, Channel 7

He comes up at us
up the steel rungs, the hand rails
onto the roof,
Looks around him.

Raises himself
large torsoed, muscular – Jack Palance or Mitchum.
Now the expected chase over the warehouse.

But tonight he is masked
by an idiot face of rubber – dreams on dreams.
Below him police like archers
poise behind their speakers and screaming whistles
as spotlights open
a sweeping arc through fog.

Like a swimmer onto the concrete side of a pool
he pulls up
here
onto this roof
for a minute.
His damaged eyes flash out: 'Where is she?'

Careening, runs at us.

I dream they have inserted footage
from an older movie
where shots ring out
and we are still falling.

Valery Nash

Television-Movie

The monster is loose.
This is an emergency area.
Leave your homes.

There is no time
to gather your belongings.
The highways are jammed,
the trains, derailed.
The planes have crashed
and the bridges are collapsing.
There is no escape.

Aunt Harriet has fallen down,
trying to escape.
The baby is hysterical.
The radio's broken.
The neighbors are gone.
Susie forgot her doll.
I can't find the insurance papers.
The monster has knocked over
the Tower of London.
The Empire State Building
is breaking in half.
Everyone is drowning
in Times Square.

In Tokyo
all the poor people
have fallen into a crevasse
which is now closing up,
even on United States citizens.
The ship's piano is rolling
across the ballroom floor.
The cargo is crushing the coolies.
The Army is out of ammunition.
The President has declared
a national state of affairs.
The almanacs were wrong.
The computers were in error.
Where will it all end?

The baby has stopped crying.
You hold her now; I'm tired.
Aunt Harriet wants to stay
one more week.

I can't say no. You tell her.
The radio repairman will come for sure
— if he can make it.
The neighbors said it's too loud.
Fix Susie's doll: the squeak's gone.
The insurance papers
are in the bottom left-hand drawer
right where you put them.
If they're not there,
keep looking.
Will you get paid tomorrow?
Did you mail my letter?
Did you set the alarm?

The monster is dead.
He is never coming back.
And if he does come,
someone will kill it.
And we will go on
just like always.
There is no escape.

Kirby Congdon

Watching War Movies

Always the same: watching
World War II movies on TV,
landing barges bursting onto

islands, my skin crawls —
heat, dust — the scorpion
bites again. How I deceived

myself. Certain my role would
not make me killer, my unarmed
body called down fire from

scarred hills. As life took
life, blood coursed into
one stream. I knew one day,

the madness stopped, I'd make
my pilgrimage to temples,
gardens, serene masters of

a Way which pain was bonding.
Atoms fuse, a mushroom cloud,
the movie ends. But I still

stumble under camouflage, near
books of tranquil Buddhas by the
screen. The war goes on and on.

Lucien Stryk

A Contemporary Film of Lancasters in Action

To see them bombing up
and wheeling off into the dusk,
nose to tail, queueing, turning for the take-off,
like long-jumpers each one coming up
stationary
before they begin the run before the jump,
piloted by volunteer bank clerks.
Is my emotion bogus or inflationary?

I was never a hero,
the shark's tooth, boar's tusk,
seeming less frightening than this kind of flying,
for all kinds of courage rated zero,
admiringly
I admit they did what I could never,
sleepwalkers showing a sleepless courage –
long flights to firework climax, untiringly.

Obstinate, I survive
and, writing in this summer musk,

I say they were the patient venturing lions
And I the mean dog that stayed alive;
we owe them
every valedictory mark of respect
(bravery's facing such boring dangers)
that we can possibly, too late, show them.

Gavin Ewart

Still

I watch you mouthing angry words like somebody
in water behind glass, noting how your faults,
most of all, are magnified in close-up.
Your skin ripples loose along your cheek-bones
as if you were about to shrug it off.
On my side, I no longer try to emulate
that underwater swimmer in the fifties film,
smiling, open-mouthed, as she approached
her technicolor lover and embraced him,
entangling arms and legs with his
and neither of them struggling to escape.
They seemed perfectly at home in a fish-tank
as in a fairy-tale, the water striped
with sunlight and her hair spun out like silk.
Even in the stills tonight, although they are
no longer larger-than-life, having shrunk to fit
the TV screen, and even though they both died
in between, their smiles are still as smooth as celluloid.
Watching them together, I could almost believe
that in order to stay happy-ever-after
we also should have learnt how not to breathe.

Sylvia Kantaris

Late Late Show

Movies, the Old Law. TV is the New
Wherein the dead who did our phantasies
Have stolen back into the living room
To do their thing again. Boxed in the bad
Resurrections of Hell, in a seamy air
And silver drizzle of shifting shape and shade,
Witnessed without terror and without pity,
Eternal return unrolls itself anew.

The stars and the members of unremembered casts
Are spared the selfish indifference of the selves
Kept up past bedtime by their early lives
Become our late ones, moving in a light
So swiftly scanning it can keep them up
As long as the old show stays on the road,
Addressing its advertisements for life
To us the living, while even their dead die.

Howard Nemerov

The Midnight Movie

Garland dances, Peck and Heston fight
To a draw in a moon-washed meadow.
Late night movies pit
Our substance against their shadow.

The heroes have not changed. Bogart still wears
His trench coat, Dooley Wilson plays
As Time Goes By. Their spent years
Go more slowly than our days.

Between us and them
There's no closing up; the distance is
The same before and after the programme.
We never meet face to face.

It's just as well. Those lovers kissing now
Lie deep in Forest Lawn, their profiles
Mangier than twenty years ago
When we admired them from the stalls.

The television set is haunted:
Not by the tenants, but the hosts.
We turn the reels of what we wanted,
Watched by our own ghosts.

Philip Oakes*

Future Shock

Eight hundred lifetimes, fifty thousand years:
In the eight hundredth lifetime greater change
Than all the others put together; hence
What Alvin Toffler christened 'future shock',

Which I've no lifetime left to have to bear.
Not that surprises don't still sometimes come,
Usually in art, and even agreeable.
I'm glad they keep repeating on TV

Jacqueline Bisset eating a single Shreddie,
Clad only in pyjama-top. And now
The hard-up Channel 4 brings back an age
When I myself faced the outstretched unknown –

Subtitle in *Riders of the Purple Sage*
That cried: 'I love you, Lassiter. Roll the stone.'

Roy Fuller*

Endings

Setting the VCR when we go to bed
to record a night owl movie, some charmer we missed,
we always allow, for unprogrammed unforeseen,
an extra half hour. (Night gods of the small screen
are ruthless with watchers trapped in their piety.)
We watch next evening, and having slowly found
the start of the film, meet the minors and leads,
enter their time and place, their wills and needs,
hear in our chests the click of empathy's padlock,
watch the forces gather, unyielding world
against the unyielding heart, one longing's minefield
laid for another longing, which may yield.
Tears will salt the leftover salad I seize
during ads, or laughter slow my hurry to pee.
But as clot melts toward clearness a black fate
may fall on the screen; the movie started too late.
Torn from the backward-shining of an end
that lights up the meaning of the whole work,
disabled in mind and feeling, I flail and shout,
'I can't bear it! I *have* to see how it comes out!'
For what is story if not relief from the pain
of the inconclusive, from dread of the meaningless?
Minds in their silent blast-offs search through space
– how often I've followed yours! – for a resting-place.
And I'll follow, past each universe in its spangled
ballgown who waits for the slow-dance of life to start,
past vacancies of darkness whose vainglory
is endless as death's, to find the end of the story.

Mona Van Duyn

NOTES

'Movies on TV: 1982' (Fuller). Born 1923 in Amsterdam, New York, Lucille Bremer enjoyed a brief Hollywood career in the 1940s, her best-known role being as the eldest daughter in the Vincente Minnelli musical, *Meet Me In St Louis*. The book consulted by Fuller is *Halliwell's Filmgoer's Companion*, first published in 1965 as *The Filmgoer's Companion* by Leslie Halliwell (1929–1989) and regularly updated. (424)

'*The Man Who Knew Too Much*' (Wojahn). *The Man Who Knew Too Much* (1934) established Alfred Hitchcock's mastery of the thriller. He remade it in Hollywood in 1956 with James Stewart and Doris Day in the roles created by Leslie Banks and Edna Best. (424)

'Big Sue and *Now Voyager*' (Duffy). In the archetypal Warner Brothers women's movie, *Now Voyager* (1942, director Irving Rapper), dull spinster Bette Davis is advised by her shrink Claude Rains to try a cruise and has a doomed affair with fellow passenger Paul Henreid. Henreid's special skill lay in lighting two cigarettes at the same time, and Davis famously said: 'O Jerry, don't let's ask for the moon. We have the stars.' (425)

'Dependants' (Hofmann). Directed by Jules Dassin from a script by Richard Brooks, *Brute Force* 1947 is a classic *film noir*, one of the last great 'big house' movies. The six convicts sharing a cell and experiencing flashbacks to what put them inside are Burt Lancaster, John Hoyt, Howard Duff, Jack Overman, Whit Bissell and Jeff Corey. Lancaster leads a revolt against a sadistic warder played by Hume Cronyn. (426)

'Sky Diving' (Reed). In John Frankenheimer's *The Gypsy Moths* (1969), Burt Lancaster, Gene Hackman and Scott Wilson play a trio of itinerant stunt parachutists jumping out of bi-planes to entertain rural audiences in the middle west during the 1930s. (428)

'*The Godfather* Returns to Color TV' (Clampitt). *The Godfather* (1972) is the first film in a trilogy directed by Francis Ford Coppola about the Corleone family gangster dynasty founded in New York by the Sicilian immigrant Don Corleone (Marlon Brando). (430)

'The Midnight Movie' (Oakes). The moonlit fight between Gregory Peck as the peace-loving sea-captain, engaged to the rancher's daughter, and Charlton Heston as the jealous chief ranch-hand takes place in the William Wyler Western *The Big Country* (1958). Forest Lawn, referred to here and in other poems, is of course the celebrated Los Angeles cemetery where many movie people are buried. (436)

'Future Shock' (Fuller). Jacqueline Bisset took her breakfast in a pyjama top as Steve McQueen's girlfriend in *Bullitt* (1968, director Peter Yates). Zane Grey's novel *Riders of the Purple Sage* was filmed in 1918 starring William Farnum, in 1925 featuring Tom Mix, and as a sound movie in 1931 with George O'Brien. (437)

ACKNOWLEDGEMENTS

For permission to reprint copyright material the publishers gratefully acknowledge the following:

Sheil Land Associates Ltd for 'A night out' from *A Small Desperation* by Dannie Abse, published by Hutchinson & Co. 1968, Copyright © 1968 by Dannie Abse; Hirt Music Inc. for 'Miss Scarlett, Mr Rhett and Other Latter-Day Saints' from *Just Give Me a Cool Drink of Water 'fore I Diiie* by Maya Angelou; Faber & Faber Ltd for 'Kid' from *Kid* by Simon Armitage; Georges Borchardt Inc. and Carcanet Press Ltd for 'Daffy Duck in Hollywood' from *Houseboat Days* and *Selected Poems* by John Ashbery, Viking Penguin and Carcanet Press Ltd for 'Forties Flick' from *Self-Portrait in a Convex Mirror* and *Selected Poems* by John Ashbery, Copyright © 1974 by John Ashbery, Alfred A. Knopf, Inc. and Carcanet Press Ltd for 'The Phantom Agents' from *Hotel Lautréamont* by John Ashbery, Copyright © 1992 by John Ashbery; Curtis Brown & John Farquharson for 'Werewolf Movies' from *Poems 1976–1986* by Margaret Atwood, published by Virago Press in 1992, Houghton Mifflin Company and Oxford University Press Canada for 'Werewolf Movies' from *Selected Poems II: Poems Selected & New 1976–1986* by Margaret Atwood, Copyright © 1986 by Margaret Atwood; Faber & Faber Ltd for 'I Am Not A Camera' from *Epistle to a Godson* by W. H. Auden, and Random House Inc. for 'I Am Not a Camera' from *W. H. Auden: Collected Poems*, ed. by Edward Mendelson, Copyright © 1972 by W. H. Auden; Sterling Lord Literistic, Inc. for 'Jim Brown on the Screen' and 'A New Reality is Better than a New Movie!' from *Hard Facts* by Amiri Baraka, Copyright © 1975 by Amiri Baraka; Barbara Watson for 'First News Reel: September 1939' from *A House under Old Sarum* by Joan Barton; the author and University of Chicago Press for 'Soundstage' from *The Enemy Joy* by Ben Belitt, Copyright © 1964 by Ben Belitt; Bloodaxe Books Ltd for 'Ode to Groucho' and 'To Celebrate Eddie Cantor' from *Marvin Bell: Complete Poems*; the author and Spoon River Press for 'Bogey' from *Seems* by Lee Berkson and 'marilyn' from *Away from Home* by Lee Berkson; Farrar, Straus & Giroux, Inc. and Faber & Faber Ltd for 'Dream Song #7', 'Dream Song #9', 'Dream Song #222', 'Dream Song #363' from *The Dream Songs* by John Berryman, Copyright © 1969 by John Berryman; *The New Yorker* for 'To Mr Mack Sennett, on his Animated Pictures' by Maurice Bishop, Copyright © 1949 by The New Yorker Magazine, Inc.; Dodd, Mead and Company for 'Hollywood and Vine' and 'The Faceless One' by Don Blanding from *Mostly California*, 1948; Kenneth Rosen for 'The Flicker' and 'Reservation Special' by Lew Blockcolski from *Voices of the Rainbow: Contemporary Poetry by American Indians*, Seaver Books 1975, Copyright © by Kenneth Rosen;

ACKNOWLEDGEMENTS

William Heinemann Ltd and Dutton, New American Library, Penguin Books USA Inc. for 'Film Epic' from *The Man Behind You* by Carl Bode, Copyright © 1959, 1960, renewed © 1987 by Carl Bode; *Punch* magazine for 'On British Films' by John Basil Boothroyd; the author for 'Stumptown Attends the Picture Show' from *Shooting Rats at the Bibb County Dump* by David Bottoms, published by William Morrow 1980; Princeton University Press for 'In Defense of Poetry' from *For Louis Pasteur* by Edgar Bowers, Copyright © 1989 by Princeton University Press; the author and Carcanet Press Limited for 'Turkish Delight' from *Sleeping Rough* by Charles Boyle, Copyright © 1987 by Charles Boyle; The Helen Brann Agency for 'Mrs Myrtle Tate, Movie Projectionist' from *Rommel Drives On Deep into Egypt* and 'The Sidney Greenstreet Blues' from *The Pill Versus the Springhill Mine Disaster* by Richard Brautigan, Copyright © 1989 by Richard Brautigan; *Punch* magazine for 'Sunday Observance' from *Punch*, 11 January 1956, by Anthony Brode, Copyright © 1956 by *Punch* magazine; Mrs Harry Brown for 'This is Merely Part of the Studio Tour' and 'Travel Film in Technicolor' by Harry Brown, published by Martin Secker & Warburg Ltd, London 1948; Rosica Colin Ltd for 'Ode to Felix' from *Alan Brownjohn: Collected Poems*, published by Hutchinson & Co., Copyright © 1988 by Alan Brownjohn; Temblor Books and the author for 'Double Sonnet for Mickey' and 'Monster Karloff' by Gerald Burns; the author for 'Ode to Fellini' from *Odes* by Paul Carroll, published by Big Table Publishing, 1969; University Press of New England for 'Grace at the Atlanta Fox', 'A Descent from San Simeon', 'A Song in Subtitles' from *Watchboy, What of the Night?* by Turner Cassity, Copyright © 1966 by Turner Cassity; Lousiana State University Press for 'Skin Flick' from *The World Between the Eyes* by Fred Chappell, Copyright © 1963, 1964, 1966, 1969, 1970, 1971 by Fred Chappell, and for 'Caligari by Dreamlight' from *First and Last Words* by Fred Chappell, Copyright © 1989 by Fred Chappell; the author for 'John Garfield' from *On Tour With Rita* and 'Reflections on a Bowl of Kumquats' from *A Short History of the Island of Butterflies* by Nicholas Christopher; Faber & Faber Ltd and Alfred A. Knopf, Inc. for '*The Godfather Returns to Color TV*' from *What the Light was Like* by Amy Clampitt, Copyright © 1985 by Amy Clampitt; the author for 'Final Farewell' by Tom Clark; BOA Editions, Ltd. for 'Come Home From the Movies' from *Good Woman: Poems and a Memoir, 1969–1980* by Lucille Clifton, Copyright © 1987 by Lucille Clifton; the author for 'Television-Movie' by Kirby Congdon from *Juggernaut*, published by Interim Books in 1966; the author for 'Dédée d'Anvers' and 'Film Revival: Tales of Hoffman' from *New and Collected Poems* by Robert Conquest, Copyright © 1988 by Robert Conquest; the author for 'Eddie's at the Movies Again', 'Old Movies' and 'The Westerners' from *Old Movies*, 'Leicester Square 1974' and 'The Movie Beauties' from *Oh Those Happy Feet*, and 'Casablanca' from *Here's Looking At You, Kid* by John Cotton; the author and Chatto & Windus Ltd, for 'Talkies' from *Talkies* by Robert Crawford, Copyright © 1992 by Robert Crawford; Marion Boyars Ltd and New Directions Publishing Corp.

for 'Bresson's Movies' from *Windows* by Robert Creeley, Copyright © 1990 by Robert Creeley; Michael Cudlipp for 'Chicks at the Flicks' and 'Patriotism' from *Bouverie Ballads* by Percy Cudlipp (Eyre & Spottiswoode 1955); MacGibbon & Kee and Liveright Publishing Corporation for 'death is more than' from *The Complete Poems 1913–62* by e. e. cummings and from *IS 5 poems* by e. e. cummings, edited by George James Firmage, Copyright © 1985 by e. e. cummings Trust, Copyright © 1926 by Horace Liveright, Copyright © 1954 by E. E. Cummings, Copyright © 1985 by George James Firmage; Sinclair-Stevenson Ltd for 'Newsreel' from *The Complete Poems of C. Day Lewis*; Writers' Guild of America, West, Inc. for 'Hollywood Jabberwocky' by I. A. L. Diamond, originally published in *The Screenwriter*; the author and The University of North Carolina Press for 'Bela Lugosi: Three Lines', 'The Day I Stopped Dreaming About Barbara Steele' and 'Inside Sally' from *The Day I Stopped Dreaming About Barbara Steele and Other Poems* by R. H. W. Dillard; *The New Yorker* for 'What You Have Come to Expect' by Stephen Dobyns, Copyright © 1980 by Stephen Dobyns (this poem originally appeared in *The New Yorker*); Anvil Press Poetry for 'The B Movie' from *Standing Female Nude* by Carol Ann Duffy and for 'Big Sue and *Now Voyager*' from *Selling Manhattan* by Carol Ann Duffy; Laurence Pollinger Limited and New Directions Publishing Corporation for 'Ingmar Bergman's *Seventh Seal*' from *The Opening of the Field* by Robert Duncan, Copyright © 1960 by Robert Duncan; the author and Faber & Faber Ltd for 'Valerio' and 'La Route' from *St Kilda's Parliament* by Douglas Dunn, Copyright © 1981 by Douglas Dunn, and for 'I Am a Cameraman' from *Love or Nothing* by Douglas Dunn, Copyright © 1974 by Douglas Dunn (this poem originally appeared in *The New Yorker*); 'Midweek Matinée' from *The Happier Life* by Douglas Dunn, Copyright © 1972 by Douglas Dunn; the author for 'Moving Pictures' by Alistair Elliot; the author for 'Shirley Temple Surrounded by Lions' by Kenward Elmslie from *Penguin Modern Poets 24*; Chatto & Windus, for 'A Grand Night' and 'The Pictures' from *The Terrible Shears* by D. J. Enright, Copyright © 1973 by D. J. Enright; Henry Holt and Company, Inc. for 'Dear John Wayne' from *Jacklight* by Louise Erdrich, Copyright © 1984 by Louise Erdrich; Hutchinson & Co., UK Ltd, for 'A Contemporary Film of Lancasters in Action' from *The New Ewart 1980–1982* by Gavin Ewart; Russell & Volkening, Inc. and Harcourt, Brace & Co. for 'Continuous Performance' from *Afternoon of a Pawnbroker* by Kenneth Fearing and 'Mrs Fanchier at the Movies' from *Stranger at Coney Island* by Kenneth Fearing, Copyright © 1944 by Kenneth Fearing, renewed 1971, 1972 by Kenneth Fearing; Indiana University Press for 'St. Agnes' Eve' from *New and Selected Poems* by Kenneth Fearing, Copyright © 1956 by Kenneth Fearing; Methuen London and Peake Associates for 'Alphaville and after' from *The Crystal Owl* by Alison Fell; the author for 'Mae West' from *Stars in My Eyes* by Edward Field (this poem originally appeared in *The New Yorker*); the author for 'At the Regal' from *August Autumn* by Duncan Forbes; the author for 'Charlton Heston' by Elliot Fried, from *The Altadena Review 1980*; the Estate of Robert Frost,

ACKNOWLEDGEMENTS

Jonathan Cape Ltd and Henry Holt & Co. for 'Provide, Provide' from *The Poetry of Robert Frost*, ed. Edward Connery Latham; Collins Harvill for 'Bright Reel Theatre', 'Future Shock' and 'Rosebud' from *Available for Dreams* by Roy Fuller; Martin Secker & Warburg for 'On the Demolition 1980 of the Roxy', 'Movies on TV: 1982' and 'On Seeing the Leni Riefenstahl Film of the 1936 Olympic Games' from *New and Collected Poems 1934–84* by Roy Fuller; the author for 'Goodbye, Old Paint, I'm Leaving Cheyenne' by George Garrett; *The New Yorker* for 'Movie Actors Scribbling Letters Very Fast in Crucial Scenes' by Jean Garrigue, Copyright © 1972 by The New Yorker Magazine, Inc.; Penguin Books Ltd and HarperCollins Publishers, Inc. for 'The Blue Angel' from *The Collected Poems* by Allen Ginsberg, Copyright © 1985 by Allen Ginsberg; The University of North Carolina Press for 'Hoppy' from *Cabin Feaver* by Edwin Godsey; the author for 'In Person: Bette Davis' from *Altamira* by Laurence Goldstein; Copper Beech Press for 'Vertigo, A Sequel' and 'A Film Review in the Form of a Poem' from *The Three Gardens* by Laurence Goldstein; David Higham Associates for 'Ballade for a Wedding' by Graham Greene from *Punch* magazine, 18 April 1956; *The New Yorker* for 'The Hustler de Paris' by Debora Greger, Copyright © 1992 by Debora Greger (this poem first appeared in *The New Yorker*); *The New Yorker* for 'They Were All Like Geniuses' by Horace Gregory, Copyright © 1940 by The New Yorker Magazine, Inc.; the author for 'Grenadine' by Susan Griffin; Anvil Press Poetry for 'Elegy for Jean Cocteau' from *Arrangements* by Harry Guest; Peters Fraser & Dunlop for 'Flying Down to Rio' and 'Continuous' from *Selected Poems* by Tony Harrison, published 1984 by Penguin & Viking, Copyright © 1984 by Tony Harrison; Faber & Faber Ltd for 'Losing Touch' by Tony Harrison from *Projections*, ed. John Boorman and Walter Donohue; Louisiana State University Press for 'Why That's Bob Hope' from *Fish, Flesh & Fowl* by William Hathaway, Copyright © 1985 by William Hathaway; the author for 'Still Life' by James Hazard; Faber & Faber Ltd and Farrar, Straus & Giroux Inc. for 'A Shooting Script' from *The Haw Lantern* by Seamus Heaney, Copyright © 1987 by Seamus Heaney; David Higham Associates and Carcanet Press for 'On the Demolition of the Odeon Cinema' from *Collected Poems* by John Heath-Stubbs, Copyright © 1988 by John Heath Stubbs; Rogers Coleridge & White Ltd and Jonathan Cape for 'Stakeout on High Street' from *Wish You Were Here* by Adrian Henri, Copyright © by Adrian Henri; Lousiana State University Press for 'In the Days of Rin-Tin-Tin' from *Hang-Gliding from Helicon, New and Selected Poems 1948–1988* by Daniel Hoffman, Copyright © 1974, 1975, 1976, 1977, 1978, 1979, 1980, 1981, 1982, 1983, 1984, 1985, 1986, 1987, 1988 by Daniel Hoffman; Faber & Faber Ltd for 'Dependants' and 'Shapes of Things' from *Nights in the Iron Hotel* by Michael Hofmann; the author for 'The Movie' by John Hollander, Copyright © 1979 by John Hollander, and for 'Movie-Going' and 'To the Lady Portrayed by Margaret Dumont' from *Movie-Going and Other Poems* by John Hollander, Copyright © 1962, 1990 by John Hollander; the author for 'Blue Films' by Geoffrey Holloway from *New Poetry – An Arts Council Anthology*; the

ACKNOWLEDGEMENTS

Estate of the author and Jonathan Cape Ltd for 'A War Film' by Teresa Hooley from *Scars Upon My Heart*; Faber & Faber Ltd for 'The Lost World' from *The Complete Poems* by Randall Jarrell; the author and Chatto & Windus for 'Marilyn and You' from *In the Hothouse* by Alan Jenkins; the author and David Higham Associates for 'Two Deaths' from *Collected Poems* by Elizabeth Jennings, Copyright © 1961 by Elizabeth Jennings; the author for 'The Earth: To Marilyn' from *Uranium Poems* by Judith Emlyn Johnson (formerly Judith Johnson Sherwin), Copyright © 1968 by Judith Johnson Sherwin; the author and W. W. Norton & Co. for 'The Blob Speaks to its Mother' from *How the Dead Count* by Judith Emlyn Johnson; Indiana University Press for 'Why I Like Movies' from *Black Sister*, ed. Erlene Stetson, by Patricia Jones; the author for 'Lines Written in Dejection' from *High Spirits* by Neil Jordan, Copyright © 1988 by Neil Jordan; Bloodaxe Books for 'Still' from *Dirty Washing: New & Selected Poems* by Sylvia Kantaris (Bloodaxe Books, 1989); New Directions Publishing Corp. for 'Patriotic Ode on the Fourteenth Anniversary of the Persecution of Charlie Chaplin' from *Solitudes Crowded with Loneliness* by Bob Kaufman, Copyright © 1965 by Bob Kaufman; University of Nebraska Press and Faber & Faber Ltd for 'Subtitle' from *Collected Poems* by Weldon Kees, Copright © 1975 by University of Nebraska Press; George Braziller Inc. for 'Buster Keaton & the Cops' from *Song in a Strange Land* by George Keithley, Copyright © 1954 by George Keithley; Sterling Lord Literistic, Inc. and City Lights Books for 'To Harpo Marx' by Jack Kerouac from *Playboy* magazine, July 1959, Copyright © 1959 by Jack Kerouac; Cleveland State University Poetry Center for 'Silent Movie' from *Sarah Bernhardt's Leg* by David Kirby, Copyright © 1983 by David Kirby; the author for 'Garbo Goodbye' and 'Haiku' by James Kirkup, Copyright © 1992 by James Kirkup, for 'Pasolini' and 'On Pasolini's *Teorema*' by James Kirkup, Copyright © 1987 by James Kirkup, and for 'The Fallen Star' from *A Spring Journey* by James Kirkup, Copyright © 1956 by James Kirkup; the author for 'Dick Powell' by Ron Koertge; Viking Penguin for 'At a Private Showing in 1982' from *The Long Approach* by Maxine Kumin, Copyright © 1982 by Maxine Kumin (this poem first appeared in *The New Yorker*); the author for 'Godard's Women' by Jeanne Lance; Anthony Lejeune for 'Cross My Heart', '*Charley's Aunt*', 'Aloma of the South Seas', 'Heart Failure' and '*Humoresque*' by C. A. Lejeune; New Directions Publishing Corporation for 'Triple Feature' from *Collected Earlier Poems 1940–1960* by Denise Levertov; Andrei Codrescu for 'A Gothic Gesture' by Steve Levine from *American Poetry since 1970: Up Late*, ed. Andrei Codrescu; the author for 'Elegy for an Actor Drowned in Time of War' by Maurice Lindsay; Polygon Books for 'In the Cutting Room' and 'Fin' from *Dreaming Frankenstein and Collected Poems* by Liz Lochhead; the author for 'judy garland' from *POOP and other poems* by Gerald Locklin; BOA Editions Ltd. for 'Saturday Afternoon at the Movies' from *John Logan: The Collected Poems*, Copyright © 1989 by the John Logan Literary Estate, Inc.; Faber & Faber Ltd for 'Scar-Face' and 'Harpo Marx' from *History* by Robert Lowell; the author for 'Moguls and Monks' from *Africa and the Marriage of Walt Whitman and Marilyn Monroe* by Lewis Mac Adams; Faber & Faber Ltd for 'The News-Reel' from *The Collected Poems of Louis MacNeice*; Bloodaxe Books Ltd for 'Girl in Films' from *The Tale of the Mayor's Son* by Glyn Maxwell (Bloodaxe Books, 1990); *The New Yorker* for 'Good Times' by Robert Mazzocco, Copyright © 1992 by Robert Mazzocco (this poem originally appeared in *The New Yorker*); the author for 'Snow White Meets the Wolfman' by Leon McAuley, originally published in *Trio 4*, Copyright © 1985 by Leon McAuley; New Directions Publishing Corporation for 'La Plus Blanche' from *Michael McClure: Selected Poems*, Copyright © 1986 by Michael McClure; Henry Holt and Company, Inc. for 'Into the Movies' from *Quiet Money* by Robert McDowell, Copyright © 1987 by Robert McDowell; University Press of Florida for 'Buster Keaton' from *Plain Air* by Michael McFee (Gainesville, Fla.: University of Central Florida Contemporary Poetry Series, xii, 1983); Peters Fraser & Dunlop Group Ltd for 'The death of John Berryman in slow motion' from *Holiday on Death Row*, 'The Filmmaker' from *Watchwords*, and 'If Life's a Lousy Picture, Why Not Leave Before the End' from *Melting into the Foreground* by Roger McGough; the author for '15th Raga/For Bela Lugosi' by David Meltzer; the author for 'Stan Laurel' by John Mole, originally published in the *Spectator*; Viking Penguin for 'Rescue with Yul Brynner' from *The Complete Poems of Marianne Moore*, Copyright © 1961 by Marianne Moore, renewed © 1989 by Marianne Craig Moore; the author and Carcanet Press Limited for 'Five Poems on Film Directors' from *Collected Poems* by Edwin Morgan; David Higham Associates for 'Elegy for Arthur Prance – The Man Who Taught the Stars to Dance' from *A Winter Visitor* by Pete Morgan; Estate of Howard Moss for 'Horror Movie' from *A Winter Come, A Summer Gone* by Howard Moss, and *The New Yorker* for 'Movies for the Home' by Howard Moss, also from *A Winter Come, A Summer Gone* and first published in *The New Yorker*, Copyright © 1960 by The New Yorker Magazine, Inc.; Faber & Faber Ltd and Wake University Press for 'The Weepies' from *Why Brownlee Left* by Paul Muldoon; the author for 'One Picture is Worth a Thousand Words' and '*Paradise Lost*' by Paul Munden from *Poetry Introduction 7* (Faber & Faber 1990) and for 'Gutting the ABC' by Paul Munden; the author and Raven Arts Press for 'Cinema' from *The Way the Money Goes* by Aidan Murphy; Little, Brown and Company and Curtis Brown Ltd, New York, on behalf of the Estate of Ogden Nash, for 'Notes for a Documentary in Search of a Sponsor' from *There's Always Another Windmill* by Ogden Nash, Copyright © 1965 and 1968 by Ogden Nash (this poem first appeared in *Traveler's World* magazine), for 'Viva Vamp, Vale Vamp' from *Everyone But Thee and Me* by Ogden Nash, Copyright © 1960 and 1962 by Ogden Nash; Curtis Brown Ltd, New York, for 'Mae West' from *The Primrose Path* by Ogden Nash, Copyright © 1935 by Ogden Nash; the author for 'Working for Dr No' and 'The End of the Late Show, Channel 7' by Valery Nash; Margaret Nemerov for 'Mousemeal' from *New and Selected Poems* by Howard Nemerov (University of Chicago Press, 1960) and for 'Late Late Show' from

ACKNOWLEDGEMENTS

Collected Poems by Howard Nemerov (University of Chicago Press, 1978); the author for 'Stars in an Oldie' from *The Window Game* by John Normanton; the author and André Deutsch for 'The Midnight Movie' from *Selected Poems* by Philip Oakes, and the author for 'A Report from the Chairman' by Philip Oakes; Bloodaxe Books for 'A Matinée' from *The Frighteners* by Sean O'Brien (Bloodaxe Books, 1987); Grove Weidenfeld for 'To the Film Industry in Crisis' from *Meditations in an Emergency* by Frank O'Hara, Copyright © 1957 by Frank O'Hara, Alfred A. Knopf, Inc. for 'An Image of Leda' and 'Vincent and I Inaugurate a Movie Theater' from *The Collected Poems* by Frank O'Hara, Copyright © 1971 by Maureen Granville–Smith, Administratrix of the Estate of Frank O'Hara; City Lights Books for 'Ave Maria', 'Fantasy' and 'Poem (Lana Turner)' from *Lunch Poems* by Frank O'Hara, Copyright © 1964 by Frank O'Hara; Alfred A. Knopf, Inc. for 'The Death of Marilyn Monroe' from *The Dead and the Living* by Sharon Olds, Copyright © 1983 by Sharon Olds; Ellen Levine Literary Agency, Inc. and Alfred A. Knopf, Inc. for 'King Kong Meets Wallace Stevens' and 'Late Movies with Skyler' from *The Cinnamon Peeler* by Michael Ondaatje, Copyright © 1989, 1992 by Michael Ondaatje; Collins Harvill for 'Shades of Grey' from *The Stripped Bed* by Michael O'Neill, Copyright © 1990 by Michael O'Neill; Jonathan Williams, Highlands, North Carolina, for 'Flowers for Luis Buñuel' from *The Suicide Room* (no. 17 in the *Jargon* series) by Stuart Perkoff; Sheil Land Associates and Chatto & Windus for 'Merging', 'The Mirror Crack'd', 'Night London' and 'Old Extras' from *Sky Ray Lolly* by Fiona Pitt-Kethley, Copyright © 1986 by Fiona Pitt-Kethley, and Sheil Land Associates for 'Bond Girl' from *The Perfect Man* by Fiona Pitt-Kethley, Copyright © 1989 by Fiona Pitt-Kethley; Sir Rupert Hart-Davis and the Estate of William Plomer for 'Not Where We Came In' from *Collected Poems* (1973) by William Plomer; the author for 'Carmen Miranda' by Frank Polite; the author for 'Claudette Colbert by Billy Wilder' from *Lion Lion* by Tom Raworth, Copyright © 1970 by Tom Raworth, and for 'You Were Wearing Blue' and 'I Mean' from *The Relationship* by Tom Raworth, Copyright © 1966 by Tom Raworth; the author for 'On Seeing a Movie Based on President Kennedy's Life', 'The Red Shoes', 'Firestarter', 'Movies (For Jane Goodall)' by David Ray; Chatto & Windus for 'Double Feature' from *Evagatory* by Peter Reading; the author for 'Sky Diving' and 'Poison Light' from *New and Collected Poems* by Ishmael Reed; W. W. Norton & Company for 'Newsreel' from *The Fact of a Doorframe, Poems Selected and New 1950–1984* by Adrienne Rich, Copyright © 1984 by Adrienne Rich; Doubleday and Faber & Faber Ltd for 'Double Feature' from *The Collected Poems of Theodore Roethke*, Copyright © 1942 by Commonweal Publishing Co.; the author for 'Walker Evans' Atlanta' from *Death Valley* by Alan Ross, Copyright © 1980 by Alan Ross; the author for 'Nobody Dies Like Humphrey Bogart' by Norman Rosten; William L. Rukeyser for 'Movie' from *Waterlily Fire, Poems 1935–1963*, Copyright © 1963 by Muriel Rukeyser; University Press of New England for 'Bijou' from *The Window* by Vern Rutsala, Copyright © 1960 by

Vern Rutsala; the author for 'Poem for a Cinema Organist' from *The Kingdom of Atlas* by Lawrence Sail, Copyright © 1980 by Lawrence Sail; the author for 'A few lines about film buffs, critics and those of us who consume the stuff' by Andrew Salkey; Harcourt Brace Jovanovich, Inc. for 'Landscape' from *Good Morning, America* by Carl Sandburg, Copyright © 1928 and renewed 1956 by Carl Sandburg; Southern Poetry Review for 'Drive In Movie' by Gary Sange, Copyright © 1992 by Gary Sange; George Sassoon for 'Picture-Show' from *Collected Poems 1908–1956* by Siegfried Sassoon; the author for 'Autobiographical Note', 'War Movie Veteran' and 'Film Shooting' from *The Collected Poems 1950–1992* by Vernon Scannell, Copyright © 1992 by Vernon Scannell; the author for 'Pasolini' from *The Love of Strangers* by Michael Schmidt; Catherine J. Scott for 'To Mourn Jayne Mansfield' and 'Kong Was King' by Alexander Scott; Estate of Robert Service (M. Wm. Krasilovsky attorney), for 'To G.K.' and 'Johnny Wayne and Randy Scott' from *Collected Verse* by Robert Service, Copyright © 1960 by Dodd Mead & Co.; the author for 'The Border' and 'The Good Guy' from *The Border* by Kita Shantiris (Bombshelter Press, 1984; 'The Good Guy' was originally published by Poetry and the Modern Language Association); Wieser & Wieser, Inc., New York, for 'Hollywood' from *Persons, Places and Things* by Karl Shapiro, and 'Movie' and 'Movie Actress' from *V Letter and Other Poems* by Karl Shapiro, Copyright © 1985 by Karl Shapiro; *The New Yorker* for 'The Shirt' by Roger Shattuck, Copyright © 1983 by Roger Shattuck (this poem originally appeared in *The New Yorker*); the author for 'Orson Welles, Are You Listening?' from *The Landscape of Contemporary Cinema*, and for 'Homage to Walter Hill's Hard Times' by William David (Bill) Sherman; the author for 'B Movie' by Robert Siegel, Copyright Robert Siegel; Franklin Watts, Inc., New York, for 'Why don't you get transferred, Dad?' from *Caviare at the Funeral* by Louis Simpson, Copyright © 1980 by Louis Simpson; Martin Secker & Warburg and Little, Brown and Company for 'Rosedale Theater, 1938', 'First NY Showing', 'Les Enfants de Thalia', 'The Cinematographers, West Cedar Street' and '*Cahiers du Cinéma*, 1956' from *Hello, Darkness* by L. E. Sissman, Copyright © 1969, 1970 by L. E. Sissman; the author for 'Twice As Many Gorillas' from *Monsters* by Jack Skelley; the author for 'Ride the High Country' from *The Carnivore* by David Slavitt; the Canadian Publishers, McClelland & Stewart, Toronto, for 'Far West' from *The Classic Shade* by A. J. M. Smith; the author for 'Brief Encounter', 'It's All True' and 'The Fall of the House of Hitchcock' by Jules Smith, first published in *Bête Noire* magazine; James MacGibbon and New Directions Publishing Corporation for 'The Film Star' from *The Collected Poems of Stevie Smith*, Copyright © 1972 by Stevie Smith; the author for 'Old Movie Stars' from *Plain Talk: Epigrams, Epitaphs, Satires, Nonsense, Occasional, Concrete and Quotidian Poems*, by William Jay Smith, published by Center for Book Arts, 1988, Copyright © 1973, 1988 by William Jay Smith, Charles Scribner's Sons, an imprint of Macmillan Publishing Company, for 'Movies for the Troops' from *Collected Poems 1939–1989* by William Jay Smith, Copyright © 1940, 1942, 1944, 1945,

ACKNOWLEDGEMENTS

© 1990 by William Jay Smith; the author and New Directions Publishing Corporation for 'On *Imagerie*: Esther Williams', formerly called 'Only in the Milkiest Emulsions' from *Voyaging Portraits* by Gustaf Sobin, Copyright © 1988 by Gustaf Sobin; the author for 'The Truly Great' from *Collected Poems 1928– 1985* by Sir Stephen Spender (published by Faber & Faber Ltd and Random House, Inc.); the author for 'Marilyn' from *Letters from Exile & Other Poems* by Lawrence P. Spingarn; the author for 'A Toast' by Charles Stetler (this poem originally appeared in *The Wormwood Review*); the author and Phoenix Literary Agency for 'Mentioning James Dean' from *Crimes of Passion* by Terry Stokes, Copyright © 1973 by Terry Stokes; the author for 'War Movie: Last Leave, 1944' by Patricia Storace (first published in *Ploughshares*) and for 'Requiem for a Producer' by Patricia Storace; Curtis Brown Ltd for 'Newsreel' and 'Reel One' from *Heroes Advise Us* by Adrien Stoutenburg; BOA Editions Ltd for 'Documentary' from *Signatures* by Joseph Stroud © 1982 by Joseph Stroud; Ohio University Press for 'Watching War Movies' from *Collected Poems 1953–1983* by Lucien Stryk; Coffee House Press for 'Movies Left to Right' from *Four Incarnations* by Robert Sward (this poem first appeared in *The New Yorker*), Copyright © 1992 by Robert Sward; The Literary Estate of May Swenson for 'The James Bond Movie' by May Swenson, Copyright © 1968 by May Swenson; the author for 'In Memoriam Busby Berkeley' by George Szirtes from *Poetry Introduction 4*, Copyright © 1978 by George Szirtes; Hubert Nicholson as Executor of the Estate of A. S. J. Tessimond for 'Chaplin' and 'Hollywood' by A. S. J. Tessimond; Bill Mohr, Momentum Press, for 'Gift of a Magic Lantern to Plato' from *Waking the Waters* by Jack W. Thomas; Peterloo Poets for 'Full Supporting Programme' from *Fables for Love: Poems New & Selected* by Bill Turner, Copyright © 1985 by Bill Turner; Alfred A. Knopf, Inc. and Victor Gollancz Ltd for 'The Newlyweds', 'In Memoriam' and 'Popular Revivals' from *The Carpentered Hen and Other Tame Creatures* (Knopf) by John Updike, Copyright © 1955, 1958 by John Updike, and from *Hoping for a Hoopoe* (Gollancz) by John Updike, Copyright © 1954, 1955, 1956, 1957, 1958 by John Updike, and Alfred A. Knopf, Inc. and Penguin Books Ltd for 'Home Movies' from *Midpoint and Other Poems* by John Updike, Copyright © 1969 by John Updike, 'Movie House' from *Telephone Poles and Other Poems* by John Updike, Copyright © 1963 by John Updike, and 'L.A.' from *Facing Nature* by John Updike, Copyright © 1985 by John Updike; the author for 'Endings' by Mona Van Duyn (this poem originally appeared in *The Yale Review*); *The Hudson Review* for 'Arizona Movies' by Michael Van Walleghen from *The Hudson Review*, Vol. XXIX, No. 3 (Autumn 1976), Copyright © 1976 by The Hudson Review, Inc.; the author for 'The Shooting of John Dillinger Outside the Biograph Theater, July 22, 1934' by David Wagoner; Curtis Brown Ltd for 'Villanelle for Harpo Marx' from *A Word Carved on a Sill* by John Wain; the author for 'Point of View' from *Jiggery-Pokery*, ed. A. Hecht and J. Hollander, by Chris Wallace-Crabbe; G. M. Watkins for 'Elegy on the Heroine of Childhood' from *Ballad of the Mari Lwyd and Other Poems* by Vernon Watkins, Copyright

ACKNOWLEDGEMENTS

© 1945, 1947 by Gwen Watkins; *The Hudson Review* for 'Motion Pictures' by Tom Wayman from the *The Hudson Review*, Vol. XXXVII, No. 1 (Spring 1984), Copyright © 1984 by The Hudson Review, Inc.; the author for 'Further Decline of Western Civilization', 'Tarantula', 'After Not Winning the Yale Poetry Prize' (first published in *Michigan Quarterly Review*), 'He's a Nice Guy, But Always Worrying' (first published in *Poetry That Heals*, Red Wind Books) by Charles Webb, Copyright by Charles Webb; the author for 'A Day with the Foreign Legion' by Reed Whittemore; Faber & Faber Ltd and Harcourt Brace Jovanovich, Inc. for 'The Undead' from *New and Collected Poems* (F&F) and *Advice to a Prophet and Other Poems* (HBJ) by Richard Wilbur, and for 'The Prisoner of Zenda' from *New and Collected Poems* (F&F) and *The Mind-Reader* (HBJ) by Richard Wilbur; Faber & Faber Ltd and Pantheon Books for 'Beasts' from *New and Collected Poems* (F&F) and *Things of This World* (PB) by Richard Wilbur; Bloodaxe Books and Farrar, Straus & Giroux, Inc. for 'Cowboys' and 'Nostalgia' from *Flesh and Blood* by C. K. Williams (Bloodaxe Books, 1988); Farrar, Straus & Giroux, Inc. for 'The Playwright in Paradise' from *Night Thoughts* by Edmund Wilson, Copyright © 1961 by Edmund Wilson, Renewal Copyright © 1989 by Helen Miranda Wilson; the author for 'The Man Who Knew Too Much' from *Icehouse Lights* by David Wojahn, Copyright © 1982 by David Wojahn (this poem originally appeared in *The New Yorker*); the author for 'Revenge of the Pleasure Seekers' by Jeffrey C. Wright; Louisiana State University Press for 'W. H. Auden & Mantan Moreland' from *The Blues Don't Change: New and Selected Poems* by Al Young, Copyright © 1974, 1975, 1976, 1977, 1978, 1979, 1980, 1981 and 1982 by Al Young; the author for 'The Cutting Room Floor' from *Boxcars* by David Young.

Faber & Faber Ltd apologize for any errors or omissions in the above list and would be grateful to be notified of any corrections that should be incorporated in the next edition of this volume.

Index